An American Anarchist

An American Anarchist

The Life of Voltairine de Cleyre

by Paul Avrich

Princeton University Press, Princeton, New Jersey

Copyright © 1978 by Princeton University Press
Published by Princeton University Press, Princeton, New Jersey
In the United Kingdom: Princeton University Press, Guildford, Surrey

All Rights Reserved

Library of Congress Cataloging in Publication Data will be
found on the last printed page of this book

Publication of this book has been assisted by a grant from the
Publications Program, National Endowment for the Humanities.

This book has been composed in Linotype Primer

Printed in the United States of America by Princeton
University Press, Princeton, New Jersey

In Memory of Max Nettlau
1865-1944

Contents

Illustrations

(following page 136)

Preface

This biography of Voltairine de Cleyre, one of the most interesting if neglected figures in the history of American radicalism, is designed to be the first of several volumes dealing with anarchism in the United States, a project on which I have been engaged for the past six years. When I began my work, I expected to treat the entire subject between the covers of a single volume, in which Voltairine de Cleyre would occupy a modest place. My intention at the time was to produce a comprehensive history of American anarchism from its seventeenth-century origins until recent years, embracing the individualists and collectivists, the native Americans and immigrants, the pacifists and revolutionists, and their libertarian schools and colonies.

A study of this type was badly needed. For while there were a number of useful works on American socialism and American communism, the history of American anarchism remained largely unwritten. Two well-known surveys of anarchism as a whole, George Woodcock's *Anarchism* and James Joll's *The Anarchists*, contained brief accounts of the movement in the United States, in addition to a longer discussion by Max Nettlau in his multivolume history of anarchism, written half a century ago but never published in its entirety. On American anarchism itself most available studies were tendentious and unreliable. There were, however, a few creditable works, such as Eunice M. Schuster's pioneering *Native American Anarchism*, which, if largely out of date, was still of some value, and James J. Martin's *Men Against the State*, an authoritative treatment of the Individualist school, of which Josiah Warren and Benjamin Tucker were the outstanding exponents. Moreover, one of the leading Anarchist-Communists, Emma Goldman, had been the

subject of a sympathetic biography by Richard Drinnon, *Rebel in Paradise*, in addition to which *The History of the Haymarket Affair* by Henry David and *The
Mooney Case* by Richard Frost merited special attention. But much remained to be done, particularly on
the immigrant groups; and in many areas scholarly
explorations were completely lacking, sources uncol-
lected and often unknown, and historical works, with
few exceptions, encrusted with political and personal
bias.

It was considerations such as these which led me,
at the beginning of the 1970s, to contemplate the
writing of a general history of American anarchism.
At an early stage, however, my plans began to alter.
For a fuller examination of the materials at my
disposal, together with the discovery of new sources,
aroused a growing sense of the complexity of the movement, of the richness and diversity of its history. Again
and again, I encountered important figures begging to
be resurrected, tangled episodes to be unraveled,
neglected avenues to be explored—too many, it was
clear, to be treated in a single volume. A larger design
was required to do the subject justice and to in-
corporate the findings of such recently published works
as Lewis Perry's *Radical Abolitionism* and Laurence
Veysey's *The Communal Experience*, which have filled
conspicuous gaps in our knowledge of American
anarchism and enabled us to begin to separate historical legend from historical reality. To a significant
extent, moreover, the need for a general history was
met in 1976 with the publication of William O.
Reichert's *Partisans of Freedom: A Study in American
Anarchism*, a work of 600 closely printed pages with
useful bibliographical references.

I found myself, as a result, less and less inclined
to produce an exhaustive chronological history of
American anarchism. Besides, as my work progressed
it became increasingly evident that much of what had

happened in the movement had been due to the
personal characteristics of its adherents, and that the
nature of American anarchism might be profitably
explored through the lives of a few individuals who
played a central role in the movement and set the
imprint of their personalities upon it. From most existing accounts, unfortunately, one gets little understanding of the anarchists as human beings, still less of what
impelled them to embark on their unpopular and seemingly futile course. Anarchism, as a result, has seemed
a movement apart, unreal and quixotic, divorced from
American history and irrelevant to American life.

For these reasons, I have decided to tell the story
of American anarchism through the lives of selected
figures who, in large measure, shaped the destiny and
character of the movement. In arriving at this decision,
I have been guided by the assumption that by focus-
ing on key individuals, their dreams and passions,
failures and successes, weaknesses and strengths, I can
make the movement as a whole more comprehensible.
I have not, however, ignored the social and economic
developments of the age, but have tried, as the story
unfolds, to include sufficient historical background to
make the lives of the anarchists intelligible.

Of all the major movements of social reform,
anarchism has been subject to the grossest misunder-
standings of its nature and objectives. No group has
been more abused and misrepresented by the authorities or more feared and detested by the public. And
of all the misconceptions of anarchism, the one that
dies the hardest is the belief that it is inseparable from
assassination and destruction. There were, to be sure,
individuals and groups among the anarchists who
were ready to commit acts of terrorism. Yet, for all
the notoriety that they achieved, they occupied a rela-
tively small place in the movement. By the time of the
First World War, however, anarchism had acquired a
reputation of violence for its own sake that the passage

of six decades has failed to alter. The stereotype, once
created, has been endlessly recopied, so that to this
day the association of anarchism with terrorism, with
bombs, dynamite, and chaos, remains deeply embedded in the popular imagination.

But who in fact were the anarchists? What did they
actually say and do with regard to economic, social,
and political issues? How did they cope with popular
abuse and with official harassment and repression?
How did they react to problems, both social and personal, which confronted them at different stages of
their careers? What did they want and what did they
achieve? Such are the questions this study will try to
answer. Every effort will be made to portray the anarchists as they really were, rather than as they have appeared in the fantasies of policemen and journalists
and not a few historians, who have neglected to look
up the sources from which any reliable study must be
made.

Anarchism has been defined as "the philosophy of a
new social order based on liberty unrestricted by man-
made law; the theory that all forms of government
rest on violence, and are therefore wrong and harmful, as well as unnecessary."[1] As such, it will be seen,
it was not an alien doctrine, but an integral part of the
American past, deeply rooted in native soil; and though
an organized anarchist movement did not emerge in
the United States until the 1870s and '80s, the belief
in a minimum of government, as one writer has noted,
had been "a fundamental article of faith of the new
nation."[2] Indeed, an American libertarian tradition
runs back to the seventeenth century and continues to
the present day. The vision of a stateless utopia may be
discovered among the religious and political dissenters

[1] Emma Goldman, *Anarchism and Other Essays*, New York,
1911, p. 50.
[2] Charles Madison, *Critics and Crusaders: A Century of
American Protest*, 2nd edn., New York, 1959, p. 163.

of the colonial era as well as among the anti-slavery followers of William Lloyd Garrison and the communitarian enthusiasts of the antebellum period. It may also be found in the writings of Emerson, Thoreau, and other nineteenth-century figures, both well-known and obscure. "Why should I employ a church to write my creed or a state to govern me?" asked Bronson Alcott in 1839. "Why not write my own creed? Why not govern myself?"[3]

Sentiments such as these, at bottom a response to the quickening pace of political and economic centralization brought on by the industrial revolution, were by no means uncommon among New England transcendentalists and reformers. Josiah Warren, who has been called "the first American anarchist," began to evolve a coherent libertarian philosophy as early as the 1820s, while identifiably anarchist colonies can be traced back to the 1830s and 1840s, if not earlier. And with the upsurge of centralized power after the Civil War, a vigorous anarchist movement took shape, spreading across the country from Massachusetts to California. During the early 1870s, Bakuninist sections of the International Working Men's Association were established in Boston, New York, and other cities, and Americans at this time began to take part in international anarchist congresses. The influx of immigrants during the succeeding decades provided the movement with a fresh supply of recruits, and anarchist groups sprang up in every part of the country except the deep South.

In most locations these groups fell into three categories: Anarchist-Communists, who envisioned a free federation of agricultural and industrial cooperatives in which each member would be rewarded according to his needs; Anarcho-Syndicalists, who pinned

[3] Lewis C. Perry, *Radical Abolitionism: Anarchy and the Government of God in Antislavery Thought*, Ithaca, N.Y., 1973, pp. 83-84.

their hopes on the labor movement and called for workers' self-management in the factories; and Individualist Anarchists, who, distrusting any collaboration that might harden into institutional form, rejected both cooperatives and unions in favor of unorganized individuals, exalting the ego above the claims of collective entities. To these might be added the Tolstoyan and pacifist anarchists, who spurned all revolutionary activity as a breeder of hatred and violence.

Communists and syndicalists, pacifists and revolutionists, idealists and adventurers—the American anarchist movement encompassed a fascinating and often contradictory variety of groups and individuals, whose activities ranged from strikes and terrorist attacks to the dissemination of birth-control propaganda and the creation of libertarian schools. Yet, however they might differ on such questions as violence and organization, they were united in their rejection of the state, their opposition to coercion, and their faith that people could live in harmony once the restraints imposed by government had been removed. In spite of personal and factional disputes, they shared a common determination to make a clean sweep of entrenched institutions and to inaugurate a stateless society based on the voluntary cooperation of free individuals, a society without oppression or exploitation, without hunger or want, in which men and women would direct their own affairs unimpeded by any authority.

This vision, to all appearances, differed little from that of the Marxists: a world in which the free development of each was a condition for the free development of all and in which no man would be master of his brother. The Marxists, however, did not regard the millennium as imminent. They foresaw an intervening stage of proletarian dictatorship that would eliminate the last vestiges of capitalism. The anarchists, by contrast, were opposed to the state in any form. Refusing to temporize with political or economic power, they poured contempt on intermediate stages, partial reforms, and palliatives or compromises of any sort. The existing regime was rotten, and salvation could be achieved only by destroying it root and branch. Moreover, political revolutions were useless, for they merely exchanged one set of rulers for another without altering the essence of tyranny. Instead, the anarchists called for a social revolution that would abolish all political and economic authority and usher in a decentralized society of autonomous communities and labor associations, organized "from below," as they put it.

Anarchism, however, did not become a creed of the mass of industrial workers. For reasons which will be explored, it was destined to remain a dream of comparatively small groups of men and women who had alienated themselves from the mainstream of American society. Yet they claim our attention, not only as a collection of colorful personalities, but as social and moral critics whose voices should not go unheard. They foresaw the negative consequences of "scientific" socialism and offered a continuous and fundamental criticism of all forms of centralized authority. They warned that political power is intrinsically evil, that it corrupts all who wield it, that government of any kind stifles the creative spirit of the people and robs them of their freedom. And, notwithstanding their small popular following, they played a significant part in American history and had a deep and abiding effect on American life.

Since no attempt was made to keep records of membership (anarchists issued no "party cards" and distrusted formal organizational machinery), the numerical strength of the movement is hard to determine. But it was greater than has generally been supposed. Scattered across the country, with concentrations in the larger cities, anarchists reckoned in the tens of thousands at the crest of the movement between 1880 and 1920, with 3,000 in Chicago alone during the last decades of the nineteenth century and comparable numbers in Paterson and New York. The Union of Russian Workers in the United States and Canada, in which anarchists formed the largest element, boasted 10,000 adherents on the eve of its suppression in 1919 by Attorney General A. Mitchell Palmer.

To spread their libertarian message, anarchists in the United States issued nearly 500 periodicals in a dozen languages, several of which ran for decades and achieved a high level of literary distinction, including Benjamin Tucker's *Liberty*, Johann Most's *Freiheit*, and Emma Goldman's *Mother Earth*. The Italian *L'Adunata dei Refrattari* endured for half a century, while the *Fraye Arbeter Shtime*, whose circulation exceeded 20,000 in the period before the First World War, is still in existence after eighty-seven years, the oldest Yiddish newspaper in the world. Anarchist influence was also exerted through active participation in trade unions and cooperatives, while the execution of the Spanish educator Francisco Ferrer in 1909 led to the formation in America of more than twenty anarchist schools on the model of his Escuela Moderna in Barcelona. One of these, at Stelton, New Jersey, survived for forty years, closing in 1953. Anarchists, it might be added, were involved in two of the most dramatic and controversial trials in American history, the Haymarket affair of the 1880s and the Sacco-Vanzetti affair of the 1920s, both of which had international repercussions, providing a rallying-point for radicals and liberals throughout the world. In short, a study of American anarchism is essential to an understanding of such subjects as labor and immigration, pacifism and war, birth control and sexual freedom, civil liberties and political repression, prison reform and capital punishment, avant-garde culture and art. In a larger sense, a study of American anarchism will shed interesting light on the nature of American democracy, American capitalism, and American government.

What began then as a chronological survey has become a series of interrelated studies which, taken together, will form a kind of biographical history of a movement that included figures as striking and diverse as Josiah Warren and Alexander Berkman, Benjamin Tucker and Johann Most, Emma Goldman and Voltairine de Cleyre. By assigning Voltairine de Cleyre a separate volume, I do not mean to overstate her importance. Yet for twenty-five years she was an active agitator and propagandist and, as a glance through the files of the anarchist press will show, one of the movement's most respected and devoted representatives, who deserves to be better known. Besides, there was so much rich drama in her life that a full-length biography was needed to do it justice. As a freethinker and feminist as well as an anarchist, moreover, she can speak to us today, across a gulf of seven decades, with undiminished relevance. For, in a remarkably detailed and articulate fashion, her writings anticipate the contemporary mood of distrust toward the centralized bureaucratic state. She was one of the most eloquent and consistent critics of unbridled political power, the subjugation of the individual, the dehumanization of labor, and the debasement of culture; and with her vision of a decentralized libertarian society, based on voluntary cooperation and mutual aid, she has left a legacy to inspire new generations of idealists and reformers.

Much of the documentation on which this biography is based has been hitherto unknown or unused. At every stage it has been necessary to reconstruct the story from primary sources—letters, memoirs, journals, oral testimony, and bits of information pieced together by other means. I have tried to approach these materials directly and to reach my own conclusions, even when some aspect of the subject has been touched

upon in a secondary work not marred by prejudice or
ignorance. While it is the first of a series of studies,
this volume is a self-contained biography, complete in
its own terms, which can be read as an independent
work. To some extent, however, it bears the character of a stage of a larger enterprise, in that several
strands of narrative and interpretation will be taken
up and expanded in future instalments.

It may be useful, finally, to indicate how the present
series fits into my overall program of research. My
work on the history of American anarchism, begun in
1971, will form part of a still larger investigation of
libertarian movements with which I have been occupied since my graduate years at Columbia University
from 1957 to 1961. My research at Columbia began
with a study of the factory-committee movement
during the Russian Revolution, a form of revolutionary
syndicalism in which rank-and-file workers assumed
control of their factories and shops. This led, in turn,
to a general history of Russian anarchism (published
in 1967) and to related histories of the Kronstadt rebellion of 1921 and of popular risings in Russia during
the seventeenth and eighteenth centuries.

I have not, in the intervening years, changed the
direction of my research, but have broadened its scope
to include the United States and other countries. When
the American volumes are completed, I hope to turn to
anarchism in Europe and Asia, and also to a history of
the forerunners of anarchism from ancient times to
the French Revolution. With regard to the United
States, my training in Russian and European history,
while it presents a number of difficulties, may also have
certain advantages. For it has been necessary to delve
into the European roots of American anarchism, especially of the numerous immigrant groups that were
formed during the late nineteenth and early twentieth
century. Such an approach, one hopes, will contribute
not only to our knowledge of American anarchism

itself, but of anarchism as a worldwide phenomenon between the French Revolution and the Spanish Civil War, and beyond.

During the course of my research on American anarchism, which is now largely completed, I have visited more than fifty libraries and archives in Europe and the United States, the most important of which are listed in the bibliography of this volume. To the staffs of these institutions, and especially to Rudolf de Jong, Thea Duijker, and Maria Hunink of the International Institute of Social History, Edward Weber and Helen Jameson of the Labadie Collection, Dorothy Swanson and Debra Slotkin-Shulman of the Tamiment Collection, Hillel Kempinski of the Bund Archives, and Laura V. Monti of the University of Florida, I am grateful for their kind assistance.

A subject such as this, however, especially when approached from the angle of biography, cannot be studied from documents alone. Personal contacts are essential, and I am fortunate in this regard to have come to know many of the survivors of the anarchist movement, who have allowed me to attend their meetings, to inspect their manuscripts and correspondence, and to discuss with them, at considerable length, points of mutual interest relating to anarchist history. By revealing the inner recesses of anarchist life as perhaps no other sources can, these contacts have done much to broaden and deepen my knowledge of the subject. Over the years, moreover, I have conducted more than 150 interviews with these survivors, each adding valuable details or a fresh point of view. Together, these interviews provide a unique account of the movement in the words of the participants, and in due course I shall deposit bound transcripts in major libraries for use by other students of anarchist history.

With regard to my work on Voltairine de Cleyre, I

am much indebted to several individuals who placed important materials at my disposal: William Morris Abbott, Marion Bell, Renée de Cleyre Buckwalter, William J. Fishman, Elmer Isaak, Rose Lowensohn, George H. O'Brien, Sidney E. Parker, and Grace Umrath. In addition, I have greatly profited from interviews and conversations with a number of people who knew Voltairine de Cleyre, heard her speak at meetings, or had other contacts with her and were willing to share their recollections with me: Rebecca August, Marion Bell, Zalman Deanin, Gussie Denenberg, Nellie Dick, Sam Dreen, Morris Gamberg, Emma Cohen Gilbert, Jeanne Levey, Harry Melman, Shaindel Ostroff, and Boris Yelensky.

Others who have aided me in different phases of my work, including the furnishing of information and the reading of the manuscript, are Irving Abrams, Sally Axelrod, Roger Baldwin, Fedora de Cleyre Benish, Morris Beresin, Eva Brandes, Emanuel V. Conason, Franklin de Cleyre, Hertha de Cleyre, Lincoln de Cleyre, Sonya Deanin, Richard Drinnon, Beatrice Schumm Fetz, Franz Fleigler, Charles Hamilton, Jack Frager, Millie Desser Grobstein, Anatole Freeman Ishill, Sophia Janoff (Yanovsky), Sonia Edelstadt Keene, Crystal Ishill Mendelsohn, Vladimiro Muñoz, Oriole Tucker Riché, Fermin Rocker, Ma Schmu, Ray Miller Shedlovsky, Clara and Sidney Solomon, Ahrne Thorne, and George Woodcock.

My exploration of the relevant archives was facilitated by a grant from the Research Foundation of the City University of New York and by a National Endowment for the Humanities Senior Fellowship for the academic year 1972-1973. The responsibility for this volume, however, is entirely my own.

New York   P. H. A.
June 1977

An American Anarchist

Introduction

"Nature has the habit of now and then producing a type of human being far in advance of the times; an ideal for us to emulate; a being devoid of sham, uncompromising, and to whom the truth is sacred; a being whose selfishness is so large that it takes in the human race and treats self only as one of the great mass; a being keen to sense all forms of wrong, and powerful in denunciation of it; one who can reach in the future and draw it nearer. Such a being was Voltairine de Cleyre."[1] Jay Fox's eulogy succeeds in evoking both the unique place of Voltairine de Cleyre in the history of American anarchism and the respect which she commanded among her comrades. Rudolf Rocker, who met her in London in 1903 and visited her grave in Chicago a decade later, considered her "one of the most wonderful women that America has given the world."[2] Max Nettlau, the foremost historian of the anarchist movement, described her as "the pearl of Anarchy," outshining her contemporaries in "libertarian feeling and artistic beauty."[3] Marcus Graham, editor of the journal *Man!*, called her "the most thoughtful woman anarchist of this century," while Leonard D. Abbott ranked her, along with Emma Goldman and Louise Michel, as "one of the three great anarchist women of modern times."[4] To Emma Goldman herself, in spite of much bitterness and friction

[1] Jax Fox, "Voltairine de Cleyre," *The Agitator*, July 15, 1912.

[2] Rudolf Rocker, *Johann Most: das Leben eines Rebellen*, Berlin, 1924, p. 363. Cf. Rocker's *Pioneers of American Freedom*, Los Angeles, 1949, p. 143, where he calls her "one of the most gifted women which America has produced."

[3] Max Nettlau, "En recuerdo de Voltairine de Cleyre, anarquista americana (1866-1912)," *La Protesta*, supplement, March 31, 1928; Nettlau, *La anarquía a través de los tiempos*, Barcelona, n.d. [1936?], p. 244.

[4] *Man!*, May 1935; *The American Freeman*, July 1949.

between them, Voltairine de Cleyre was "the poet-rebel, the liberty-loving artist, the greatest woman Anarchist of America."[5]

And yet, of all the major American anarchists, Voltairine de Cleyre has received the least serious attention from historians and literary scholars. Even the most elementary facts of her life are unknown to all but a handful of specialists, who themselves have perpetuated the errors and myths of previous generations.[6] Surprisingly, Voltairine de Cleyre is not so much as mentioned, let alone accorded the space she deserves, in the widely read histories of anarchism by George Woodcock, James Joll, and Daniel Guérin,[7] while the most authoritative accounts of her career (produced by Max Nettlau) remain buried in an Argentinian anarchist journal of 1928 and in an unpublished volume of Nettlau's German-language history of anarchism.[8] Nor is she represented in any of the anthologies of anarchist or feminist writings that have appeared in recent years, although her essay on "Anarchism and American Traditions," perhaps her best-known work, has been reprinted in two documentary collections of American radical thought.[9]

The reasons for this neglect are not far to seek. The most important, perhaps, are the brevity of her life

[5] Emma Goldman, *Voltairine de Cleyre*, Berkeley Heights, N.J., 1932, p. 41.

[6] Derived, for the most part, from Emma Goldman's *Voltairine de Cleyre* and Hippolyte Havel's Introduction to *Selected Works of Voltairine de Cleyre*, New York, 1914.

[7] George Woodcock, *Anarchism*, Cleveland and New York, 1962; James Joll, *The Anarchists*, London, 1964; Daniel Guérin, *Anarchism*, New York, 1970.

[8] *La Protesta*, supplement, March 31 and April 16, 1928; Volume 7 of his history of anarchism, manuscript, International Institute of Social History, pp. 53-71.

[9] Henry J. Silverman, ed., *American Radical Thought*, Lexington, Mass., 1970; Laurence Veysey, ed., *Law and Resistance*, New York, 1970.

and the difficulty of finding relevant source materials. Voltairine de Cleyre was of the same generation as Emma Goldman, Alexander Berkman, and a number of other prominent American anarchists. But she died in 1912 at the age of 45. Thus she did not live to see the First World War, the Russian Revolution, and the Spanish Civil War, which marked the high-points of anarchist activity during the twentieth century. Goldman and Berkman outlived her by a whole generation, twenty-eight and twenty-four years respectively. Her own mother survived her by fifteen years, her elder sister Adelaide by thirty-three. Because of her untimely death, ending her career abruptly in mid-course, there are few people now alive who so much as attended her lectures or met her even casually at anarchist meetings, let alone knew her on an intimate basis. And the passing of her only child in 1974 removed the last direct link; her grandchildren were all born after her death and thus have no recollection of her.

Furthermore, Voltairine de Cleyre was seldom in the public limelight during her short life. In contrast to Emma Goldman, she shrank from notoriety. Her withdrawn, retiring nature kept her out of the headlines except for a few brief periods, as in 1902, when she was wounded by an assassin, and in 1908, when she was involved in a free-speech disturbance in Philadelphia. Unlike Emma Goldman or Alexander Berkman, moreover, or Lucy Parsons or Johann Most, she was never imprisoned, although she was once arrested and brought to trial but acquitted. Though well known among the anarchists in the United States, she played no role in the international movement comparable to that of Most or Goldman or Berkman. She traveled only twice to Europe (in 1897 and 1903), and her writings, though translated into several languages, never became as widely known as the works of these other figures.

Had she been granted the financial means, the

physical constitution, and the necessary leisure for sustained writing and speaking, Voltairine de Cleyre might have emerged in the forefront of both the anarchist and feminist movements. As it was, however, she was compelled to work long hours to earn a meager living, with the result that she remained largely in the background and out of the public consciousness, gaining sudden but fleeting prominence on a few dramatic occasions. She was a brief comet in the anarchist firmament, blazing out quickly and soon forgotten by all but a small circle of comrades whose love and devotion persisted long after her death.

Today, however, even among the older generation of anarchists, Voltairine de Cleyre remains little more than a memory. But her memory possesses the glow of legend and, for vague and uncertain reasons, still arouses awe and respect. She is not rated among the major theorists or practitioners of the anarchist creed, such as Godwin or Proudhon, Stirner or Tucker, Bakunin or Kropotkin, Malatesta or Reclus. Yet she is a distinguished minor figure, a strong and unusual personality among the many interesting men and women thrown up by the anarchist movement around the turn of the century. She produced a number of essays which have enriched the literature of anarchism; and, though American born and rooted primarily in native traditions, she became, like Rudolf Rocker in London, the apostle of anarchism to the Jewish immigrants of the Philadelphia ghetto, learning to read and to some extent to speak and write the Yiddish language, in addition to her knowledge of German and proficiency in French which she acquired from her father and from the Catholic convent where she was educated.

It is not difficult, then, to understand the fascination, verging at times on reverence, that she inspired among her contemporaries, and continues to inspire among the dwindling band of survivors of the classical age of anarchism which preceded the First World War.

To Abraham Frumkin, a prominent Jewish anarchist who first heard her speak in London in 1897, her name itself had a beautiful, exotic sound that somehow fit her character and appearance.[10] But it was her writings that won her lasting acclaim among her comrades. An inspired essayist and poet, she possessed a greater literary talent than any other American anarchist. She was at pains to write well; and she put into what she wrote a voice, an era, a state of mind that nobody else has conveyed. She was, in fact, one of the most powerful and distinctive writers in the entire anarchist movement, with an individuality of mind and expression that only the very gifted possess. Her prose, distinguished, in Emma Goldman's words, by an "extreme clarity of thought and originality of expression," reflects the working of a first-rate intellect and a strong creative impulse. Leonard Abbott, associate editor of *Current Literature*, called her "a gifted and distinguished writer" whose arresting images and phrases "live vividly in my mind after forty years."[11]

She was also a voluminous writer, publishing hundreds of poems, essays, stories, and sketches, mainly on themes of social oppression, but also on literature, education, and women's liberation. Her note is distinctively American, yet she had a more universal appeal, and her prose has been translated into several languages, including French, Italian, Spanish, Russian, Chinese, German, and Yiddish. She herself was an accomplished translator, rendering into English Jean Grave's *Moribund Society and Anarchy* and Francisco Ferrer's *The Modern School*. She also produced an unfinished translation of Louise Michel's autobiography, the manuscript of which has been lost; and her translations from the Yiddish of Libin and

[10] Abraham Frumkin, *In friling fun yidishn sotsializm*, New York, 1940, p. 224.

[11] Goldman, *Voltairine de Cleyre*, pp. 39-40; *The American Freeman*, July 1949.

Peretz appeared in the early issues of Emma Goldman's *Mother Earth*.

Owing to her unfortunate personal and financial circumstances and to chronic ill health, Voltairine de Cleyre's literary potentialities were never completely fulfilled. She never published a full-length book, something she always regretted. A novel on social themes, written in collaboration with Dyer D. Lum, remained unprinted during her lifetime, and the manuscript has not survived. Nor did her shorter works reach a large audience outside the anarchist and free thought movements. A selection of her writings, edited by Alexander Berkman, was brought out by the Mother Earth Publishing Association in 1914, two years after her death, but many of her best poems and essays remain buried in obscure and hard-to-find periodicals of the late nineteenth and early twentieth century, while most of her manuscripts and letters—she was a careful and prolific correspondent—have been lost.

To a large extent, it is true, the power of her pen derived from her personal suffering and from her sympathy with the suffering of others. Yet if she had enjoyed greater physical comfort and peace of mind, she might have achieved a reputation beyond the circles of freethinkers and libertarians in which she revolved. Her failure in this regard was one of the greatest disappointments of her life. "Had she followed the line of least resistance, and forgotten her principles, she would have been famous," wrote her Scottish friend, Will Duff. "Instead she spent her tortured life in the service of an obscure cause—lecturing, teaching, and writing for Anarchist papers."[12]

To the modern reader her writing may seem at times too flowery, displaying a weakness for rhetorical flights. In this respect, it resembles the essays of the

12 William Duff, "Voltairine de Cleyre," *The Herald of Revolt*, September 1913.

French anarchist Elisée Reclus and of other romantic revolutionaries of the Victorian and Edwardian period. Yet much of what she wrote retains its vitality and originality. Her prose seems superior to the work even of Alexander Berkman, Emma Goldman, and Benjamin Tucker, who figure among the most talented anarchist writers in English, possessing a lyrical quality that the other three lacked. Nor, so far as I am aware, did any of them publish a line of poetry or fiction, of which Voltairine de Cleyre's output was prodigious. She wrote for both Tucker's *Liberty* and Goldman and Berkman's *Mother Earth*. Emma cherished her stories for their stylistic beauty and descriptive power, singling out "The Chain Gang" (which appeared in *Mother Earth* in October 1907) as a literary gem. Berkman shared this opinion. "I consider Voltairine de Cleyre one of the best short story writers in America," he wrote to Upton Sinclair, "of high idealism and clear social view. A proletarian writer."[13]

For all their elegance, however, her writings could become emotional and occasionally maudlin. They were always intensely and sometimes passionately felt, sounding a mournful note, a note of deep and overwhelming sadness. "The world is as full of weeping as the heavens are full of stars" is a not uncharacteristic line from her poems.[14] Leonard Abbott remarked: "Her voice has a vibrant and somber quality that, so far as I know, is unique in literature. Crimson as blood, black as hate, are some of her lyric utterances. Night birds flap their wings, 'the whipped sky shivers,' and the wind roars from the depths of the sea, in the ghostly visions she evokes." Her best poems, as Abbott noted, were poems of vengeance. "They are crimson and

[13] Alexander Berkman to Upton Sinclair, July 27, 1925, Berkman Archive, International Institute of Social History.

[14] Voltairine de Cleyre, "A Song in the Night," *The Herald of Revolt*, September 1913.

black; they quiver with hatred."[15] To Emma Goldman
these morbid preoccupations constituted a serious
drawback: "She saw life mostly in greys and blacks,
and painted it accordingly. It was this which prevented
Voltairine from being one of the greatest writers of her
time."[16]

Voltairine de Cleyre's writings reflected not only the
miseries of humanity at large but also her profound
personal unhappiness, the tragedy of her own existence. Her life was so littered with catastrophes and
misfortunes that Will Duff described it as "a long-
drawn-out martyrdom."[17] She was a troubled and a
troubling spirit, the woes of the world weighing heavily
upon her. On this point all her acquaintances were
unanimous. "A great sadness, a knowledge that there
is a universal pain, filled her heart," wrote Hippolyte
Havel in the Introduction to the *Selected Works*. "I feel
in her a tragic and tortured spirit," said Leonard Abbott, "one of the most tragic figures that I have ever
known."[18] Born in poverty in Michigan, she lived in
poverty in Philadelphia and died in poverty in Chicago
after weeks of agonizing pain. She suffered from
chronic physical illness and moral torment. Her life,
moreover, was jarred by a series of emotional disloca-
tions which might have destroyed a weaker nature.
Her lover and mentor, Dyer D. Lum, committed
suicide; and she herself had frequent suicidal impulses
and tried to take her own life more than once. In 1902,
when she was thirty-six, she was the victim of an assassin's bullets which nearly killed her and, by aggravat-

[15] Leonard D. Abbott, "A Priestess of Pity and Vengeance,"
The International, August 1912; Abbott, "Voltairine de Cleyre's
Posthumous Book," *Mother Earth*, October 1914.

[16] Goldman, *Voltairine de Cleyre*, p. 39.

[17] *The Herald of Revolt*, September 1913. Cf. Alden Freeman
and Harry Kelly in *Mother Earth*, July 1909 and July 1912.

[18] *The International*, August 1912; *The American Freeman*,
July 1949.

ing her already weak physical condition, left her in constant pain and shortened the remaining span of her life.

On top of all this, Voltairine de Cleyre wore herself out in the day-to-day struggle for existence and in her unremitting labors for her cause. Her earnings were insufficient to keep her in even moderate comfort; and as the years wore on and the effects of her illness, poverty, and accumulating misfortunes took their toll, she became increasingly introverted, shrinking from people and conversation. Her natural disposition toward privacy, reinforced by her physical pain, made her, in Emma Goldman's words, "taciturn and extremely uncommunicative." "I never feel at home anywhere," Voltairine wrote. "I feel like a lost or wandering creature that has no place, and cannot find anything to be at home with."[19]

There was very little joy in her life, especially in these later years. Not that she was incapable of happiness. In her youth during the 1880s and 1890s, her letters often sparkled with gaiety, and she was in general more animated and cheerful than she is sometimes depicted. Emma Goldman, in particular, exaggerates the gloomy side of her character and consequently leaves a distorted picture. Yet humor was not one of her notable attributes. For her life was too touched by sadness, at times by outright calamity, to allow more than temporary relief from her melancholy.

Although an atheist and freethinker with a "logical, analytical mind,"[20] Voltairine de Cleyre possessed a deeply religious nature. In spite of her pragmatic approach to anarchist theory and practice, she remained at bottom a zealot of sectarian temperament, ascetic, self-sacrificing, even puritan, akin to the religious heretics of the past. Had she lived in the Middle Ages,

[19] Goldman, *Voltairine de Cleyre*, pp. 37-38.
[20] Joseph Kucera, "Voltairine de Cleyre (A Character Sketch)," *Why?*, August 1913.

she might have been a Cathar or a Waldensian or a Sister of the Free Spirit. Emma Goldman speaks of the "religious zeal which stamped everything she did. . . . Her whole nature was that of an ascetic. Her approach to life and ideals was that of the old-time saints who flagellated their bodies and tortured their souls for the glory of God."[21] Educated in a Catholic convent, she once considered becoming a nun; and, in a sense, this is in fact what she did. By living a life of religious-like austerity, she became a secular nun in the Order of Anarchy, consecrating herself to her ideal. "In the service of the poor and oppressed she found her life mission," wrote Hippolyte Havel. But it was Sadakichi Hartmann, the Eurasian writer and poet, who summed it up best: "Despite the wealth of her emotions, limitless sympathies, and love for nature, her whole life seemed to center upon the exaltation over, what she so aptly called, the dominant idea. Like an anchorite, she flayed her body to utter one more lucid and convincing argument in praise of direct action. She starved and endured, and worked indefatigably for the enlightenment of the masses. She was brave, far seeing, invincible, one of the staunchest, truest, nevertiring banner-bearers of Anarchism, the great cause that to so many means the solution of the most important problem of modern society, the problem of equal rights for all."[22]

In time, Voltairine de Cleyre acquired the status of a saint. Leonard Abbott, who presided over a memorial meeting after her death and called her "one of the strongest influences in my life,"[23] named his first daughter, who died in infancy, Voltairine. Other anarchists did the same. During her own lifetime, there was a Voltairine de Cleyre Blum at the Playhouse

[21] Goldman, *Voltairine de Cleyre*, pp. 25-29.
[22] Havel, Introduction to *Selected Works*, p. 14; Sadakichi Hartmann, "Voltairine de Cleyre," *Mother Earth*, April 1915.
[23] *The American Freeman*, July 1949.

School in Brooklyn, conducted by the pioneer libertarian educators, Alexis and Elizabeth Ferm. In after
years there was a Voltairine de Cleyre Bernstein in
Chicago and a Voltairine de Cleyre Winokour in Stelton, New Jersey, both of them children of anarchists.
The main thoroughfare at Stelton, the most important
anarchist colony in America, was called Voltairine de
Cleyre Street. (The library was named after Peter
Kropotkin and the colony itself after the Spanish
educator and martyr, Francisco Ferrer.)

On the eve of the First World War, Adolf Wolff, an
anarchist sculptor and poet at the Ferrer Center in
New York, included Voltairine de Cleyre among the
heroines for his daughter to emulate:

> May you be a Judith decapitating a Holofernes,
> A Joan of Arc leading a people to victory,
> A Louise Michel fighting on the barricades,
> A Voltairine de Cleyre singing songs of revolt,
> An Emma Goldman preaching the gospel of
> rebellion.[24]

The juxtaposition of Voltairine de Cleyre with Louise
Michel was particularly apt, for the parallels between
them, down to their French names and origins, are
striking. In her religious-like passion and asceticism,
her acute sensitivity to suffering, her pity for the unfortunate and exploited, her hatred for cruelty and oppression, Voltairine de Cleyre resembled Louise Michel
—whom she met in London in 1897—more than any
other figure in the anarchist movement. Both were
teachers and poets who were militantly devoted to their
ideal. Both were wounded in assassination attempts;
and both, returning good for evil, refused to press
charges against their assailants. Both, moreover, loved
plants and animals with deep feeling. Voltairine, as
Emma Goldman noted, "would give shelter to every

[24] Adolf Wolff, *Songs of Revolution, Songs of Life, Songs of
Love*, New York, 1914, p. 15.

stray cat and dog," something it would be hard to imagine Emma herself doing. As her friend George Brown remarked, "I have never known any one who had so much sympathy for dumb animals. In fact, she made the house a hospital for misused cats and dogs," and in keeping with her Tolstoyan precepts, she would not destroy life of any kind if she could avoid it, so that "when pests invaded her rooms she captured them and carried them out."[25] In view of these similarities, it is small wonder that she should have translated Louise Michel's autobiography; and it was fitting that Leonard Abbott should have called her "a priestess of pity and vengeance," a phrase originally applied to Louise Michel by the British editor and reformer, W. T. Stead.

Voltairine de Cleyre bore an equally striking resemblance to Mary Wollstonecraft, the inaugurator of the modern women's rights movement, about whom she often wrote and lectured. As with Louise Michel, both were poets and writers and pioneering feminists and libertarians. Intense, dedicated, troubled, they both led turbulent, tragic lives and suffered untimely deaths. Intelligent and high-strung, both lived as individualists in the face of stifling convention. And yet, for all their independence of spirit and strength of character, both were vulnerable in the extreme, passing through a series of unhappy love affairs which left them with permanent scars. Both traveled to Norway to seek escape and solace; both worked as teachers and as translators of French; and both called for educational as well as political and economic reform as a cure for society's ills.

Short as it was, Voltairine de Cleyre's life spanned the classical age of anarchism between the Commune of Paris and the First World War. She was a contemporary of Emma Goldman and Alexander Berkman—two and a half years older than Emma, four years older

[25] *Mother Earth*, July 1912; *The Agitator*, July 15, 1912.

than Sasha—and her interesting relationships with both will be treated in this book. Her radical career coincided with the rise of the American anarchist movement to its fullest flowering. She lived through, and was profoundly affected by, the Haymarket hangings of 1887, the Homestead strike of 1892, and the McKinley assassination of 1901, dying a decade later, on the eve of the great war, when anarchism had reached its zenith and stood on the threshold of decline.

Her life, at the same time, stretched from America's agrarian past into its industrial and urban present. Born just after the Civil War, she witnessed the passing of the western frontier, the development of corporate capitalism, the centralization and bureaucratization of government, the convulsive changes in population and social relations, and the rise of the United States to the position of a world power, which cast a shadow over the promise of its future. To Voltairine de Cleyre and her associates, the Gilded Age seemed fraudulent, hypocritical, and ruthlessly and coarsely materialistic. It was an era of gluttony and ostentation, of unbridled economic exploitation and unparalleled political corruption, from which men and women of conscience must recoil in indignation and disgust. Together with other articulate reformers, she was attracted by the self-sufficient, noncommercial aspects of American life, the dream of every man his own master and the lost Jeffersonian ideal of autonomous villages and towns, workshops and farms, which had fallen victim to omnivorous corporate industrialism and centralized political power.

In her speeches and writings she drew up a scathing indictment of the new America of big business and money values that, swelling to monstrous proportions, confronted the world at the turn of the century. She criticized the whole range of oppressive institutions, the whole character of the new America in the making,

including nearly every feature of American life that
has again come under attack in our own time, from
militarism and expansionism to racial and sexual exploitation and rapacious industrial development, in
short, the whole "modern empire that has grown up on
the ruins of our early freedom," as she put it in one of
her best-known essays.[26]

A study of Voltairine de Cleyre's life, then, is also a
study of American society and of the American anarchist movement during its heyday—its "blossom-time,"
as Max Nettlau called it—in the decades before the
world war. My main concern, however, is biographical:
to piece together the facts of her career, to analyze her
character, her ideas, her feelings, to explain the intense
fascination which she exerted on her companions, to
depict the life which throbbed behind her writings. I
must leave to others the task of providing a specialist's
analysis of her stories and poems, for which I, as an
historian, am inadequately equipped. I would hope,
however, that the historical and biographical material
presented herein will prove useful to the scholar who
will one day undertake an evaluation of her literary
legacy.

It is not easy to discover the concealed, often sub-
conscious motives, those hidden springs of action and
behavior, which few of us understand in ourselves,
much less in others. Voltairine de Cleyre was an extremely complicated individual of a type that does not
yield its secrets readily. Therefore, while not avoiding
a discussion of her underlying motives, I shall adhere
as closely as possible to the available sources and quote
extensively from her writings, both published and
unpublished. Although documentation is occasionally sketchy—for some episodes almost nonexistent—
enough has survived to permit a reasonably complete
account of the life of this fascinating woman who,

[26] Voltairine de Cleyre, "Anarchism and American Traditions," *Selected Works*, p. 131.

in Emma Goldman's words, "was born in some obscure town in the state of Michigan, and who lived in poverty all her life, but who by sheer force of will pulled herself out of a living grave, cleared her mind from the darkness of superstition—turned her face to the sun, perceived a great ideal and determinedly carried it to every corner of her native land. . . . The American soil sometimes does bring forth exquisite plants."[27]

[27] Goldman, *Voltairine de Cleyre*, pp. 40-41.

1. Childhood

Voltairine de Cleyre grew up in the American Middle West of flat farms and little towns. She was born, as her sister describes her, "a dainty, fragile girl child,"[1] in the village of Leslie, Michigan, a year after the Civil War ended. Her rebellious character, which manifested itself at an early age, had both native and European roots. On her mother's side, she was linked to the abolitionist movement of antebellum America; on her father's, to the artisan, socialist, and free thought traditions of early nineteenth-century France. From both parents, moreover, she inherited a strong will, a stubborn nature, and a keen intellect. Her sister writes: "Our mother was a remarkable woman. Father was a brilliant man. It is no wonder Voltai was a genius."[2]

Her father, Hector De Claire, came from Lille, in northern France, where he was born in 1836. Though brought up in the Catholic faith, as a boy he became "tinged with earlier French skepticism," and by the time he was twelve, during the Revolution of 1848, he was already, like his own father, a socialist, "which is probably the remote reason for my opposition to things as they are," Voltairine remarks, for "at bottom convictions are mostly temperamental."[3] At the age of eighteen, in 1854, Hector De Claire emigrated to the United States, and both he and a brother fought in the Civil War on the side of the North, for which they were rewarded with American citizenship.

In the years before the war, Hector De Claire worked as an itinerant tailor in the European artisan manner,

[1] Adelaide D. Thayer to Joseph Ishill, November 17, 1934, Ishill Collection, Harvard.
[2] Adelaide D. Thayer to Agnes Inglis, n.d. [1934], Labadie Collection.
[3] Voltairine de Cleyre, untitled autobiographical sketch, manuscript, Wess Papers, London.

tramping from town to town in central Michigan. On March 28, 1861, two weeks before Fort Sumter and the outbreak of hostilities, he married Harriet Elizabeth Billings, who had come to Kalamazoo in 1853 from Rochester, New York, where she was born, the youngest of eight children of Pliny and Alice Billings, on December 27, 1836. Of old New England Puritan stock, her father had been an abolitionist in the "Burned-Over District" of upper New York state, where William Lloyd Garrison had stumped for the antislavery cause, and he had helped with the escape of fugitive slaves passing through Rochester on the underground railroad on their way to Canada.[4]

Hector and Harriet De Claire had three daughters, all born in Leslie, some twenty miles south of Lansing. The first, Marion, arrived on May 26, 1862. Next came Adelaide, on March 10, 1864, then Voltairine, the youngest of the three, on November 17, 1866. As a liberal and freethinker, Hector De Claire was an admirer of Voltaire, which, Voltairine tells us, prompted his choice of her name, though "not without some protest on the part of his wife, an American woman of Puritan descent and inclined to rigidity in social views." After two girls, moreover, he had been hoping for a boy. Accordingly, as Adelaide puts it, "he coined a name to fit the occasion, and called the baby Voltairine."[5]

In May 1867, the De Claires received what Adelaide calls "the greatest shock and sorrow of their lives." Marion, just five years old, was accidentally drowned. Missing her from her play, her mother went to look for her and "found her little draggled body in the river under the bridge," a tragedy, says Adelaide, which

[4] Voltairine de Cleyre, "Direct Action," *Selected Works*, pp. 227-28. See also Agnes Inglis's notes on Voltairine de Cleyre, recorded after visiting her sister Adelaide in 1934, Labadie Collection.

[5] Voltairine de Cleyre, autobiographical sketch, Wess Papers.

"may have caused many of the psychological mishaps that came to our family."[6] In their grief the parents decided to move. Hector De Claire managed to scrape together enough money to buy a small frame house at 204 South Lansing Street in St. Johns, Michigan, some forty miles to the north in Clinton County, where Voltairine's mother was to live for sixty years, until her death at the age of ninety in 1927, and Adelaide until 1945 when she died at eighty-one.

When the family moved to St. Johns, Voltai (as she came to be called) was less than a year old. She was to have no recollections of a happy, secure childhood in old agrarian America. Nor was she to be among that first generation of college-trained American women, drawn from the middle and upper classes, who threw themselves into the reform movements of the Gilded and Progressive eras. On the contrary, she was raised in extreme and unrelieved poverty, and her formal education stopped in a Catholic convent in Canada when she was seventeen. Her birth itself, she thought, coming in "the bleak mid-November of a northern winter," had set the scene for a grim existence, embittered by the want of common necessities, which her parents, hard as they tried, were unable to provide. As she wrote in an early poem:

> Bright faced joy was not for me,
> Born among the snows and pines,
> Gray faced sorrow was to be
> Imaged in my mournful lines.[7]

To assist her husband, who scratched out a meager and difficult living at his tailor's craft, Harriet De Claire herself took in sewing, so that they "managed to feed us, sparingly, and clothe us and keep us in

---

[6] Adelaide D. Thayer to Joseph Ishill, November 17, 1934, Ishill Collection.

[7] Voltairine de Cleyre, "Love's Ghost" (Pittsburgh, 1889), *The Freethinkers' Magazine*, March 1892.

school," Addie recalls. But "we were among the *very poor*. There was no 'Welfare' in those days, and to be aided by any kind of charity was a disgrace not to be tho't of. So we were all underfed, and bodily weak. Poor father could not carry the burden of our support, and mother did what she could. So did I. But it was very up-hill work."[8] To their own grinding poverty Addie attributes much of her sister's future radicalism, not to mention "the deep sympathy and understanding that she had for poverty in others." In a similar vein, Voltairine herself speaks of her compassion for the impoverished and disinherited and of "the awful degradation of the workers, which from the time I was old enough to begin to think had borne heavily upon my heart."[9]

A measure of their poverty was that Voltai and Addie were unable to buy Christmas presents during these childhood years in St. Johns. "We wanted, as all children do, to give our parents and each other something," Addie recalls, "but spending money was an unknown quantity with us. So we had to *make* our own gifts." One year Voltai made her mother a little box with a padded cover with colored beads sewn on it and a little case for Addie's crochet-hook out of a scrap of cardboard. "Poor little kiddie!" wrote Addie, when she found these articles in the attic many years later. "I think she was about nine years old then."[10]

Added to their privation was a mounting friction between the parents, which stemmed, at least in part, from their economic difficulties. As the years wore on, Hector De Claire became an increasingly bitter man and, though not without affection for his daughters, a

[8] Adelaide D. Thayer to Joseph Ishill, November 17 and December 30, 1934, Ishill Collection.

[9] Voltairine de Cleyre, "The Eleventh of November, 1887," *Free Society*, November 24, 1901.

[10] Adelaide D. Thayer to Joseph Ishill, December 30, 1934, Ishill Collection.

rather stern and demanding father. "Father's life was
such a disappointment to himself," wrote Addie to
Joseph Ishill, an anarchist printer who was assembling
her sister's manuscripts. "And mother's also. Yet, in
his way he was kind to us." Addie, at the same time,
speaks of his "impulsive nature," while Voltairine's son
Harry calls him "a petty tyrant."[11] When Voltairine was
nearly thirty and living in Philadelphia, he could still
scold her for writing to him in pencil, which displeased
him as much then, he complained, as fifteen years
before "when I brushed you up over the same thing."[12]

Their mother, too, was often out of sorts. Although
she lived to be ninety, she suffered from a chronic sinus
inflammation, which Voltairine attributed to long
stretches of malnutrition and "fifty years of depriva-
tion." She was also ungenerous with her affections,
holding back her love and not allowing it to blossom.
In her poem "To My Mother," written in 1889, Voltairine alludes to this coolness:

> Some souls there are which never live their life;
> Some suns there are which never pierce their cloud;
> Some hearts there are which cup their perfume in,
> And yield no incense to the outer air.
> Cloud-shrouded, flower-cupped heart: such is thine
>   own:
> So dost thou live with all thy brightness hid;
> So dost thou dwell with all thy perfume close;
> Rich in thy treasured wealth, aye, rich indeed—
> And they are wrong who say thou "dost not feel."[13]

[11] Adelaide D. Thayer to Joseph Ishill, February 3, 1935,
Ishill Collection; Adelaide D. Thayer to Agnes Inglis, November
5, 1934; Harry de Cleyre to Agnes Inglis, October 12, 1947,
Labadie Collection.

[12] Hector De Claire to Voltairine de Cleyre, January 16, 1895,
Ishill Collection.

[13] Voltairine de Cleyre to Harriet De Claire, May 27, 1907,
Ishill Collection; Selected Works, p. 26.

Like most mothers of her time and background, Harriet De Claire sought to guide her daughters into the conventional channels of American life. Against Adelaide's wishes, she pressed her to become a schoolteacher ("I would rather have gone into a newspaper office, but she was opposed to it"). Not that the good-natured, even-tempered Addie wished to break away, like her rebellious sister, and lead the life of an emancipated woman. She remained conservative in her political and social views and, "much to Mother's dislike," became a Baptist. "I have been quite proud of the genius of my talented sister," she wrote to Joseph Ishill, "but I am glad to be one of the 'common people' myself. Mother could never see any use, or beauty in service of this kind. She never forgave me for marrying two poor men. But they were *real* men, and I was always proud that they selected me from the world of women."[14]

Addie, however, excused her mother's shortcomings. "Don't judge her too harshly," she wrote to Agnes Inglis, curator of the Labadie Collection, for she was the youngest of eight children and "so she naturally grew up very self-centered."[15] Voltairine was less forgiving, although she remained a devoted daughter all her life, wrote and visited her mother often, and, at great sacrifice, sent her regular sums of money from her meager earnings. "I couldn't fulfil your wishes for me," she told her mother in 1907, "which were probably that I would have entertained your own principles, married some minister or doctor, or been one of them myself, and have a home, children, and a warm room for you—I mean the idea that the parent gives to the

[14] Adelaide D. Thayer to Joseph Ishill, February 3, 1935, Ishill Collection. Addie's first husband, Franklin Berry, died in 1902, her second, Judd Thayer, in 1918.

[15] Adelaide D. Thayer to Agnes Inglis, November 5, 1934, Labadie Collection.

child in youth and the youth returns to the parent in age. All that is utterly foreign to me. I have wanted even less of life than you, for myself. I have cared neither for a home nor any of its addenda. But I have wanted a whole lot of other things, and I've got some of them. I have wanted to travel and see the whole world; I've seen some. I've wanted to print the force of my will—not over-rating it—on the movement towards human liberty. And I have done that, to a certain extent. I have failed in one thing, and that was to hold a place in literature. And I think I have failed partly because I haven't cheek and persistence enough, and mostly because I've always *had* to do other things. But altogether I think I've had more satisfaction in my forty years than you in your seventy."[16]

Voltairine de Cleyre grew up to be an intelligent and pretty child, with long brown hair, blue eyes, and interesting, unusual features. She had a passionate love for nature and animals. But, already displaying the qualities that were to trouble her personal relations in later life, she was headstrong and emotional. She was "a very wayward little girl," says Addie, "often very rude to those who loved her best." Her eyes could be warm or as "cold as ice." When only four, her "indignation was boundless" when she was refused admission to the primary school in St. Johns because she was under age. She had already taught herself to read, says Addie, "and could read a newspaper at four! I have never known a child who could do that." Admitted the following year, she was "a bright pupil" and attended the school till the age of twelve. "She was very good friends with all her teachers; but especially a Mrs.

[16] Voltairine de Cleyre to Harriet De Claire, May 27, 1907, Ishill Collection.

Helen Lamphere, who had more influence over her than any one else up to that time."[17]

At home, both Voltai and Addie were voracious readers. They consumed poetry and novels—Dickens, Scott, Wilkie Collins—"but very little trash," and discussed what they read with their mother. Literature, writes Addie, was "nearly all the comfort we had." Mrs. De Claire was herself fond of poetry, especially Byron, which she read to her daughters before putting them to bed. She was "a remarkably fine reader," says Addie. "The pleasantest memory of my childhood is of Mother reading to us in the evenings." Many years later, when Addie was visiting Voltairine in Philadelphia, she told her sister that her poetry had "the ring and rhythm of Byron," to which Voltairine replied, "Can you wonder at it?"[18]

Voltairine herself began to write at a very early age. "Her little hands were not very steady or expert in the use of a pen," Addie recalls, "and her desk was a board that she had fixed up in the branches of one of our maple trees," seating herself on an adjacent limb to write or draw. Sensitive and introspective, she had an overriding need for privacy, even as a child, and often took refuge in her tree, her personal retreat, where she could think and write without being disturbed. "Our mother was determined to cut that tree down; but I fought for its life and saved it."[19]

Rummaging through the attic in 1934, Addie dis-

[17] Adelaide D. Thayer to Joseph Ishill, November 6 and 17, 1934, Ishill Collection.

[18] Adelaide D. Thayer to Joseph Ishill, December 30, 1934, Ishill Collection. In Philadelphia, Voltairine had a copy of Byron's *Poetical Works* as well as Milton's *Paradise Lost*, the poems of Dante Gabriel Rossetti, and other works now in the possession of her granddaughter, Renée de Cleyre Buckwalter.

[19] Adelaide D. Thayer to Joseph Ishill, November 17, 1934, Ishill Collection. With this letter, Addie sent Ishill a photograph of the house and of the tree where Voltairine wrote.

covered what is Voltairine's first known poem, "My
Wish," written when she was about six years old "while
sitting at her little home made table up in our north
maple tree." It consists of three short stanzas, the first
and third of which Addie copied (the second was il-
legible) and sent to Joseph Ishill:

> I wish I was a little bird
> To live up in a tree
> Or a butterfly upon a flower
> Or maybe a honey bee.

> But more than all I wish I was
> A great big man like Pa!
> And wouldn't have to stand around
> But would have a chance to jaw!

In 1936 Addie found another poem, tucked away in an
old book of her mother's. This one, written when
Voltairine was eight or nine, was called "The School-
House Over the Way":

> Here's the path to the old brick school-house
> It carries me there to-day—
> So I think I'll take this rose bud,
> To sweeten and brighten the way.

> As the dew on the bud is heavy,
> And bowed down by its weight,
> I stoop down to pick it slowly
> And condescend to fate.

> As I stoop down to pick it slowly
> And I think of the dreary way
> And the long, long mess of trouble
> I'll have 'ere the close of the day.

> At last I have reached the school-house
> The gems on the bud are gone
> But as I touch it softly
> It seems more beautiful grown.

The studies at length are over
And the examples are all done
And then there is shouting and laughter
For we're all a-going home.

My beautiful bud has wilted
For as older it grew
The beautiful faded
And took a duller hue.

But methinks it has done its duty
That beautiful little bud
And I hope we shall all learn the lesson
The lesson of doing good.

Examining these lines, one finds little of "the vein of sadness" that Hippolyte Havel discovered in Voltairine de Cleyre's early poems, "the songs of a child of talent and great fantasy," as he describes them.[20] Yet they are remarkably good for a child of her age, as her sister was quick to point out. "And to think that neither Mother, nor Father nor I realized nor recognized Voltai's beautiful spirit nor soul," wrote Addie to Agnes Inglis, to whom she sent the second poem. "I want you to see it as I do—the spontaneous out-pouring of her practical nature and reaching for beauty of expression. I cried as I read it, and am crying now as I write, to think of all the wasted years of misunderstanding, when we were children, when our childish years should have been filled with beauty, as they could have been."[21]

But beauty failed to materialize. Indeed, matters became still worse as Hector De Claire found it increasingly difficult to get work in St. Johns, where many of the residents did their own sewing. During the early 1870s, therefore, he left home and went again on the

[20] Havel, Introduction to *Selected Works*, p. 7.
[21] Adelaide D. Thayer to Agnes Inglis, February 10, 1936, Labadie Collection.

tramp, as he had done before his marriage. After a while he settled down in Port Huron, a town with more than 13,000 inhabitants and a lively trade in lumber and fish. As far as one can tell, he never returned to his wife or to the house in St. Johns. He sent home money whenever he was able. But his absence, far from relieving the tensions within the De Claire household, only compounded the unhappiness of his daughters, who "suffered much shame and sorrow in that we were children of separated parents. All the bitter pain of it was ours."[22]

In the spring of 1879 Adelaide fell seriously ill, and Voltairine was sent to live with her father, who was still working as a tailor in Port Huron. I was "very sick," recalls Addie, and mother thought that "she could not do for both of us." Voltai was twelve years old and "had developed that wilfulness that comes to most girls at that age; and Mother had neither the taste nor the strength to cope with it. So Voltai was sent to Father."[23]

A restless child on the threshold of adolescence, Voltairine was bored and fidgety in Port Huron, and extremely homesick. She missed the house in St. Johns and the rural life to which she was accustomed. She missed her mother and sister, her maple tree and chickens, her pet birds "Petie" and "Sweetie." "I don't want you to write to Pa but I think Port Huron is a nasty hole," she wrote her mother in June 1879. "I want to come back to St. Johns. I am just as homesick as can be." On Sundays her father took her to the park to listen to the bands and on the ferry boats plying between Michigan and Ontario. But her homesickness

[22] Adelaide D. Thayer to Joseph Ishill, February 3, 1935, Ishill Collection.
[23] Adelaide D. Thayer to Joseph Ishill, November 17, 1934, Ishill Collection.

grew worse every day. "I don't like a city," she wrote. "They have such times with the privies. I want to come home."[24]

Nothing further is known of the more than a year that Voltairine de Cleyre spent in Port Huron. Whether she attended school there, whether she returned for visits to St. Johns, remains obscure. In September 1880, however, her father enrolled her in the Convent of Our Lady of Lake Huron at Sarnia, Ontario, directly across the river from Port Huron. Why should a liberal and freethinker have taken such a step? According to Hippolyte Havel, Hector De Claire had "recanted his libertarian ideas, returned to the fold of the church, and [become] obsessed with the idea that the highest vocation for a woman was the life of a nun."[25] Havel, however, is mistaken. For her father did not rejoin the church until several years later, when she had already graduated from the convent. "I never heard that Father wanted her to become a nun," wrote Addie, "and can hardly believe it."[26] Nor was his object to punish his difficult child, as Havel implies, although he did hope that she would "tone up" and shed some of the "impudence and impertinence, so very prominent in her." Besides, he worked twelve hours a day, notes Agnes Inglis, "and what was he to do with an emotional high strung girl?"[27]

The convent, wrote Hector De Claire to his wife, will "refine her, so she has manners and knows how to behave herself and cure her of laziness, a love of idleness, also love of trash such as Story Books and

[24] Voltairine de Cleyre to Harriet De Claire, June 5, 1879, Labadie Collection.

[25] Havel, Introduction to *Selected Works*, p. 8.

[26] Adelaide D. Thayer to Joseph Ishill, November 17, 1934, Ishill Collection.

[27] Agnes Inglis to John Nicholas Beffel, September 2, 1947, Labadie Collection. Cf. Agnes Inglis to Joseph Ishill, n.d. [1934], Labadie Collection; and Agnes Inglis to Leonard D. Abbott, March 7, 1943, Abbott Papers, New York.

papers," and it will "give her ideas of proprieties, of order, rule, regulation, time and industry, as I doubt not you know she needs." Apart from this, however, he recognized that his daughter was gifted and wanted her to have the best education consistent with his limited means. The convent seems to have been the best school in the vicinity, where she could "get instruction in a vast amount of work, such as makes up a young woman."[28] He labored long and hard to pay her tuition and board, which cost him a thousand dollars, a very large sum for a man in his circumstances to pay. Sending her there, says Addie, nearly "crippled him financially."[29]

Voltairine de Cleyre spent three years and four months at Sarnia, from September 1880 to December 1883. In later life she looked back on this period as the saddest and darkest of her life—as a term of "incarceration." It had "a lasting effect upon her spirit," Emma Goldman observed, killing "the mainspring of joy and gaiety in her."[30] That a girl of her age, a sensitive, emotional child, suddenly removed from her family and put in a convent, should be untroubled is hardly conceivable; and though the extent of her suffering was exaggerated in retrospect, though the convent was perhaps not as dismal as her memory painted it, being wrenched from her home, from her mother and sister, was a trauma from which she never fully recovered. For the rest of her life its effects remained with her, compounding the misfortunes that accumulated as the years progressed. She never com-

[28] Hector De Claire to Harriet De Claire, September 17, 1880, Ishill Collection.

[29] Harry de Cleyre to Joseph Ishill, October 15, 1934, Ishill Collection; Harry de Cleyre to Agnes Inglis, October 28, 1934, Labadie Collection; Adelaide D. Thayer to Joseph Ishill, February 3, 1935, Ishill Collection.

[30] Voltairine de Cleyre, autobiographical sketch, Wess Papers; Goldman, *Voltairine de Cleyre*, p. 28.

pletely understood how her father, for whom she had considerable affection, could have abandoned her to such a situation; nor could she forgive him for doing so.

After a few weeks at the convent she decided to run away. Escaping before breakfast, she crossed the river to Port Huron. From there, as she had no money, she began the long trek to St. Johns on foot. After covering seventeen miles, however, she realized that she would never make it all the way home, so she turned around and walked back to Port Huron and, going to the house of acquaintances, asked for something to eat. They sent for her father, who took her back to the convent.

By any standard the regimen at the convent was severe. The girls got up at 5:45 every morning, made their beds, then went downstairs to say prayers. Admitted as a Protestant (her mother was a Presbyterian), Voltairine was not compelled to recite them, and she was permitted access to the Bible, which, according to her son, "was denied to those of the Catholic faith." Yet she had to remain with the others "on our knees ½ an hour." Breakfast was at 7, dinner at 12, supper at 5, with classes from 9:30 to 11:30 and 1:30 to 4:30, conducted by the nine nuns of the convent, Carmelites of the Order of the Holy Names of Jesus and Mary. Sister Mary Médard, wrote Voltairine many years later, "was the only little sister who sympathetically kissed me when all the rest were frowning."[31]

The pupils at Sarnia were allowed to write home only once every two weeks. As Hector De Claire informed his wife, all letters, papers, and books were "strictly under the surveillance of the mother superior, so in writing to [Voltairine], govern yourself accordingly and do not abuse me nor the Nuns, nor the Town

[31] Harry de Cleyre to Joseph Ishill, October 28, 1934; Voltairine de Cleyre to Harriet De Claire, September 25, 1880; Voltairine de Cleyre to Mary Hansen, December 6, 1909, Ishill Collection.

or the British Government for if you do, she'll never
get the letters."[32] In this connection, Addie records an
incident which reveals a good deal both about the convent and about her sister: "Once I wrote to her, I suppose a silly letter as girls often write to each other.
I'm sure there was no harm in it—but the nuns kept it
from her, but in plain sight, until our Father should
come over from Port Huron, and tell them what to do
with it. I believe it was a week or more. You know in
those schools all the mail is read by the nuns first.
Well, when Father came he saw no harm in the letter and let her have it. Then she wore it in her belt
until it wore out!" Addie then vents her indignation:
"Oh that horrible, accursed convent! She was there
about three years I think, and came away a nervous
wreck. She was very self willed I suppose, and she was
unmercifully punished—and such inhuman punishment! She hardly dared mention these things; but told
me that at one time, for a week, she was made to go
out for 'recreation,' with the others, but they were forbidden to speak to her. Think of that, for an over-
sensitive, nervous child to endure!"[33]

As the weeks passed, however, Voltai's homesickness abated, if it did not dissipate completely. At first
she was "terribly disgusted and lonesome," wrote Hector De Claire to his wife on September 17, 1880, but
"this week she is all right, and after kicking against the
rules all last week is now beginning to laugh at the
antics she had cut up, and comes down peacefully."[34]
A few days later Voltairine was allowed to visit her
father in Port Huron. While there she took the opportunity to write to her mother "because I don't want the
sisters to read my letter." The convent, she now confided, was "a very nice place. I learn physiology,

[32] Hector De Claire to Harriet De Claire, September 17, 1880,
Ishill Collection.

[33] Adelaide D. Thayer to Joseph Ishill, November 17, 1934,
Ishill Collection.

[34] Ishill Collection.

Physical Geography, mythology, French, Music, writing and Manners. They wanted me to study Arithmetic but I wouldn't. To-morrow there is a confirmation and I am going to sing for the Bishop. Don't be scared for fear I shall be a Catholic for the nuns are ladies and force their religion on no one." Voltai still missed St. Johns, however, and sent her love to Addie "and to my maple tree and chickens. They sent me my birds but only Petie was alive. Poor little Sweetie was dead."[35]

After a difficult initial adjustment, Voltairine settled down to work. She began to excel in her studies—especially in language and music—and soon was at the head of her class. By October 24th, three weeks before her fourteenth birthday, she was writing to her mother in an almost happy frame of mind and in a style which already shows a literary gift well above the ordinary for a girl of her education and background: "The convent is a dear little home. It is a regular little mansion built in the Gothic style surrounded by grand old pines that are always singing sad soft music for us. It commands a fine view of the lake. The grounds in front are beautifully laid out. When you enter the gate you pass under to [sic] large trees and up a gravelled walk which divides into two, three times and the inner two are around a heart-shaped flower-bed. There are also flower-beds all down the sides of the path."[36]

For all its austerity, then, the convent had its compensations. It gave Voltairine a solid training in writing and music; she perfected her French and learned to play the piano, by which she afterwards supported herself. Hippolyte Havel is mistaken when he writes that during her years at Sarnia she had little communication with her parents. On the contrary, she saw a good deal of her father and wrote to her mother as often as the rules allowed. The surviving letters show her to

[35] Voltairine de Cleyre to Harriet De Claire, September 25, 1880, Ishill Collection.

[36] Ishill Collection. See also Voltairine de Cleyre to Adelaide D. Thayer, October 9, 1881, Labadie Collection.

have been in tolerably good spirits, and "certainly no
'despair,' " as Agnes Inglis notes.[37] And if she found the
convent cold and confining, there were a few sympathetic teachers, above all Sister Médard, who took an
interest in such a talented, unusual child; and she kept
in touch with them for many years after her graduation—with Sister Médard and one or two others until
the end of her life.

In some respects at least, Voltairine's aversion to
Catholicism diminished during her stay at the Sarnia
school. She was attracted by the aesthetic and ethical
side of the church—the caring for the poor and suffering, the ideal of brotherhood and love—and at one
point, says her son, even "considered becoming a nun
of the Carmelite order." She herself tells us that "by
early influences and education I should have been a
nun, and spent my life glorifying Authority in its most
concentrated form, as some of my schoolmates are doing at this hour within the mission houses of the Order
of the Holy Names of Jesus and Mary."[38] A poem composed during her years at the convent reveals the
strength of her religious preoccupations:

> There's a love supreme in the Great Hereafter,
>   The buds of Earth are bloom in Heaven,
> The smiles of the world are ripples of laughter
>   When back to its Aidenn the soul is given,
> And the tears of the world, though long in flowing,
>   Water the fields of the bye-and-bye;
> They fall as dews on the sweet grass growing,
>   When the fountains of sorrow and grief run dry.
> Though clouds hang over the furrows now sowing
>   There's a harvest sun-wreath in the After-sky.

[37] Agnes Inglis to Joseph Ishill, November 22, 1949, Ishill
Collection.

[38] Harry de Cleyre to Agnes Inglis, October 12, 1947, Labadie
Collection; Voltairine de Cleyre, "The Making of an Anarchist,"
The Independent, September 24, 1903; *Selected Works*, p. 155.

No love is wasted, no heart beats vainly,
  There's a vast perfection beyond the grave;
Up the bays of heaven the stars shine plainly—
  The stars lying dim on the brow of the wave.
And the lights of our loves, though they flicker and
      wane, they
  Shall shine all undimmed in the ether nave.
For the altars of God are lit with souls
  Fanned to flaming with love where the star-wind
      rolls.

But she was too self-willed and independent to be con-
fined by any religious order; and as she wrestled with
the questions of the existence of God and the divinity
of Jesus, the "old ancestral spirit of rebellion" reas-
serted itself. "I never dared God," she writes. "I always
tried to propitiate him with prayers and tears even
while I was doubting his existence; I suffered hell a
thousand times while I was wondering where it was
located."[39]

For a time the struggle continued, both within herself and against the convent authorities. "How I pity
myself now, when I remember it," she wrote in 1903,
twenty years after her graduation, "poor lonesome little soul, battling solitary in the murk of religious
superstition, unable to believe and yet in hourly fear
of damnation, hot, savage, and eternal, if I do not in-
stantly confess and profess! How well I recall the bitter
energy with which I repelled my teacher's enjoinder,
when I told her that I did not wish to apologize for an
adjudged fault, as I could not see that I had been
wrong, and would not *feel* my words. 'It is not necessary,' said she, 'that we should feel what we say, but
it is always necessary that we obey our superiors.' 'I will
not lie,' I answered hotly, and at the same time
trembled lest my disobedience had finally consigned
me to torment!"[40]

[39] *Selected Works*, pp. 10, 155, 289.   [40] *Ibid.*, pp. 155-56.

So firm was her will, as she clung to her father's secularism and to her own understanding of truth, that the sisters finally despaired of any attempt to win her over. "In the heart of Catholicism," she writes, "the child of fourteen became a freethinker, and frequent and bitter were the acts of rebellion and punishment engendered by the gradual growth of the notion of individual right as opposed to the right of inflexible rule. It was only after repeated insubordination and subsequent, partial submission, that she was finally allowed to go before the examiners and awarded the gold medal of the institution."[41]

But the convent had levied its toll. Five weeks before her graduation, worn out by the struggle and plagued by recurrent attacks of "catarrh" which she had inherited from her mother, Voltairine suffered a physical collapse. She was sent home for a rest, after being warned, according to Hippolyte Havel, "that she would find her every movement watched, and that everything she said would be reported to them. The result was that she started at every sound, her hands shaking and her face as pale as death."[42] When her respite was over, she returned to Sarnia to complete her studies. On December 20, 1883, she submitted her graduation essay on "The Fine Arts," a remarkable prose-poem written in her beautiful calligraphic script. The next day, December 21st, she was graduated with the gold medal of the convent, which she greatly prized and which she continued to wear for many years after her departure.[43]

For all the unhappiness it caused her, Voltairine's

[41] Voltairine de Cleyre, autobiographical sketch, Wess Papers.

[42] Havel, Introduction to *Selected Works*, p. 9.

[43] Her graduation essay is preserved in the Labadie Collection. The gold medal, now in the possession of her granddaughter, is inscribed, "Graduating Honors Conferred on Voltairine de Claire, December 21st, Convent of Our Lady of Lake Huron, Sarnia, Mother Apollonie, Sup." There are photographs of her in 1891 and 1897 with the medal around her neck.

experience in the convent did much to shape the strength of her character in later life. She had faced severity and hardship and had risen above them. She left the convent a doubter, if not yet an outright infidel, eager for ideas more congenial to her rebellious temperament. Her revulsion against religious dogma and the doctrine of absolute obedience, so deeply implanted by those years at Sarnia, were to evolve into a generalized hatred of authority and obscurantism in all their manifestations. "I struggled my way out at last," she recalls, "and was a freethinker when I left the institution, three years later, though I had never seen a book or heard a word to help me in my loneliness. It had been like the Valley of the Shadow of Death, and there are white scars on my soul yet, where Ignorance and Superstition burnt me with their hellfire in those stifling days. Am I blasphemous? It is their word, not mine. Beside that battle of my young days all others have been easy, for whatever was without, within my own Will was supreme. It has owed no allegiance, and never shall; it has moved steadily in one direction, the knowledge and assertion of its own liberty, with all the responsibility falling thereon. This, I am sure, is the ultimate reason for my acceptance of Anarchism. . . ."[44]

[44] *Selected Works*, p. 156.

2. The Making of an Anarchist

Voltairine de Cleyre was seventeen years old when she left Sarnia and returned to her home in St. Johns. What kind of work was she to do? For an inexperienced girl in rural Michigan, trained in no craft or profession, the choices were narrowly limited. Her education at the convent, she tells us, had left her "utterly unfitted for the practical, commercial world which rates young women by their capacities for counting change." Accordingly, life became "immediately a desperate struggle with Hunger," as it had been before she left for Port Huron in 1879.[1] To earn a living, she offered lessons in "music, French and fancy penmanship,"[2] thus beginning the career in private teaching by which she was to support herself for the rest of her life. Addie, at this time, was also a teacher, in the St. Johns public school, while their mother continued to take in sewing. As for Hector De Claire, he left Port Huron not long after Voltai's graduation, returned to the Catholic church, and moved from town to town plying his tailor's craft. In 1895 we find him in Flint, between Port Huron and Lansing. Drifting westward, he eventually wound up in Milwaukee, Wisconsin, where he died, at the Soldiers' Home in Woods, in 1906.

Toward the end of 1885, after nearly two years at St. Johns, Voltairine went to live for several months with an aunt in Greenville, Michigan, continuing to give lessons in music and handwriting. Her departure for Greenville opened a new period in her life. She was nineteen years old and, in a limited way at least, this was her first venture out into the world. Leaving her childhood behind her, along with the remains of her religious faith, she proclaimed herself a freethinker,

[1] Voltairine de Cleyre, autobiographical sketch, Wess Papers.
[2] Adelaide D. Thayer to Joseph Ishill, November 17, 1934, Ishill Collection.

dedicated not to God but to man. To celebrate the occasion, she wrote her first important poem, "The Burial of My Past Self," which concludes with the following lines:

> And now, Humanity, I turn to you;
>   I consecrate my service to the world!
> Perish the old love, welcome to the new—
>   Broad as the space-aisles where the stars are
>   whirled![3]

During the next few years, Voltai threw her energies into the free thought movement. She was in fact to remain a lifelong secularist and anti-Catholic, writing for free thought periodicals and lecturing before free thought organizations long after anarchism had displaced atheism as her primary ideological commitment. For between the anarchist and free thought movements there was a close and longstanding affinity. Both shared a common anti-authoritarian viewpoint and a common tradition of secularist radicalism stretching back to Thomas Paine and Robert Owen, heroes to atheists and anarchists alike. Nearly all anarchists were freethinkers; and many, like Voltairine de Cleyre, first came to anarchism through the free thought movement, in which they constituted a militant left wing within the local clubs as well as the regional and national federations. They were unyielding in their rejection of church as well as state—"my two *bêtes noires*," Bakunin had called them—for both religious and secular authority were repugnant to the libertarian spirit, and "Neither God Nor Master" has been an effective summation of the anarchist message.

In Voltairine's case, plunging into the free thought movement was part of her struggle to liberate herself from the shackles of religious tyranny. In this struggle, the goals of personal and social freedom became

[3] *Selected Works*, p. 17.

inextricably intertwined, so that, recoiling from the
discipline and obscurantism of the convent, she began
to identify her own emancipation with that of humanity as a whole. Her poems of this period, especially
"The Christian's Faith" and "The Freethinker's Plea,"
both written in 1887, show her wrestling free of the
lingering effects of the convent, completing the burial
of her "past self." At the same time, her idealism was
turning outward, from the cloister to society, from the
convent to the world.

Moving in 1886 to Grand Rapids, Michigan, Voltairine took a room at 54 Kent Street and began to
write for a small free thought weekly called *The Progressive Age*, of which she soon became the editor.
Here, over the name of "Fanny Fern," borrowed from
a popular writer of the period, she published her first
articles and stories. (Her pen names in later years included "Fanny Forrester" and "Flora Fox.") Meanwhile, as a token of her new identity, her real name
evolved by rapid stages from Voltairine De Claire to
Voltairine de Claire then finally (from 1887 or 1888)
Voltairine de Cleyre.[4]

Grand Rapids also became Voltairine's base for lecturing engagements. For small fees she addressed the
local free thought circuit in Grand Rapids, Kalamazoo,
and other Michigan towns and, in the spring of 1887,
recited a temperance poem "all over Montcalm
county."[5] Being a former pupil in a convent, she was
a particularly effective speaker, as she could talk from
firsthand experience, like the runaway slaves who addressed abolitionist gatherings before the Civil War.
"I know of what I speak," she told an audience in November 1887. "I spent four years in a convent, and I

[4] The rest of the family, except for her son Harry, continued
to spell it De Claire, though after Voltairine's death her mother
sometimes signed her name Harriet de Cleyre.

[5] Voltairine de Cleyre to Adelaide D. Thayer, January 16,
1888, Ishill Collection.

have seen the watchwords of their machinations. I have seen bright intellects, intellects which might have been brilliant stars in the galaxies of genius, loaded down with chains, made abject, prostrate nonentities. I have seen frank, generous dispositions made morose, sullen, and deceitful, and I have seen rose-leaf cheeks turn to a sickly pallour, and glad eyes lose their brightness, and elastic youth lose its vitality and go down to an early grave murdered—murdered by the church."[6]

For Voltairine de Cleyre's generation public lectures and recitals were an important cultural phenomenon, the equivalent of the radio, the motion picture, the television show of later years. The railroads provided convenient transportation for public speakers, and the growing cities and towns provided eager audiences. Hundreds, even thousands, might flock to a lecture hall, sometimes traveling long distances to hear a celebrated orator. And it was as a speaker that Voltairine first made her mark in the radical movement, though she was not of the flamboyant, histrionic school of orators who overwhelm their audiences with tirades of venom or irony and capture them by main force. She differed in this respect from, say, Emma Goldman or Johann Most, being closer to Peter Kropotkin, whose speeches, as Stepniak observed, produced "an immense impression; for when feeling is so intense it is communicative, and electrifies an audience."[7]

This was also Voltairine de Cleyre's effect on her listeners. She considered herself "more of a lecturer than an orator, and more of a writer than either," to quote her own rather modest description. "I am not an orator," she insisted, "and I have a good deal of contempt for extemporaneous speaking, as a rule. It's so disjointed and loaded with repetition. So I usually

[6] Voltairine de Cleyre, "Secular Education," *The Truth Seeker*, December 3, 1887.

[7] Stepniak [S. M. Kravchinsky], *Underground Russia*, London, 1883, p. 99.

write my stuff."[8] Having committed her speech to paper, she would read it to the audience, a method, complained one listener, that "invariably detracts from the personal power of the performer."[9] But this was a minority opinion. Steadily building her argument, she was an intense figure on the platform, "her pale face lit up with the inner fire of her ideal," noted Emma Goldman, who found her lectures always carefully prepared, brilliant in form and presentation, and "richly studded with original thought."[10] As Jay Fox similarly observed, "she had the power of holding one with her eloquence while she packed his mind full of ideas." And her words carried conviction. "The even delivery, the subdued enthusiasm of her voice, the abundance of information, thought and argument, and the logical sequence of the same made a deep impression on me," wrote Sadakichi Hartmann, who attended a lecture she gave on Mary Wollstonecraft at the Manhattan Liberal Club in 1894. Beyond this, her unusual manner and appearance heightened the overall impression. George Brown heard her speak in Chicago in 1887 or 1888: "She was then a young girl, queerly dressed and with two long thick plaits of hair hanging down her back. When on platform she wore a sort of Roman toga, and the effect was queer and unique."[11] Small wonder that, after one of her speeches in 1888, "a good kind old man came to me and made me promise to deliver his funeral oration."[12]

As her reputation increased, Voltairine went farther afield, into Ohio and Pennsylvania, making repeated tours on behalf of the American Secular Union, a na-

[8] Voltairine de Cleyre, autobiographical sketch, Wess Papers.
[9] Walter Starrett, untitled manuscript, Ishill Collection.
[10] Goldman, *Voltairine de Cleyre*, pp. 9, 32.
[11] *The Agitator*, July 15, 1912; *Mother Earth*, April 1915 and July 1912.
[12] Voltairine de Cleyre to Adelaide D. Thayer, February 7, 1888, Ishill Collection.

tionwide free thought organization. After speaking in Alliance, Ohio, in 1888, she was invited to deliver the annual Paine memorial lecture there the following year. By 1890 she had addressed rationalist groups as far west as Chicago and Topeka and as far east as Philadelphia and Boston. After each of these trips she would return to her room in Grand Rapids or to her aunt's house in Greenville (where she spent Christmas in 1887) or else would stay in St. Johns with her mother and sister, who were always happy to see her, although they frowned upon her radicalism and her unconventional life. "Her opinions and mine were very much out-of-step," noted Addie, "so we said little about them to each other."[13]

Nor would Voltai alter her behavior to suit her family's notions of propriety. "If I advocate new and strange ideas," she told her mother in December 1887, "it is because I think them *right*. They are no strangers to me; I have had the same thoughts for more than two years; but out of respect for your feelings never mentioned them until lately. That I did so now is because I think you *ought to know*."[14] In spite of their differences, however, Voltai was always glad to be home, though after the hubbub of Boston or the silent majesty of western Pennsylvania the Michigan prairie might seem a letdown. "No more blue, dim heights down which the cloud tears tremble and drip and fall in hard gleaming crystals," she wrote in March 1888 in her florid but beautiful prose of that period, "where the sobbings of the rocks are hushed in frozen music; where hill rises over hill in its mad, steep staircase to the stars, and the sun flashes down its cohorts of golden lancers through the jutting teeth, the cavernous hollows, the darting ravines, of the wild Alleghenies.

[13] Adelaide D. Thayer to Joseph Ishill, November 17, 1934, Ishill Collection.

[14] Voltairine de Cleyre to Harriet De Claire, December 18, 1887, Ishill Collection.

Here, in our broad, fair, level fields of southern Michigan, hemmed in by the sweet-toned thunder of our deep lakes alone, we lose the grandeur of the mountains. But one sublime peak which caps them all stands out as clear and bright to us as fair—the height of science, over whose majestic brow is bursting the glory of the new day, when all shall be truth seekers, when none shall walk blindfold, and knowledge be the savior of mankind."[15]

Young as she was, Voltairine had become a crusader for free thought worthy of her namesake, although her eighteenth-century rationalism was overlaid with a patina of nineteenth-century romanticism and utopianism. As a speaker she found herself in growing demand throughout the East and Middle West; and, apart from her work on *The Progressive Age*, she contributed numerous articles and poems to such leading secularist publications of the day as *The Boston Investigator*, *The Freethinkers' Magazine*, *The Truth Seeker*, and *Freethought*. Having buried her past self, she felt an intoxicating sense of freedom and was enjoying her new independence to the hilt. "I do see a lot of misery," she wrote her sister from Pittsburgh, where she addressed a free thought gathering in January 1888, "misery enough to make one's blood stand still in the veins. But there are many beautiful things too—many wonderful sweet things in this world."[16]

Not least among these were the young men whom she met, including "my latest—my Pittsburgh lover." But there was also the theater, the opera, the reception following her talk. "O say! I danced! I did, I did, I did. At the ball after the oration I danced waltzes, quadrilles, schottisches and oh!—'it makes me tired'!" On soberer occasions she visited the Carnegie Iron Works

[15] Voltairine de Cleyre, "Pennsylvania Conventions and Ohio Workers," *The Truth Seeker*, March 24, 1888.

[16] Voltairine de Cleyre to Adelaide D. Thayer, February 7, 1888, Ishill Collection.

and the Western Penitentiary, where the "clock-work regularity and oppressive stillness of the place" reminded her of the convent, although the inmates were some of "the finest looking men I have ever seen."[17] It was there, less than five years later, that Alexander Berkman would begin his fourteen-year imprisonment after shooting Henry Clay Frick.

In December 1887, a few weeks before her lecture in Pittsburgh, Voltairine de Cleyre took part in a Paine Memorial Convention at Linesville, "an out-of-the-way corner of the earth among the mountains and snowdrifts of Pennsylvania." She herself spoke on Paine in the afternoon, while in the evening she sat in the audience to hear Clarence Darrow, the rising midwestern lawyer, deliver an address on socialism, which she found as "unique and as pleasing as it was unexpected." Darrow's speech, in fact, came as a revelation: "It was my first introduction to any plan for bettering the condition of the working-classes which furnished some explanation of the course of economic development, and I ran to it as one who has been turning about in darkness runs to the light."[18]

A letter to her mother, written a few days after the convention, reveals the impact of Darrow's address. In withering terms Voltai denounces the "coal-kings" and "salt-owners" who monopolize the market, create unemployment, and mercilessly exploit their workers. "It is so strange to me that you are so afraid of anarchy and socialism," she declares. "I am neither one nor the other and the methods of the former are abhorrent to me. But why, why does the whole world point to anarchy as the great evil when (no later than two weeks ago) the Lehigh Valley Coal and Iron Syndicate

[17] *Ibid.; The Truth Seeker*, March 24, 1888.
[18] *Selected Works*, p. 157; *The Truth Seeker*, March 24, 1888.

(nice, law-abiding people) turned out their helpless
starving miners who had struck for a little better wages
than 75¢ and $1.00 a day, and (in violation of the
foreign contract labor law) have imported 3,500 Bel-
gians, to work their mines." The banks and oil compa-
nies—she is writing a month after the Haymarket hangings—"either buy out or starve out all competition" and,
together with the "land thieves," have done "an incal-
culable amount more of damage than Spies, Parsons,
Lingg, Engel, Fischer, Fielden, or Schwab ever thought
of."[19]

So deeply was Voltairine impressed by Darrow's
words that, before the year was out, she adopted the
socialist label. More than that, her essays and speeches
began to contain a social message, beyond the question
of individual conscience and religious liberty which
had preoccupied her since the convent. Free thought,
while still important, was not enough, and "her natural
tendencies drew her into the world movement towards
the emancipation of the disinherited classes."[20] From a
rejection of the church she was advancing toward a
rejection of all domination, secular as well as religious,
economic as well as political. In due course, the struggle between skepticism and faith became submerged
in the larger struggle between freedom and authority
as a whole.

Socialism, however, was but a step, a temporary
way-station, in her drift toward full-fledged anarchism,
the belief that all forms of government should be
abolished. Only six weeks after the Linesville convention she found herself hard pressed to defend her new
faith before a debating society in Pittsburgh, where a
Russian Jew named Mozersky, an anarchist "and a bit
of a Socrates," questioned her into "all kinds of holes,
from which I extricated myself most awkwardly, only

[19] Voltairine de Cleyre to Harriet De Claire, December 18,
1887, Ishill Collection.
[20] Voltairine de Cleyre, autobiographical sketch, Wess Papers.

to flounder into others he had smilingly dug while I was getting out of the first ones." It was her first encounter with the Russian Jewish anarchists among whom she was to live for more than two decades, and it stimulated her to undertake an intensive study of the sources of anarchist theory and practice. Most important among these was Benjamin Tucker's *Liberty*, the leading anarchist journal of the day, which convinced her, in the motto of Proudhon on its masthead, that "Liberty is not the Daughter but the Mother of Order." As she mastered the doctrines of anarchism, she found herself irresistibly drawn to them; and though she was quick to shed the individualistic economic gospel advocated by Tucker's circle, anarchism itself remained with her and "broadened, deepened, and intensified itself with years."[21]

Under the impact of Tucker's journal, she cast the socialist label aside. As Emma Goldman explains, her "inherent love of liberty could not make peace with State-ridden notions of Socialism."[22] But the chief factor in her conversion to anarchism was the execution on November 11, 1887, of Albert Parsons, August Spies, George Engel, and Adolph Fischer. The Haymarket tragedy, she tells us, marked "the specific occasion which ripened tendencies to definition."[23]

The Haymarket affair, one of the most famous incidents in the history of the anarchist movement, began on May 3, 1886, when the Chicago police fired into a crowd of strikers at the McCormick Reaper Works, killing and wounding several men. The following evening, the anarchists held a protest meeting near Haymarket Square. Toward the end of the meeting, which had proceeded without incident, rain began to fall and the crowd started to disperse. The last speaker, Samuel Fielden, was concluding his address when a contingent

[21] *Selected Works*, p. 157.
[22] Goldman, *Voltairine de Cleyre*, p. 16.
[23] *Selected Works*, p. 156.

of police marched in and ordered the meeting to be closed. Fielden objected that the gathering was peaceful and that he was just finishing up. The police captain insisted. At that moment a bomb was thrown. One policeman was killed and nearly seventy were injured, of whom six later died. The police opened fire on the crowd, killing at least four workers and wounding many more.

Who threw the bomb has never been determined. What is certain, however, is that the eight men who were brought to trial, Albert Parsons, August Spies, George Engel, Adolph Fischer, Louis Lingg, Samuel Fielden, Oscar Neebe, and Michael Schwab, were not responsible. Six of them, in fact, were not even present when the explosion occurred, and the other two were demonstrably innocent of throwing the bomb. Moreover, no evidence was produced to connect the defendants with the bombthrower. Yet all eight were found guilty, the verdict being the product of perjured testimony, a packed jury, a biased judge, and public hysteria. In spite of petitions for clemency and appeals to higher courts, five of the defendants were condemned to death and the others to long terms of imprisonment. On November 10, 1887, Lingg committed suicide in his cell with a cigar-shaped explosive smuggled to him by a friend. The following day, November 11th, Parsons, Spies, Engel, and Fischer were hanged.[24]

The five Chicago anarchists became martyrs. Their pictures were displayed at anarchist meetings; every year, November 11th was observed in their honor; and the last words of Parsons and Spies—"Let the voice of the people be heard!" and "There will come a time when our silence will be more powerful than the voices you strangle today!"—were often quoted in anarchist speeches and writings. Six years later, in 1893, the

[24] Henry David's *The History of the Haymarket Affair*, New York, 1936, remains the most authoritative account.

imprisoned men, Fielden, Neebe, and Schwab, were pardoned by Governor John P. Altgeld, who criticized the judge for conducting the trial "with malicious ferocity" and found that the evidence had not shown that any of the eight anarchists were involved in the bombing.

The Haymarket affair–the unfairness of the trial, the savagery of the sentences, the character and bearing of the defendants–fired the imagination of many young idealists and won more than a few to the anarchist cause. Among them was Voltairine de Cleyre. As with Emma Goldman, Alexander Berkman, and many others, the event remained permanently embedded in her consciousness. Haymarket runs like a scarlet thread through her writings, both published and unpublished. She dedicated a poem to Governor Altgeld when he pardoned Fielden, Neebe, and Schwab, and yet another after his death in 1902. She wrote a poem to Matthew M. Trumbull, a distinguished Chicago attorney who had defended the anarchists in two incisive pamphlets and appealed to the state for clemency. For the epigraph of her poem "The Hurricane" she quoted the prophecy of Spies: "We are the birds of the coming storm." Nearly every year she took part in memorial meetings to her comrades, delivering moving and deeply felt orations, the most powerful of her career.

At the time of the explosion in May 1886, Voltai was nineteen years old. She was living in St. Johns and had not yet embarked on her radical course. Glimpsing the newspaper headlines–"Anarchists Throw Bomb in Crowd in the Haymarket in Chicago"–she joined the cry for vengeance. "They ought to be hanged!" she declared, words over which she agonized for the rest of her life. "For that ignorant, outrageous, blood-thirsty sentence I shall never forgive myself," she confessed on the fourteenth anniversary of the executions, "though I know the dead men would have forgiven me, though I know those who love them forgive me.

But my own voice, as it sounded that night, will sound
so in my ears till I die—a bitter reproach and shame."[25]

No sooner had the pronouncement escaped from her
lips than she regretted it. When Addie responded in
agreement, "Voltai didn't like it; she didn't like the way
my words rang in her ears."[26] As the case unfolded, she
followed it with feverish excitement. At length she
came to the conclusion that "the accusation was false,
the trial a farce, that there was no warrant either in
justice or in law for their conviction; and that the hanging, if hanging there should be, would be the act of a
society composed of people who had said what I said on
the first night, and who had kept their eyes and ears
fast shut ever since, determined to see nothing but rage
and vengeance."[27]

Around this time, moreover, her lectures took her to
Chicago and brought her into contact with friends of
the condemned men, who reinforced her conclusions
regarding "the infamy of the trial and the judgment."
Hoping until the end for mercy, she felt a crushing disappointment, an overwhelming sorrow, when the men
were finally hanged. Her early compassion for Jesus—
"cursed for all his love; thanked with the cross"[28]—was
transferred to her martyred comrades, for whom the
gallows had replaced the crucifix as the instrument and
symbol of repression. Embracing their ideal as her
own, she became an anarchist for life; and in an effort of expiation she set out to investigate their beliefs,
to learn all she could of what they had preached. "Little by little I came to know that these were men who
had a clearer vision of human right than most of their
fellows; and who, being moved by deep social sympathies, wished to share their vision with their fellows,

[25] *Free Society*, November 24, 1901; *Selected Works*, pp. 164-
65.

[26] Frumkin, *In friling fun yidishn sotsializm*, p. 242.

[27] *Selected Works*, pp. 165-66.

[28] Voltairine de Cleyre, autobiographical sketch, Wess Papers.

and so proclaimed it in the market place," she writes. "It was the message of these men (and their death swept that message far out into ears that would never have heard their living voices), that all [piecemeal reforms] are folly. That not in demanding little, not in striking for an hour less, not in mountain labor to bring forth mice, can any lasting alleviation come; but in demanding much—all—in a bold self-assertion of the worker to toil any hours he finds sufficient, not that another finds for him—here is where the way out lies."[29]

So it was that Voltairine de Cleyre embraced the anarchist creed and was launched on her new life as one of its most devoted apostles. The spirit of revenge, she declares, "accomplished its brutal act." But had it lifted its eyes from its work, "it might have seen in the background of the scaffold that bleak November morning the dawn-light of Anarchy whiten across the world."[30]

The year 1888 marked a major turning point in Voltairine de Cleyre's life. Not only was it the year in which she became an anarchist and wrote her first anarchist essays. It was also the year in which, while on the lecture circuit, she met the three men who played the most critical roles in her life: T. Hamilton Garside, with whom she fell passionately in love; James B. Elliott, by whom she had her only child; and Dyer D. Lum, with whom her relationship, being intellectual and moral as well as physical, transcended those with Garside and Elliott, yet ended, like the others, in tragedy.

Of Garside we know very little. A former evangelical preacher, he was a fluent, magnetic speaker who had come to the United States from Scotland, converted to

[29] *Selected Works*, pp. 166-67.
[30] *Ibid.*, p. 171.

socialism, and lectured for the Knights of Labor and
other working-class groups. Emma Goldman, who met
him around 1890 during a textile strike in which he
was an agitator, describes him as being "about thirty-
five, tall, pale, and languid-looking. His manner was
gentle and ingratiating, and he resembled somewhat
the pictures of Christ."[31] Voltairine too, in her poem
"Betrayed," speaks of "his tender mouth and Christ-
like eyes" and his voice "as sweet as the summer wind
that sighs through the arbors of Paradise."[32] Twenty-
one when she first encountered him in Philadelphia,
she thought him the most attractive man she had ever
met.

Dyer Lum, who had far more experience of life than
Voltairine, considered Garside vain and self-indulgent.
Moreover, he told her as much; but, swept off her feet,
she disregarded his warnings and ran off with her ir-
resistible lover. Lum understood Voltairine's vulnerabil-
ity to a man of Garside's character and knew what
must inevitably result from such an adventure. His
worst expectations were fulfilled. Garside, for all his
charm and glib phrasemaking, proved to be superficial,
egotistical, and callous. Tiring of Voltairine after a few
months, he abruptly abandoned her. Her pain and dis-
illusionment were shattering. For Garside had aroused
all the passion of which her intense nature was
capable. She had experienced, for the first time
perhaps, the joyous power of love, so that the collapse
of the affair left her deeply wounded, her pride as well
as her emotions suffering dearly.

Indeed, she had been so overwhelmed by her feelings for Garside, and so overcome by his rejection,
that she never quite got over it, as poem after pathetic
poem bears witness. Yet these poems—"Betrayed,"
"Waiting," "Love's Ghost," "The Toast of Despair," "And

[31] Emma Goldman, *Living My Life*, New York, 1931, p. 57.
See also Rocker, *Johann Most*, p. 369.
[32] *Selected Works*, p. 27.

Thou Too" are the most important—failed to purge her of the anguish which, a friend noted, Garside had "most heartlessly and deceptively" caused her. In search of solace, she returned to her home in St. Johns, where Addie remembers her, in great distress, "wringing her hands and pacing up and down in the garden, her long, long hair streaming down to her feet behind her as she paced in the garden."[33] A few years later Voltai cut off her hair and began to dress more plainly. Garside in due course dropped out of the movement and disappeared without a trace.

But for the support of Dyer Lum, the consequences might have been even more tragic. An older man (twenty-seven years Voltai's senior, he had been married and separated and had two grown children), Lum did not possess Garside's seductive attractiveness for a girl of twenty-one. But his character was cast in a stronger mold than that of Garside or of Voltai's later lovers, who tended to be weak and undependable. From the time of their meeting in 1888 until his death five years later, Lum was the main stabilizing force in her life, "her teacher, her confidant and comrade." Voltairine calls him "the brightest scholar, the profoundest thinker of the American Revolutionary movement."[34]

Under Lum's tutelage, her mind developed, her outlook broadened, her understanding of anarchism matured and ultimately crystallized into a coherent philosophy. At the same time, there grew up between them a great love and a strong and unshakable friendship that lasted until his death. The extent of their physical relationship remains unclear. That they were at least intermittent lovers is evident from their poems

[33] Jay Chaapel, in a note appended to the manuscript of "Love's Ghost," Ishill Collection; Agnes Inglis, notes on Voltairine de Cleyre, Labadie Collection.

[34] *Selected Works*, p. 12; Voltairine de Cleyre, "Dyer D. Lum," *Freedom*, June 1893.

and letters, yet throughout the five years that they
knew each other they appear to have lived apart,
Voltairine in Philadelphia, Lum mostly in New York;
and it is hard to say how often they met, though Lum
did go down to see her from time to time and at one
point belonged to an anarchist reading group of which
Voltairine was also a member.

Yet, like Mary Wollstonecraft and William Godwin,
they chose to maintain separate quarters. Why they
did so must remain a mystery. Perhaps they cherished
their privacy more than constant intimate contact, or
feared, indeed, that such contact might spoil their
relationship. At any rate, the force of their love, which
deepened with time, is beyond dispute. "I have 'got it'
strong," confessed Lum in October 1889. Less than a
year later he published a turbulent love poem to his
"Irene," as he called her, "so dear, so pure, so fair," to
which she replied in kind. Encountering Lum, she
remarks, was "one of the best fortunes of my life."[35]

A native American of old New England stock, Dyer
Daniel Lum was born at Geneva, New York, in the
heart of the "Burned-Over District," on February 15,
1839. On his father's side he was descended from
Samuel Lum, a Scotsman who came to America in
1732. His great-grandfather on his mother's side,
Benjamin Tappan, was a Minute Man in Northampton,
Massachusetts, during the revolutionary war, and
Lum's grandfather was a brother of Lewis and Arthur
Tappan, the well-known abolitionists, and of Benjamin
Tappan, Jr., a freethinker and United States Senator.[36]

Lum himself became an abolitionist at an early age,
and with the outbreak of the Civil War he enlisted as

[35] Dyer D. Lum to Voltairine de Cleyre, October 1, 1889,
Ishill Collection; *Twentieth Century*, July 10, 1890; *Mother
Earth*, January 1907.

[36] Dyer D. Lum, autobiographical sketch, manuscript, May
13, 1892, Ishill Papers, Gainesville; Voltairine de Cleyre, "Dyer
D. Lum," *The Freethinkers' Magazine*, August 1893.

a volunteer in the 125th New York Infantry to fight for the emancipation of the slaves. After twice escaping from Confederate prisons, he transferred to the 14th New York Cavalry, rising from private to captain owing to bravery in combat. In later years, however, he was to refer to his army service as a period "when I risked my life to spread cheap labor over the South."[37] Voltairine de Cleyre writes of his change of heart: "I remember how Dyer D. Lum used to relate his war experiences in the great civil conflict of 1861-65, during which he sincerely believed himself to be fighting for the emancipation of the negroes; but twenty years after he plainly perceived it had turned out to be a Northern manufacturers' game, with the inevitable commercial result—concentration, centralization; surrender of historical tradition (State sovereignty), the nucleus of a formidable military power," with the net result being "a limited gain for the negro and an unlimited loss for the white man."[38]

After Reconstruction, Lum entered Massachusetts politics, running unsuccessfully for Lieutenant-Governor with Wendell Phillips, the celebrated abolitionist and reformer, on the Greenback ticket in 1876. A solitary photograph shows him as a real Yankee with a long mustache and penetrating eyes, every inch the former cavalry officer. Now a bookbinder by trade, he plunged into the early labor movement, served briefly as secretary to Samuel Gompers, and turned to radical agitation in 1877, the year of the great railroad strike, becoming secretary of a Congressional committee to inquire into "the depression of labor." In 1880 he was appointed to a national committee to press for the eight-hour day before Congress, serving with Albert R. Parsons and forming a friendship that lasted until the latter's execution.

[37] *Liberty*, July 16, 1887.
[38] Voltairine de Cleyre, "American Notes," *Freedom*, August 1898.

By 1884, however, both Lum and Parsons had lost
their faith in legislation and discarded state socialism
for anarchism. When Parsons started *The Alarm*, Lum
became a frequent contributor, succeeding to the
editorship a week before Parsons was hanged. Lum
was an immensely prolific writer, publishing a dozen
books and pamphlets as well as hundreds of essays and
poems in a variety of radical journals. In addition to
The Alarm, he wrote for Benjamin Tucker's first anarchist magazine, *The Radical Review*, and afterwards
for *Liberty*, his pieces including a moving poem to
Wendell Phillips, his former running-mate and mentor.[39] Covering a wide range of subjects, from money
and land reform to ethics and religion, he dabbled in
Buddhism and oriental philosophy and admired the
cooperative economic ventures of the Mormons, whom
he defended against their detractors.[40]

Lum, by the same token, took an eclectic approach
to anarchism, establishing ties with both wings of the
movement, the individualist and the socialist. A champion of unity among the quarreling factions, he
adopted a middle position on the vexed question of
property, which only drew the fire of both contending
camps and ended by embroiling him in the very
disputes he was attempting to conciliate. Victor Yar-
ros, associate editor of *Liberty*, called Lum's economic
doctrines "neither fish nor flesh,"[41] a view with which
Tucker himself concurred. "It is very amusing, and at
the same time painful to see Lum twist in the Alarm,"
wrote Tucker to Joseph A. Labadie. ". . . I now despise
him more than I did before."[42]

[39] Dyer D. Lum, "Wendell Phillips's Grave," *Liberty*, June
20, 1885.
[40] Dyer D. Lum, *Utah and Its People*, New York, 1882; Lum,
Social Problems of Today, Port Jervis, N.Y., 1886. See also
Liberty, December 26, 1885 and April 17, 1886.
[41] *Liberty*, January 14, 1888.
[42] Benjamin R. Tucker to Joseph A. Labadie, January 16,
1888, Labadie Collection.

Lum, for his part, scorned the ultra-egoists of the Stirner school who contributed to Tucker's journal, "dung-beetles," he called them, who thought only of themselves and cared not a rap for society as a whole.[43] Where Tucker, moreover, was largely removed from labor and industrial affairs, Lum, in Voltairine de Cleyre's words, "spent the greater part of his life in building up workmen's unions, himself being a hand worker, a book-binder by trade." Thus while Lum denounced scabs as "social traitors," Tucker rushed to defend the "starving wretches" who "prefer low wages to begging or stealing or dying in the streets."[44]

And yet, for all their differences, Lum and Tucker had more in common than either might have cared to admit. So much, in fact, that Lum's writings continued to make occasional appearances in the columns of *Liberty*, even during his tenure as editor of *The Alarm*, when their polemical exchanges were at their most vehement. As fellow adherents of Proudhon's mutualist doctrines, they both defended individual autonomy against collectivist encroachments, whether from the statist or the anarchist camp. Thus Lum, who admired Johann Most in other respects, came to share Tucker's belief that his collectivist economics "logically leads to and rests upon authority."[45] No less than Tucker, moreover, he saw in state socialism, and especially its Marxist variety, the seeds of what Spencer, in a famous phrase, called "the coming slavery." "The great field of Individualistic warfare will be in the future when our Collectivist friends have fully generated their Bismarckian web," Lum predicted in 1889. "Then the

[43] Dyer D. Lum to Voltairine de Cleyre, March 11, 1891, Ishill Collection; Voltairine de Cleyre, "Dyer D. Lum," *Selected Works*, p. 291.

[44] Voltairine de Cleyre, "Anarchism," *Selected Works*, p. 111; *Liberty*, May 24, 1890.

[45] Voltairine de Cleyre, "Economics of Dyer D. Lum," *Twentieth Century*, December 7, 1893.

issue will be squarely drawn between the two paths, one leading to increased dependence and collective mediocrity, the other to manly self-reliance and individual incentive." In 1892, a year before his death, he reproached Lucy Parsons, the widow of his Chicago comrade, with adopting the communist label in her new anarchist journal, *Freedom*.[46]

Voltairine de Cleyre followed her mentor's teachings in economic matters, rejecting both communism and collectivism in favor of mutualism and voluntary co-operation, as outlined in Lum's pamphlet *The Economics of Anarchy*. She was also profoundly influenced by Lum's ethical theories—like Kropotkin, he believed that anarchism had an underlying moral basis —and saw to the posthumous publication of his most important essays on the subject.[47] On other matters, however, they were "far from being in perpetual accord, even on vital points; for example, the position of women as it is and as it should be, upon which question, as might naturally be expected, the pupil took a more pronounced view than the teacher."[48]

On the whole, however, pupil and teacher were remarkably alike in temperament as well as social outlook. Both possessed intense, rebellious natures combined with a passionate, perhaps a fanatical, dedication to their ideal. Both were native Americans with ancestral roots in New England puritanism and abolitionism. Both were accomplished essayists and poets and translators of French anarchist classics. Both were eclectic in their ideology, mingling individualist with socialist components, which they embodied in a

[46] *The Individualist*, August 24, 1889; Dyer D. Lum to Lucy E. Parsons, March 21, 1892, *Freedom* (Chicago), April 1892.

[47] Dyer D. Lum, "The Basis of Morals" and "Evolutionary Ethics," *The Monist*, July 1897 and July 1899.

[48] Voltairine de Cleyre, autobiographical sketch, Wess Papers.

long social and philosophical novel on which they collaborated but which remained unpublished. Ascetic and self-sacrificing, both were deeply sympathetic with the laboring poor and with the newly arriving immigrants who crowded into America's cities. Both, however, were melancholy spirits who, tormented by economic and psychological pressures, led profoundly troubled lives. And both died before their time—Lum by his own hand—in exceedingly unhappy circumstances.

Beyond all this, both were deeply affected by the Haymarket executions, which stirred their most powerful emotions and haunted their dreams as no other event in their lifetime. In Lum, Voltairine found a direct link to the martyred anarchists. A close friend of all five victims, Spies, Engel, Fischer, and Lingg, as well as Parsons, Lum revived *The Alarm* a few days before the executions, having sold his bookbindery in Port Jervis, New York, and come to Chicago to fight for the condemned men. Day after day he visited them in prison and "would have gone to the scaffold" by their side, as Voltairine maintains.[49] After the executions, he refused to shake the hand of the leader of the Knights of Labor ("There's blood on it Powderly") who had denounced the anarchists as "bombthrowers." For the remaining years of his life Haymarket dominated his thoughts. He published a book-length history of the case, brief biographies of the defendants, and a series of deeply felt poems in their memory, which Joseph Ishill brought together as a pamphlet in 1937.[50]

Lum, however, has been one of the most neglected and misunderstood figures in the history of the anarchist movement. "In disposition," wrote a friend, "Mr.

[49] Voltairine de Cleyre, "The Fruit of the Sacrifice," *The Rebel*, November 20, 1895.

[50] *Selected Works*, p. 288; Dyer D. Lum, *In Memoriam, Chicago, November 11, 1887*, Berkeley Heights, N.J., 1937.

Lum was most amiable; in the character of his mind, he was philosophical; in mental capacity, he was at once keen and broad." To Henry David, the able chronicler of the Haymarket affair, he stood "intellectually head and shoulders above most of the Chicago revolutionaries."[51] But there was another side of Lum's character that has previously remained undisclosed. For beneath the calm, academic exterior burned the flame of an uncompromising rebel for whom violence, including terrorism, was a necessary, indeed an inevitable, weapon in the struggle against government and capital. Indebted to Garrison and Phillips, he also possessed much of the old abolitionist fire of John Brown, for whom his admiration was boundless and like whom he was willing—in fact yearning—to lay down his life for the cause of human emancipation.

After a closer look at his career, with its dynamite plots and secret codes, he comes to resemble a character out of the subterranean world described by Henry James in *The Princess Casamassima* and Joseph Conrad in *The Secret Agent*. "I am just uncultured and savage enough to confess to *hatred* as *la grande passion* of my contradictory psychological anatomy," he confides to Voltairine de Cleyre. "I am slow to wrath, but when I get mad it sticks and feeds on everything till it becomes full grown hatred. Ah! That is a passion I can understand. . . . Even as a child—and I have both paternal and maternal assurance that I was a 'bad boy' —I often got up at night before I had got in my teens to watch the storm. Once my mother found me with face glued to the glass in wild exultant mood, looking through blackness to see the lightning's flash. I was spanked and tucked in and lay awake with the storms inside raging like a prairie fire, consuming and blackening alike." On another occasion he writes: "So you acknowledge a wild nature too. I knew you had

[51] *Liberty*, April 15, 1893; David, *History of the Haymarket Affair*, p. 141.

it–I could see it–and for that reason the psychological attraction was greater."[52]

Apart from Voltairine herself, only Emma Goldman seems to have had any inkling of the complexity of Lum's nature, which she but imperfectly understood. "One marvels that so intense a person as Voltairine could have been infatuated with a man like Lum," she wrote to Joseph Ishill, "but although he seemed dry on the surface I rather think he had considerable depth. He certainly had a beautiful spirit as I am able to testify from my own acquaintance with the man."[53] But there was more to Lum than even Emma Goldman suspected. Not only was he an anarchist, but he also called himself a "Social Revolutionist," favoring militant resistance against tyranny and exploitation.[54] In his article on "The Social Revolution," in his poem "Les Septembriseurs, September 2, 1792," in his eulogy of Julius Lieske, hanged for assassinating the police chief of Frankfurt, he glorified the heroes who act rather than contenting themselves with words. "There is more education in a single event than in years of agitation by press and speech," he told a friend.[55] In the Chicago *Alarm*, a year before the Haymarket explosion, he appealed to "the wage slaves of America" to arm themselves against their oppressors, arguing that those in power yield only to force, which alone can alter entrenched social conditions and relieve the workers of their misery.[56]

[52] Dyer D. Lum to Voltairine de Cleyre, July 4, 1890, September 19 and October 1, 1889, Ishill Collection.

[53] Emma Goldman to Joseph Ishill, September 28, 1927, Ishill Collection.

[54] Dyer D. Lum, "Why I Am a Social Revolutionist," *Twentieth Century*, October 30, 1890.

[55] *The Commonweal*, October 24, 1891; *Free Society*, February 3 and August 11, 1901; Rocker, *Johann Most*, p. 213.

[56] Dyer D. Lum, "To Arms: An Appeal to the Wage Slaves of America," *The Alarm*, June 13, 1885; reprinted on April 24, 1886, ten days before Haymarket.

Lum, as Voltairine de Cleyre notes, was "in all of his writings the advocate of resistance, the champion of rebellion," believing in revolution "as he believed in cyclones; when the time comes for the cloud to burst it bursts, and so will burst the pent up storm in the people when it can no longer be contained."[57] "I am glad the 4th of May occurred," he told her, referring to the Haymarket incident. Despite the consequences for his comrades, he had "shed no tears." Nor did he accept the *agent provocateur* hypothesis put forward by some of his associates to account for the explosion, insisting that it was "puerile" to attribute the bomb to the Pinkertons or police. He was convinced—possibly he knew it for a fact—that it came from the anarchist movement itself, even if the condemned men were not responsible.[58]

And yet, being an uncompromising opponent of the state, he counseled Parsons and the others against petitioning the governor for clemency. "Die, Parsons," he said, when his friend asked his advice on the matter. Five days before the executions he exulted over their unyielding behavior. "*The four will not sign* or compromise their position," he wrote in an oddly frivolous manner. "I saw them yesterday and they are firm. Spies is now de-Spies (I beg pardon). Only terrorism—I honestly believe—will save them now."[59]

Lum's seemingly heartless attitude cost him more than a few friends within the movement: "I was taunted everywhere with 'wishing their death'; that skinful of sentiment Nina Van Zandt repeated it to

[57] *Selected Works*, p. 287; *Freedom*, June 1893.

[58] Dyer D. Lum to Voltairine de Cleyre, April 1, 1890, Ishill Papers, Gainesville; *The Alarm*, December 29, 1888.

[59] *Selected Works*, p. 288; Dyer D. Lum to Joseph A. Labadie, November 6, 1887, Labadie Collection. "No one helped them more than I to reject all proffers of mercy," he later wrote. Lum to Voltairine de Cleyre, March 1, 1891, Ishill Papers, Gainesville.

Spies. I did and I didn't: I wanted their honor to the cause and they saved it, to hell with life without that, and they agreed with me! Most and Lucy Parsons believe me a cold 'hair splitter.' So be it." To Joseph Labadie he wrote shortly after the hangings: "I am very sorry you take their deaths so hard—can't you realize that it was nothing but an episode in our work? I do— Perhaps my nearness to them and seeing and feeling their enthusiasm gives me a different feeling."[60]

Yet, as has been noted, he would gladly have joined them on the scaffold. Indeed, he was yearning for a martyr's death, after the example of John Brown. In a letter to Lum, George A. Schilling, the Chicago labor leader, lays bare this hidden obsession: "It is impossible to eradicate the infatuation from which you suffer. The trouble is you want to be with Engel, with Spies and Parsons, stand a crown upon your forehead and a bomb within your hand; you want to be a martyr and fill a martyr's grave."[61]

With this in mind, one is fascinated to discover that it was Lum who smuggled in the dynamite cigar with which Lingg committed suicide in his cell. The popular story, recorded by Charles Edward Russell and repeated by Frank Harris in his novel *The Bomb*, was that Lingg's girlfriend had conveyed the deadly instrument to her lover. Voltairine de Cleyre, who knew otherwise, alludes to this in a speech on the twentieth anniversary of the hangings: "the public may believe that Lingg's sweetheart gave him a bomb to kill himself with, if it likes. I do not." In another Haymarket

[60] Dyer D. Lum to Voltairine de Cleyre, April 1, 1890, and March 1, 1891, Ishill Papers, Gainesville; Lum to Joseph A. Labadie, December 26, 1887, Labadie Collection.

[61] George A. Schilling to Dyer D. Lum, September 2, 1888, Schilling Papers, University of Chicago. In her obituary of Lum, Voltairine writes: "His early studies of Buddhism left a profound impress upon all his future concepts of life, and to the end his ideal of personal attainment was self-obliteration—Nirvana." *Freedom*, June 1893.

speech she refers to the "dynamite cartridge given him in a cigar by a friend." The friend was Dyer D. Lum, as she told her son Harry, who relayed the information to Agnes Inglis many years later.[62]

But few were inclined to believe it. "I doubt very much that Dyer D. Lum was the type of man who would be party to such a conspiracy," wrote the secretary of the Pioneer Aid and Support Association, which erected the Haymarket Monument in Chicago's Waldheim Cemetery. Agnes Inglis agreed, suggesting that the prison authorities themselves were responsible for Lingg's death, a dubious hypothesis which Alexander Berkman demolishes in a letter to Emma Goldman: "I don't think it's plausible. They knew well enough that Lingg would have to hang, why then should they want to kill him before that? On the other hand Lingg was probably the kind of man who'd prefer to die by his own hand."[63]

Besides, as must now be clear, Lum was precisely the sort of man who would have delivered the cartridge. He himself refers obliquely to the episode in a letter to Voltairine de Cleyre.[64] To enable Lingg to cheat the hangman and at the same time enhance his heroic image was Lum's manifest intention. Five years later, by the same token, he planned to smuggle poison to Alexander Berkman, should Berkman have been given the death penalty for shooting Frick. For Homestead, he believed, had rung the bell "summoning us to our places in the great drama." Before a public audience

[62] Voltairine de Cleyre, "November Eleventh, Twenty Years Ago," *Mother Earth*, November 1907; de Cleyre, "November 11th," Wess Papers; Harry de Cleyre to Agnes Inglis, December 29, 1947, Labadie Collection.

[63] Irving S. Abrams to Agnes Inglis, February 1, 1949, Labadie Collection; Alexander Berkman to Emma Goldman, June 21, 1934, Berkman Archive. Cf. David, *History of the Haymarket Affair*, p. 474.

[64] Dyer D. Lum to Voltairine de Cleyre, March 1, 1891, Ishill Papers, Gainesville.

in New York City he defended Berkman's act, because "when another has done a thing of which you approve as leading in the direction of your own aspirations, it is your duty to share the effects of the counterblast his action may have provoked."[65] The following spring he became "the moving spirit" of the native-born anarchists behind a drive to secure the reduction of Berkman's twenty-two-year prison sentence. It was with poison, incidentally, that he ended his own life a few weeks later.

Beyond this, yet another important episode emerges from Lum's hitherto obscure activities. In November 1887, with the German anarchist Robert Reitzel, he began to organize a plot to blow up Cook County Jail in an effort to liberate his comrades. ("Only terrorism will save them now," he had written to Joseph Labadie.) The escape was planned for the 10th, on the eve of the scheduled hangings—"Annie Laurie Day," Lum later called it after the song Parsons sang that night in his cell. At the last moment, however, the conspiracy was abandoned. " 'The boys,' in the shadow of death, stopped it," Lum confided to Voltairine. "They said their deaths were better—and they died." As Lingg had told him: "Work till we are dead. The time for vengeance will come later." "I swore then, and to them," Lum writes, "that while I carried out their instructions, if I ever got in, the word would be to unchain the dogs. And out of the number I know, the 'resources of civilization' [i.e., dynamite] would be called into requisition. A man with a purpose, who is indifferent to life, who is not *mortgaged*, could stir up—well—what?"[66]

[65] Voltairine de Cleyre to Alexander Berkman, July 10, 1906, Berkman Archive; Dyer D. Lum, "The Higher Law," *Solidarity*, August 13, 1892; *Selected Works*, pp. 288-89; Goldman, *Living My Life*, p. 110.

[66] Dyer D. Lum to Voltairine de Cleyre, November 10, 1891, Ishill Collection, Harvard; Lum to Voltairine de Cleyre, March 1, 1891, Ishill Papers, Gainesville.

As late as 1892, nearly five years after the executions, Lum still harbored vague plans to strike back at the authorities. Mesmerized by notions of the purifying value of violence, he had an uncontrollable urge for reprisal. From his letters to Voltairine de Cleyre, he seems to have been contemplating a suicide plot, an act of "propaganda by the deed," to avenge his fallen comrades. "Now don't think I am insane," he wrote, "even if I have a dominant purpose. None who knows me (superficially) would think it; a happy, joking, indifferent fellow." Voltairine, who at this point rejected violence and only later came to sympathize with Lum's position, tried to dissuade him. But Lum, addressing her sardonically as "Moraline" and "Gush-erine," derided her pacifist arguments which permitted sentiment to interfere with hard necessity: "Yes, you and Tolstoi are right. Let us pray for the police here and the Tzar in Russia."[67]

Not that Lum himself was destitute of sentiment. Far from it. "Underneath the cold logician who mercilessly scouted at sentiment," writes Voltairine, "underneath the pessimistic poet that sent the mournful cry of the whip-poor-will echoing through the widowed chambers of the heart, that hung and sung over the festival walls of Life the wreathes and dirges of Death; underneath the gay joker who delighted to play tricks on politicians, police and detectives; was the man who took the children on his knees and told them stories while the night was falling, the man who gave up a share of his own meagre meals to save five blind kittens from drowning; the man who lent his arm to a drunken washerwoman whom he did not know, and carried her basket for her, that she might not be arrested and locked up; the man who gathered four-leafed clovers and sent them to his friends, wishing them 'all the luck which superstition attached to them'; the man whose heart was beating with the great com-

[67] Dyer D. Lum to Voltairine de Cleyre, March 1, 1891, and February 28, 1893, Ishill Papers, Gainesville.

THE MAKING OF AN ANARCHIST

mon heart, who was one with the simplest and poorest."[68]

Yet he was determined to make good his "pledge," as he called it, to Lingg, Parsons, Spies, Engel, and Fischer. "I never lost sight of my purpose. I will raise the money and carry out my part of the programme. I am cold, relentless, unflinching. If any fools get in the way, so much the worse for them. In this sentiment cuts no figure. And this time a poster will let people know the 'police' did not do it—as Mrs. Parsons said before. If done, and I think it will work, as we use chemicals, the responsibility will be assumed in posters on the walls. Now, my own darling, rise above personal feeling, damn self, and *be thyself*. I have written enough—for you will never get another such letter from your old bear—Dyer D. Lum."[69]

In the end, however, Lum failed to execute his plan. Instead, he sank into a deep psychological depression, unable to eat or sleep, his mind in constant turmoil, his life a bitter struggle against poverty. Moving to a flop-house on the Bowery, he fell to heavy drinking and, his insomnia worsening, took opiates to fall asleep. Late at night, under the influence of alcohol and drugs, he wrote his last letters to Voltairine, rambling, agitated, almost incoherent. He was driving himself toward the grave. "My brain needs rest," he says at one point. "Oh! how I do long for rest and hate the sight of pen and paper."[70] In this distracted mood he fled to his ancestral home at Northampton, but, failing to find respite from the moral and financial pressures that assailed him, returned to his lodgings on the Bowery. There a friend encountered him in September 1892, seven months before his death: "He came trudging

[68] *Selected Works*, p. 294.

[69] Dyer D. Lum to Voltairine de Cleyre, March 1, 1891, Ishill Papers, Gainesville. See also Lum to Voltairine de Cleyre, February 5, 1892, Ishill Collection, Harvard.

[70] Dyer D. Lum to Voltairine de Cleyre, July 28, 1891, Labadie Collection.

along the street, soft felt hat carelessly slung on one side, blue flannel shirt and red necktie, a suit of well worn homespun clothes, a pair of well worn shoes, and a large bundle of papers and writings under his arm; looking at no one, caring for nothing save the propaganda of Anarchism."[71]

At length, Voltairine de Cleyre tells us, Lum "seized the unknown Monster, Death, with a smile on his lips." After a "farewell look into a friend's eyes, he went out into the April night and took his last walk in the roar of the great city."[72] Then, returning to his room, he swallowed a fatal draft of poison.

Voltairine had sensed that the end was approaching when she wrote her poem "You and I" in 1892. A reply to Lum's "You and I in the Golden Weather," it hints of the brevity of life and the nearness of death, a central theme of her writings:

You and I, in the sere, brown weather,
    When the clouds hang thick in the frowning sky,
When rain-tears drip on the bloomless heather,
Unheeding the storm-blasts will walk together,
    And look to each other—You and I.

You and I, when the clouds are shriven
    To show the cliff-broods of lightnings high;
When over the ramparts, swift, thunder-driven,
Rush the bolts of Hate from a Hell-lit Heaven,
    Will smile at each other—You and I.

You and I, when the bolts are falling,
    The hot air torn with the earth's wild cries,
Will lean through the darkness where Death is
    calling,
Will search through the shadows where Night is
    palling,
    And find the light in each other's eyes.

[71] G.W.R. in *The Commonweal*, May 13, 1893.
[72] *Selected Works*, pp. 289, 295.

You and I, when black sheets of water
  Drench and tear us and drown our breath,
Below this laughter of Hell's own daughter,
Above the smoke of the storm-girt slaughter,
  Will hear each other and gleam at Death.

You and I, in the gray night dying,
  When over the east-land the dawn-beams fly,
Down in the groans, in the low, faint crying,
Down where the thick blood is blackly lying,
  Will reach out our weak arms, You and I.

You and I, in the cold, white weather,
  When over our corpses the pale lights lie,
Will rest at last from the dread endeavor,
Pressed to each other, for parting—never!
  Our dead lips together, You and I.

You and I, when the years in flowing
  Have left us behind with all things that die,
With the rot of our bones shall give soil for growing
The loves of the Future, made sweet for blowing
  By the dew of the kiss of a last good-bye![73]

Yet Lum's death, on April 6, 1893, came as a terrible blow. "Mine the wrung heart, mine the clasped, useless hands," she wrote at the town where she was speaking when the news arrived. As her lover and mentor, Lum had been the most important figure in her life, her guide through an acutely critical period, when she desperately needed support. "His genius, his work, his character," she wrote a year after his passing, "was one of those rare gems produced in the great mine of suffering and flashing backward with all its changing lights the hopes, the fears, the gaieties, the griefs, the dreams, the doubts, the loves, the hates, the sum of that which is buried, low down there, in the human mine."[74]

[73] *Ibid.*, pp. 42-43. Lum's "You and I" appeared in *Truth*, February 1890.

[74] Voltairine de Cleyre, "In Memoriam," *Twentieth Century*, May 4, 1893; *Selected Works*, p. 284.

3. Philadelphia

Besides Garside and Lum, a third man, James B. Elliott, entered Voltairine de Cleyre's life in 1888. In June of that year, Voltairine came to Philadelphia on her first visit. Invited to speak before the Friendship Liberal League, a leading free thought organization in the city, she was met at the railroad station by Mr. Longford, its secretary, and by Mr. Elliott, "a whole entertainment committee in himself." They conducted her to the meeting hall where, she says, "I have never addressed a finer audience of men and women."[1] Indeed, she was so favorably impressed that she returned the following year and made the city her home.

Voltairine remained in Philadelphia the greater part of her adult life, from 1889 to 1910, when she moved to Chicago less than two years before her death. The young woman who arrived in the great eastern city—then the third largest in America, with more than a million inhabitants—was far from being the melancholy figure that we will know a decade later. Yet the underlying features were already in evidence. Lonely, vulnerable, she had not yet recovered from her affair with Garside when she was thrown together with Mr. Elliott, whose company had so amused her the previous year.

Born in Philadelphia in 1849, James B. Elliott, like Dyer D. Lum, was considerably older than Voltai, who had not yet reached her twenty-third birthday when she took up quarters in the rooming house on Wallace Street where Elliott, a carpenter, lived with his mother. Elliott, while not an anarchist, was an ardent freethinker. He lectured for the Philadelphia Ethical Society as well as for the Friendship Liberal League and wrote articles and reviews for *The Truth Seeker*, *Freethought*, and other rationalist publications. A wor-

[1] Voltairine de Cleyre, "The Quaker City," *The Truth Seeker*, July 28, 1888.

shiper of Thomas Paine, he had visited all the known homes of his idol in the United States, Canada, and England and accumulated a large collection of Paine memorabilia. After the turn of the century he became secretary of the Paine Memorial Association and of the Paine Historical Association of America.[2]

Voltairine's union with Elliott was of short duration. Because she refused to become domesticated, as Elliott desired, theirs was "not a happy companionship,"[3] and it soon came to an end, although they remained on more or less friendly terms—when Voltairine was away on the lecture circuit, it was still "dear Jimsky" who took care of her pets and plants—and she continued to live in the same house (even boarding with Mrs. Elliott) for several years after they had ceased to be lovers. In 1896, moreover, we find Elliott visiting Voltai's mother in St. Johns and building an extension to her house. Their acquaintance dissolved only in 1910, when Voltai moved to Chicago. Elliott remained in Philadelphia for the rest of his life, dying in 1931 in his eighty-second year.[4]

On June 12, 1890, Voltairine bore Elliott her only child, a son called Harry.[5] For the young mother, however, it was not a happy occasion. "I think I hardly laughed once for the year preceding and accomplishing his birth," she later recalled. "I was as weak and sick as possible, and decidedly given to books in the few min-

---

[2] James B. Elliott, biographical questionnaire, Labadie Collection. See also his letters to Henry Bool, April 1, 1902, and to John B. Andrews, December 13, 1907, Labadie Collection.

[3] Agnes Inglis to S. E. Parker, November 21, 1949, courtesy of S. E. Parker, London.

[4] *The Truth Seeker*, August 1931; Agnes Inglis to Joseph Ishill, July 18, 1934, Ishill Collection.

[5] Born Vermorel Elliott (presumably after Auguste Vermorel, martyr of the Paris Commune), which he shed for Harry de Cleyre.

utes free from physical torture."[6] Moody and irritable, in chronic illness and desperate need of privacy, she could not face the task of raising a child. Leaving him with the Elliotts, she went off to Kansas to lecture for the Woman's National Liberal Union, a free thought society. For almost a year she remained in Kansas, mostly in the town of Enterprise, tutoring and writing to supplement her lecture fees, until she could muster the will and physical strength to return to Philadelphia.[7]

Thus, as Emma Goldman observes, the one child that Voltairine de Cleyre brought into the world "had not been wanted."[8] Yet we must not judge her too harshly. For neither physically nor emotionally nor yet financially was she able to cope with the responsibilities of motherhood. After her return to Wallace Street, she and her son remained almost strangers, though she lived just down the hall or, afterwards, in the immediate neighborhood. As Voltairine's granddaughters have said, "he just did not fit into her life, her plans, at all. . . . She had things she wanted to do with her life, and he was not part of them."[9]

For a while she gave Harry piano lessons, but stopped because he would not work at it hard enough. On the whole, she let him fend for himself, giving him a small weekly allowance which, from the age of ten, he had to supplement by going to work. "He always has 'the blues,' poor laddie," wrote Addie, who took pity on the boy. "It is his unfortunate inheritance." Childless herself, Addie asked her sister if she could have him, and Voltai replied: "It is nothing to me, what Elliott

[6] Voltairine de Cleyre to Lillian Harman, November 21, 1905, Harman Papers, San Francisco.

[7] See Voltairine de Cleyre to Harriet De Claire, November 16, 1890, Labadie Collection.

[8] Goldman, *Voltairine de Cleyre*, p. 35.

[9] Interviews with Fedora de Cleyre Benish and Renée de Cleyre Buckwalter, May 22 and April 28, 1975.

does with his boy." But Elliott, says Addie, refused to give him up.[10]

Mechanically inclined, Harry grew up with a love of machines. At sixteen he enrolled in automotive school, at his mother's expense, but would not apply himself to study any more than he would practice the piano as a child. Disgusted, Voltairine refused to pay for any further schools, complaining to her mother that Harry never finished more than half the course.[11] Added to this, the stigma of illegitimacy had its effect. Throughout his life, Harry referred to himself as a "bastard." Voltairine herself, while in Kansas, composed a poem called "Bastard Born"; and surely she was thinking of her own child—perhaps also of herself—when she wrote of the "little babies, helpless, voiceless little things, generated in lust, cursed with impure moral natures, cursed, prenatally, with the germs of disease, forced into the world to struggle and to suffer, to hate themselves, to hate their mothers for bearing them, to hate society and be hated by it in return.[12]

Yet, in spite of her neglect, Harry loved his mother with an intensity that never abated. It was her name, not his father's, that he took; and he called his first daughter Voltairine. Emma Goldman is less than just in her speculations about Harry twenty years after his mother's death: "He went his way. He is today probably one of the 100% Americans, commonplace and dull."[13] Although he did not become an anarchist and he lacked his mother's creative gifts, his letters reflect more than

[10] Adelaide D. Thayer to Agnes Inglis, January 24, 1937, Labadie Collection; Adelaide Thayer to Joseph Ishill, February 3, 1935, Ishill Collection.

[11] Voltairine de Cleyre to Harriet De Claire, May 27, 1907, Ishill Collection.

[12] Voltairine de Cleyre, "Sex Slavery," *Selected Works*, pp. 343-44. "Bastard Born" (*Selected Works*, pp. 36-41) was written in Enterprise, Kansas, in January 1891, and first published in the Chetopha, Kansas, *Democrat*, May 2, 1891.

[13] Goldman, *Voltairine de Cleyre*, p. 36.

a little of her intelligence and independent spirit. A housepainter near Philadelphia, he became, like both his parents, a devotee of Thomas Paine (his daughter, in turn, wrote a prize essay at school about Paine). He was at his mother's bedside when she died, and in later years he wanted all the time to talk about her, worshiping her memory (her *Selected Works* became "his Bible") and proud of "her stubborn defense of those being oppressed."[14]

When Voltairine de Cleyre returned from Kansas in the fall of 1891, several young anarchist immigrants, Jewish cigar and textile workers, asked her for help with their English, and she began to teach them in the evenings after they came home from the factory. She charged a modest fee, fifty cents a lesson when she went to their homes and twenty-five cents when they came to her. As her clientele increased, this provided her with a meager living, augmented by lessons in music and, on occasion, in French and mathematics.

The poverty of the Philadelphia immigrants was more acute than any Voltairine herself had known as a child. "I will send you some of their compositions to read sometimes," she wrote her mother. "There are times when I can't speak for keeping back the tears when I am correcting them; they are mostly so pathetic —always on one subject—the misery of the poor."[15] Teaching these working-class immigrants, Voltairine herself eked out a shabby existence, living amid dreary and wretched surroundings, working extremely hard and taxing her body to the utmost. She had no great love for teaching. She did it rather as a means of earning a living, having no other training or profession

[14] Renée de Cleyre Buckwalter to Paul Avrich, May 19, 1975; Lincoln de Cleyre to Paul Avrich, May 5, 1975.

[15] Voltairine de Cleyre to Harriet De Claire, March 20, 1894, Labadie Collection.

nor any formal education beyond what she had received at the convent. From Dr. Joseph H. Greer, an
anarchist physician in Chicago, she once sought advice
about the possibility of studying law, but she soon gave
up the idea.[16]

Thoughout these early years in Philadelphia, then,
she lived in great privation. She occasionally made a
bit of extra money by translating or by publishing an
essay or poem in a nonanarchist journal (the anarchist journals paid no fees). But she possessed few
articles of clothing ("I haven't bought a dress in three
years," she wrote her mother in December 1893), ate
very little, and lived austerely in a poor section of the
city, populated largely by Jews, Germans, Russians,
and Poles, with a small bedroom and a sitting room
for her teaching. Her near starvation diet, says one of
her pupils, Nathan Navro, coupled with the constant
work and the strain it involved, aggravated her old
illness and shortened her life by "allowing the chronic
disease to make terrible inroads on her constitution."[17]
When Sadakichi Hartmann paid her a visit, she received him in a plain white dress and bare feet in a
frugally furnished room. Sadakichi borrowed two dollars, which he failed to return, and she never forgave
him. "Very likely," he remarks, "she had worked hard
for it, and I needed it merely for the entertainment of
some 'beer' comrades and had forgotten all about it a
few hours later."[18] Voltairine had no patience with
parlor or saloon anarchism, both of which Sadakichi
practiced.

After a few years, however, her financial situation

[16] Voltairine de Cleyre to Harriet De Claire, January 22/23,
1894, Labadie Collection. Dr. Greer was a Vice President of the
American Secular Union.

[17] Voltairine de Cleyre to Harriet De Claire, December 1,
1893, Labadie Collection; Nathan Navro, untitled manuscript
on Voltairine de Cleyre, Ishill Collection.

[18] *Mother Earth*, April 1915.

improved, and she was able, during the middle 1890s, to put her lover, Samuel Gordon, through medical school while sending regular sums (two or three dollars with almost every letter) to her mother. She also managed to buy a piano on the instalment plan. She loved music passionately, says Emma Goldman, and was "an artist of no small measure."[19]

Throughout these years, Voltairine lived and worked mostly with Jews. She had hundreds of Jewish comrades, hundreds of Jewish pupils, and two (possibly more) Jewish lovers. After Philadelphia she spent her last years in Chicago with a Jewish couple, Jacob and Anna Livshis. Living among these Jewish immigrants, she grew to admire their ability and dedication, their passion for learning, their toiling long hours in the factory during the day then reading and studying at night, above and beyond their activity in the radical movement, which consumed a major part of their energies. More than any other group, she came to believe, the Jews had served as "movers in the social revolution." They were, she told Nathan Navro, "the most liberal minded and active comrades in the movement, as well as the most transcendental dreamers."[20] Her poem "The Wandering Jew," written in 1894, was suggested, she tells us, "by the reading of an article describing an interview with the 'wandering Jew,' in which he was represented as an incorrigible grumbler. The Jew has been, and will continue to be, the grumbler of the earth—until the prophetic ideal of justice shall be realized: 'BLESSED BE HE.' "[21]

Voltairine had little difficulty in overcoming the

[19] Goldman, *Voltairine de Cleyre*, p. 19. See also Voltairine de Cleyre to Joseph J. Cohen, n.d. [1908 or 1909], Cohen Papers, Bund Archives.

[20] *Mother Earth*, September 1906; Navro manuscript, Ishill Collection.

[21] *Selected Works*, p. 58.

differences in background and ideology that divided her from her new comrades, who found this young American woman who had come to live with them and teach them an exotically fascinating personality, a "beautiful spirit," as they often put it. For Christmas 1893 two of her young pupils presented her with Ernest Renan's *History of the People of Israel* in a handsome two-volume edition. "It cost them $5.00, poor 'children of Israel,' and they are only cigar-makers," she wrote to her mother.[22] In her essay on "The Making of an Anarchist," written in 1903, she sums up her experiences among the Jews: "In those twelve years that I have lived and loved and worked with foreign Jews I have taught over a thousand, and found them, as a rule, the brightest, the most persistent and sacrificing students, and in youth dreamers of social ideals. While the 'intelligent American' has been cursing him as the 'ignorant foreigner,' while the short-sighted working-man has been making life for the 'sheeny' as intolerable as possible, silent and patient the despised man has worked his way against it all. I have myself seen such genuine heroism in the cause of education practiced by girls and boys, and even by men and women with families, as would pass the limits of belief to the ordinary mind. Cold, starvation, self-isolation, all endured for years in order to obtain the means for study; and, worse than all, exhaustion of body even to emaciation—this is common. Yet in the midst of all this, so fervent is the social imagination of the young that most of them find time besides to visit the various clubs and societies where radical thought is discussed, and sooner or later ally themselves either with the Socialist Sections, the Liberal Leagues, the Single Tax Clubs, or the Anarchist Groups. The greatest Socialist daily in America is the Jewish *Vorwaerts*, and the most

[22] Voltairine de Cleyre to Harriet De Claire, January 27, 1894, Labadie Collection.

active and competent practical workers are Jews. So they are among the Anarchists."[23]

At the same time, however, she was troubled by the tendency of more than a few of her Jewish comrades to immerse themselves in the competition of American life, to succeed within the existing system by making money in business or the professions rather than devoting their lives to the cause of social emancipation, as Kropotkin advised in his *Appeal to the Young.* Voltairine writes: "As the years pass and the gradual filtration and absorption of American commercial life goes on, my students become successful professionals, the golden mist of enthusiasm vanishes, and the old teacher must turn for comradeship to the new youth, who still press forward with burning eyes, seeing what is lost forever to those whom common success has satisfied and stupefied." That her own lover, Gordon, was to follow this path surely accentuated her disappointment. When she visited London in 1897, she complained to Kropotkin that many anarchists, after a few years of activity, would leave the movement. He replied: "Let them go; we have had the best of them."[24]

In the process of teaching her comrades English, Voltairine acquired a respectable command of Yiddish, placing herself in the small company of non-Jewish anarchists—Rudolf Rocker is the outstanding example —who worked among the Jews and learned their language. To her mother she expressed a desire to study Hebrew and Russian as well,[25] but apparently did not progress very far in these languages. In Yiddish, by contrast, she reached the point where she could read it and understand it without difficulty and

[23] *Selected Works*, p. 159.

[24] *Ibid.*, pp. 159-60. See also Harry Kelly, Introduction to Thomas B. Eyges, *Beyond the Horizon*, Boston, 1944.

[25] Voltairine de Cleyre to Harriet De Claire, February 25, 1894, Labadie Collection.

also speak it, if only haltingly. She followed the Jewish anarchist press, read the *Fraye Arbeter Shtime* every week, and "enjoyed it," says its editor, Saul Yanovsky.[26]

She herself contributed several articles in English to the *Fraye Arbeter Shtime* and other Yiddish journals, which Yanovsky and Joseph Cohen, one of her Philadelphia pupils, translated into Yiddish. Carefully going over their work, she once threatened to withhold further contributions should Yanovsky cut or otherwise tamper with her writing, whose integrity must under no circumstances be infringed. "If at any time you undertake to lop out things from my work," she warned, "that will be the last time you will have a chance to. If you don't like a thing, return it; but *don't edit it.*"[27] In 1906 and 1907, she herself translated the Yiddish of Z. Libin and I. L. Peretz for Emma Goldman's *Mother Earth*, notably "Hofenung un Shrek" (Hope and Fear), Peretz's powerful essay on social democracy. Her letters to Yanovsky and Cohen are peppered with Yiddish words and phrases ("matsos," "vundermensh," "telerel fun himl") in a clear and correct Yiddish script; and she experimented with writing whole pieces, only one of which, an unfinished story called "In dem Shoten fun der Livunen" (In the Shadow of the Moon), has been preserved.[28]

A few of Voltairine de Cleyre's pupils—Nathan Navro, Samuel Gordon, Joseph Cohen—made sufficient progress with their lessons to publish in the English anarchist press. Navro, a young cigarmaker who first came to her for lessons in 1896, contributed poems to *Free Society*, the foremost revolutionary anarchist

[26] Saul Yanovsky to Joseph Ishill, September 30, 1930, Ishill Collection.

[27] Voltairine de Cleyre to Saul Yanovsky, April 27, 1911, Ishill Collection.

[28] Labadie Collection. She also took to addressing her sister Addie as "Dear Sisterle," with the affectionate Yiddish ending.

paper in America around the turn of the century. Addie met Navro while visiting her sister in 1898 and thought him "a fine man and a good friend." Voltairine's son describes him, similarly, as "a man whose integrity is unquestioned" and who, unlike some other of his mother's admirers, was "free of petty jealousies." Voltairine herself once called him "the best character I have ever known in all this world." Owing to her influence, he eventually gave up the factory to study music; and his unfailing friendship, which lasted, in his own words, "until the day of her death,"[29] stands in contrast to the faithlessness of Garside and, as we shall see, of Gordon.

Joseph Jacob Cohen, a young man of energy and intelligence, entered her life a bit later, arriving from Russia in the spring of 1903. A cigarmaker like Navro, he was bent on mastering English and went to Voltairine for help. "I had the honor and privilege to be her pupil for many years and cherish her memory dearly," he wrote to Max Nettlau, the Austrian historian of anarchism.[30] Cohen's daughter, sixty years later, could still remember accompanying her mother and father to Voltairine's apartment on North Marshall Street. Her impressions remain sharp and convey a remarkable portrait: "Both my parents, who were immigrants, learned English from Voltairine de Cleyre, and though I was only a small child when they were taking lessons from her, my memories are quite vivid. (My own first language was Yiddish, and I can remember standing up in my crib and reciting a Yiddish poem, but my parents were determined on learning English,

[29] Adelaide D. Thayer to Joseph Ishill, February 3, 1935; Harry de Cleyre to Joseph Ishill, October 15, 1934; Voltairine de Cleyre to Harriet De Claire, September 14, 1901; Navro manuscript, Ishill Collection.
[30] Joseph J. Cohen to Max Nettlau, May 17, 1932, Nettlau Archive, International Institute of Social History.

so my Yiddish dropped away very quickly.) When they went to her apartment for lessons they would take me along, and I sat in her lap as she taught them. My whole understanding of 'elegance' goes back to Voltairine. It was the first time I saw a room with curtains, with little pieces of décor, though nothing expensive of course. She herself had an ascetic kind of beauty. And she smelled very good, like lavender. She wore a dark long-sleeved dress, and every gesture of hers had a kind of beauty—especially in contrast to Emma Goldman, whom I always found repulsive. . . . I used to sit in Voltairine's lap and play with the things on her desk while she gave my mother English lessons. Her rooms were the first and, for many years, the only ones I knew in which there were things that were in them just for the love of things. All the other places where people I knew lived were barely functional. But here there were soft chairs and little tables with things on them. And her desk! There was a crystal ball with snow flakes—not like the cheap things we later saw—it was a fairy tale like thing. And pens of sea-shell nacre shaped like feathers, and little painted dishes or vases. These were the things she let me play with. . . . I knew when [father] carried me on his shoulders and chanted 'The Raven' and 'The Bells' and 'Annabel Lee'—and when he read the 'Just So Stories'—that they were part of his lessons with Voltairine. And 'Riki-Tiki-Tavi,' which is a favorite I have read to children and grandchildren, still has an echo in my mind of my father's voice and Voltairine's corrections. . . . The word 'elegance' has always had something of Voltairine in it —her hands, the tall curtained windows, the things that were there for love, not for use. That is what I remember."[31]

[31] Interview with Emma Cohen Gilbert, White Plains, N.Y., September 23, 1974; Emma Cohen Gilbert to Paul Avrich, April 20, 1975.

Cohen, a "strong and able man," as his friend Harry Kelly describes him,[32] quickly emerged as a leading figure in the Jewish anarchist movement. Voltairine's faith in his abilities—"I don't know just *what* you'll accomplish, but you'll accomplish something, if you don't kill yourself trying," she wrote him in 1911— was not misplaced. Not only was he the driving force of the Radical Library Group and the Modern School movement in Philadelphia, but he went on to become a founder of the Stelton Colony, the editor of the *Fraye Arbeter Stime*, a founder of the Sunrise Colony in Michigan, and the author of four books and many articles which chronicle these ventures in which he played so central a part.[33]

Samuel H. Gordon, a third Jewish anarchist and cigarmaker, became not only Voltairine de Cleyre's pupil but also her lover. Born in Russia in 1871, he was twenty-one when he emigrated to Philadelphia in 1892 and joined the Knights of Liberty (Ritter der Frayhayt), the oldest and most important Jewish anarchist group in the city, inspired by Johann Most, of whom Gordon became an ardent disciple. In 1893, ten months after his arrival, Gordon went to Voltairine for help with his English. For this handsome young comrade, five years her junior, she felt an immediate physical attraction, more powerful than any she had experienced since her liaison with Garside. Ripe for love and companionship, she poured out on Gordon all her unused store of passion. Presently, her "Pussy mine," as she affectionately called him, was sharing her quarters and assisting with her radical propaganda. He was also acquiring a good enough command of

[32] Harry Kelly to Max Nettlau, March 29, 1921, Nettlau Archive.

[33] Joseph J. Cohen, *The House Stood Forlorn*, Paris, 1954; *In Quest of Heaven*, New York, 1957; *Di yidish-anarkhistishe bavegung in Amerike*, Philadelphia, 1945; and (with Alexis C. Ferm) *The Modern School of Stelton*, Stelton, N.J., 1925.

English for Voltairine to invite him, on March 27, 1894, to speak on the subject of "Revolution" before the Ladies' Liberal League, a free thought group of which she was a founder.[34]

Her involvement with Gordon, however, was to become another in the series of unhappy love affairs that disrupted her life. She was soon to discover that his love was less absorbing than her own; and, as it turned out, he was the type of young enthusiast about whom she complained to Kropotkin: his ardor for anarchism (along with that for his teacher) cooled with the achievement of material success. From her own slender earnings she managed to put him through medical school (he received his diploma in 1898), only to find that, like Garside, he was irresponsible and self-indulgent. Because he disliked her pets, she had to lock her kitten in the coal bin, and it broke the window and escaped. "Poor little thing," she later wrote. "I can see his bright, terrified eyes and his white paw trying desperately to get back through the crack after I had buttoned the coal-house door; and I never saw him again!"[35]

Nervous and irritable, Voltairine was herself far from easy to live with, and her relationship with Gordon was a stormy one, marred by petty jealousies and suspicions. They "hammered away at each other after the manner of young radicals with an excess of energy," she writes in a story based on her experience with Gordon. At one point (the date is uncertain) they quarreled so bitterly that afterwards they both

[34] Samuel H. Gordon, *Revolution: Its Necessity and Its Justification*, Philadelphia, 1894. According to Will Duff, the lecture was actually written by Voltairine de Cleyre herself; and from its style and references to Parsons and Lum, it is probable that, if not the sole author, she at least had a hand in it. See Will Duff to Joseph Ishill, November 23, 1931, Ishill Collection.

[35] Voltairine de Cleyre to Mary Hansen, December 6, 1909, Ishill Collection.

took poison. A friend, Dr. Morgan, sent Voltai to Horn and Hardart for black coffee "that made me vomit terribly." Gordon was given medicine, but the next day his stomach was burned up, his lips were black, and "we were both like rags."[36]

According to Voltairine, Gordon was angry because she rejected "the regular program of married life," that is, "exclusive possession, home, children, all that."[37] But she would not now accept the role of traditional wife and housekeeper any more than she had done with Elliott. "If you want me back I shall come all the sooner if you treat me as a free woman and not as a slave," she wrote Gordon from London in 1897. "Last summer I wanted to enslave you—at least so much that my days and nights were tears because you preferred other people to me, though theoretically I know I was wrong. I will never, *never* live that life again. It is not worth while *living* at that price. I would rather die here in England and never see your beautiful face again than live to be the slave of my own affection for you. I will never, let come what will, accept the condition of married slavery again. I will not do things for you; I will not *live* with you, for if I do I suffer the tortures of owning and being owned."[38]

Partly because of Gordon, Voltairine de Cleyre became involved in a long and bitter controversy with Emma Goldman, which was to last until the end of her life. Voltairine and Emma first met in August 1893, a time of acute economic depression, when Emma came to Philadelphia to address a rally for the unemployed.

[36] *Ibid.*; Voltairine de Cleyre, "Harry Levetin," Ishill Collection, published in *Free Vistas*, 1 (1933).

[37] Voltairine de Cleyre to Adelaide D. Thayer, September 14, 1900, Ishill Collection.

[38] Voltairine de Cleyre to Samuel H. Gordon, n.d. [1897], Cohen Papers.

"I had heard about this brilliant American girl," writes
Emma, "and I knew that she had been influenced, like
myself, by the judicial murder in Chicago, and that
she had since become active in anarchist ranks." Emma
had long wanted to meet her, but found her ill in bed
from the "catarrh" which she had developed in early
childhood and which had grown continually worse over
the years. Despite her illness, however, Voltairine attended the rally, and when Emma was arrested as
she mounted the platform, Voltairine took her place
and delivered a rousing protest against the suppression
of free speech. "I thought it splendid of her to have
gone to the meeting from a sick-bed and to have
spoken in my behalf," says Emma. "I was proud of her
comradeship."[39]

Emma's detention had been requested by the New
York police department. For before coming to Philadelphia she had addressed a mass meeting in Union
Square where, like Louise Michel, who was prosecuted
in 1883 for exhorting the poor of Paris to take bread,
she had urged her listeners, many of them jobless, to
"demonstrate before the palaces of the rich; demand
work. If they do not give you work, demand bread. If
they deny you both, take bread. It is your sacred
right!"[40] The next day she had left for Philadelphia.
But, pursued by a warrant from New York, she was
quickly extradited, tried for inciting to riot, and sentenced to a year on Blackwell's Island.

The two young women next saw each other four
months later, when Voltairine came to New York to
address a meeting to protest Emma's imprisonment.
Her speech, "In Defense of Emma Goldman and the
Right of Expropriation," delivered on December 16,
1893, compared Emma to Jesus and her judge to
Pontius Pilate and upheld the claims of individual conscience against the sham legality of "hypocrites, ex-

[39] Goldman, *Living My Life*, p. 124.
[40] *Ibid.*, p. 123.

tortionists, doers of iniquity, robbers of the poor, blood-partakers, serpents, vipers, fit for hell!" Thomas Paine had declared that "men should not petition for rights but take them." Voltairine agreed. For "constitutional rights," "natural rights," "inalienable rights" were merely an abstract fiction. "Unless the material conditions for equality exist, it is worse than mockery to pronounce men equal." Only the spirit of rebellion, the spirit which animated Emma Goldman, *will emancipate the slave from his slavery, the tyrant from his tyranny—the spirit which is willing to dare and suffer.*"[41]

After her speech, Voltairine visited Emma on Blackwell's Island with Emma's lover, Edward Brady. They talked, recalls Emma, of anarchism and of Berkman's imprisonment, the "things nearest to our hearts." "Ever since I had come into the anarchist movement I had longed for a friend of my own sex, a kindred spirit with whom I could share the inmost thoughts and feelings I could not express to men, not even to Ed. Instead of friendship from women I had met with much antagonism, petty envy and jealousy because men like me. . . . The coming into my life of Voltairine de Cleyre held out the hope of a fine friendship."[42]

Returning to Philadelphia, Voltairine wrote Emma "wonderful letters of comradeship and affection." She suggested that "on my release I come straight to her. She would make me rest before her fire-place, she would wait on me, read to me, and try to make me forget my ghastly experience." Soon afterwards, however, an incident occurred which shattered their blossoming friendship. Voltairine wrote to say that she was coming on another visit, accompanied by her companion Gordon. Gordon, however, was a disciple of

[41] *Selected Works*, pp. 205-19. In the pamphlet edition of this speech, published in Philadelphia in 1894, the date of its delivery and the spelling of Emma's surname are incorrect.

[42] Goldman, *Living My Life*, p. 157.

Most, who had repudiated Berkman's attempt on Frick, for which Emma could never forgive him. When Emma was in Philadelphia, Gordon had denounced her "as a disrupter of the movement, charging me with being in it only for sensational ends. He would not participate in any meeting where I was to speak."[43]

Accordingly, Emma wrote Voltairine that she would prefer not to see Gordon. "I was permitted only two visits a month; I would not give up Ed's visit, the other being taken up by near friends." Deeply hurt, Voltairine stopped writing. In October 1894, when she was again in New York to lecture on Mary Wollstonecraft, Emma, less than two months out of prison, was in the audience, but the two did not speak. Nor did they speak when Emma came to lecture in Philadelphia in 1896. That year, however, Emma wrote to Voltairine for help in securing a reduction of Berkman's twenty-two-year sentence. Voltairine promptly replied with a public appeal on his behalf, but sent it to Brady rather than Emma. "For a moment I felt angry at what I considered a slight," says Emma, "but when I read the document, my wrath melted away. It was a prose poem full of moving power and beauty. I wrote her my thanks without reference to our misunderstanding. She did not reply."[44]

With two such strong and divergent personalities as Emma and Voltairine, conflict was perhaps inevitable. They did, it is true, share certain common features. Both were unusually talented women, strong-minded and strong-willed. Both were militant anarchists and feminists and prolific speakers and writers. Harry Kelly, who knew them both well, wrote: "Voltairine de Cleyre and Emma Goldman will always stand out in my mind as the two most notable women it was ever my good fortune to meet. Widely different

[43] *Ibid.*, pp. 157-58.
[44] *Ibid.*, pp. 176-77; Voltairine de Cleyre to James B. Elliott, October 8, 1894, Labadie Collection.

in racial background, character, temperament, and
education, they had two attitudes in common—love of
freedom and dauntless physical and moral courage."[45]

Yet a clash was latent from the outset. For Voltairine
differed from Emma as poetry differs from prose. Or,
as their friend Carl Nold put it, comparing their
performance on the lecture platform, Emma tried to
attract her listeners with a base drum while Voltairine
did it with a violin. "I have not a tongue of fire as
Emma Goldman has," Voltairine once said. "I cannot
'stir the people'; I must speak in my own cold,
calculated way." Not that she envied Emma, as some
of their comrades maintained. Such allegations were
utter "nonsense."[46] But she did not approve of dramatic
oratory. Nor did she highly regard Emma's written
work. She herself was a more versatile craftsman,
composing poems and stories as well as essays and
speeches. Her writing, too, was more lyrical in style
and more philosophical in content than Emma's,
whose first book, *Anarchism and Other Essays*, she
uncharitably dismissed as "a very poor thing, an incoherent collection of badly written lectures," as she
confided to Joseph Cohen. "There is *force* in them; that
is their one quality of value. Don't tell it to the others,
but the reviews are making her insufferably vain over
it." Emma, for her part, underrated Voltairine's
"Anarchism and American Traditions," which was
published in her own *Mother Earth*.[47]

Beyond this, there were other, more personal
grounds for conflict. Each had small regard for the

[45] Harry Kelly, "Roll Back the Years: Odyssey of a Libertarian," unpublished autobiography, Tamiment Collection,
VI: 4.

[46] *Selected Works*, p. 214; Voltairine de Cleyre to Saul Yanovsky, March 29, 1911, Ishill Collection.

[47] Voltairine de Cleyre to Joseph J. Cohen, March 8, 1911,
Cohen Papers; Emma Goldman to Alexander Berkman, May 27,
1934, Goldman Archive, International Institute of Social
History.

other's physical attractions, still less for the men who succumbed to them. "Poor Voltairine," wrote Emma to Berkman, "with all her greatness she had a petty streak when it came to other women. . . . Voltairine could never forgive me two things, my dislike of that dog Gordon who sapped her dry and then cast her away, and Brady's love for me."[48] Voltairine had an especially low opinion of Ben L. Reitman, Emma's companion after Brady, "a white-fleshed, waxy-looking doctor," as Max Eastman describes him, "who thought it radical to shock people with crude allusions to their sexual physiology." Most of Emma's friends agreed that Reitman was "the most vulgar and impossible man they'd ever met."[49] Berkman found him "politically and socially confused," while Margaret Anderson, editor of *The Little Review*, maintained that he "wasn't so bad if you could hastily drop all your ideas as to how human beings should look and act." As for Voltairine, Reitman himself says that she "used to hate me as frankly as I loved her." "My God, Emma, how can you stand Ben?" she asked when they were again on speaking terms.[50]

To Voltairine, moreover, Emma herself was dumpy and unattractive. Emma, by the same token, considered Voltairine, with her spiritual and ascetic nature, as totally unappealing to men. Yet most of Voltairine's contemporaries—a number of whom I have interviewed at length—were struck by her unusual beauty and feminine charm. It was only in later years that she covered herself with "ungainly clothes," to

---

[48] Emma Goldman to Alexander Berkman, December 23, 1927, Berkman Archive.

[49] Max Eastman, *Enjoyment of Living*, New York, 1948, p. 424; *The Road to Freedom*, September 1931; Ben L. Reitman to Leonard D. Abbott, June 15, 1940, Abbott Papers.

[50] Richard Drinnon, *Rebel in Paradise*, Chicago, 1961, p. 123; Ben L. Reitman, "Following the Monkey," unpublished autobiography, Reitman Papers, University of Illinois, Chicago Circle.

quote Emma's phrase; and even then men and women found her, with her slender figure, soft brown hair, and piercing blue eyes, attractive and pleasing to look at.

It was not only Emma's looks and choice of companions that troubled Voltairine. It was her whole style of life, flamboyant and self-indulgent in Voltairine's view, to which she ultimately objected. Emma was too much in the limelight, too much a "public figure" for Voltairine's ascetic tastes. "E. G. has *cheek*—millions of it—and you know what Barnum said about the American people, 'they like to be humbugged'—Anarchism's no exception," she wrote in 1898. Under Emma's influence, she feared, added to that of Lucy Parsons, the movement was losing its soul.[51]

Voltairine, by contrast, was inflexible, almost fanatical, in her personal code of behavior and self-denying righteousness. And she expected the same of her comrades. Her criticisms of Emma and Reitman for staying in expensive hotels and eating expensive meals[52] resemble young Berkman's sermons against squandering money on material pleasures. "I was tired of having the Cause constantly thrown in my face," Emma reacted. "I did not believe that a Cause which stood for a beautiful ideal, for anarchism, for release and freedom from conventions and prejudice, should demand the denial of life and joy. I insisted that our Cause could not expect me to become a nun and that the movement should not be turned into a cloister. If it meant that, I did not want it. 'I want freedom, the right to self-expression, everybody's right to beautiful things.' Anarchism meant that to me, and I would live it in spite of the whole world—prisons, persecution, everything. Yes, even in spite of the condemnation of

[51] Voltairine de Cleyre to William and Margaret Duff, May 21, 1898, Ishill Collection; Voltairine de Cleyre to Elizabeth Turner Bell, n.d. [1898], Bell Papers, Los Angeles.

[52] Voltairine de Cleyre to Joseph J. Cohen, October 15, 1910, Cohen Papers.

my own closest comrades I would live my beautiful ideal."[53]

For Voltairine de Cleyre anarchism was a serious business. There was little joy in it, just as there was little joy in her private life. She suffered neither pseudo-revolutionaries nor hangers-on gladly. She was a true believer, a puritan, who resented Emma Goldman's "bourgeois" extravagances just as she resented Sadakichi Hartmann's sponging for drink. "I have been told," remarked the British anarchist Thomas Keell, "that she was a difficult woman to work with as she set a higher standard for the movement than the all too human comrades were ready to accept."[54] She was disturbed by the middle-class values which seemed to be penetrating anarchist circles. When *Mother Earth* announced a special issue in honor of Kropotkin's seventieth birthday, Voltairine, despite her admiration for her old comrade, demurred. "About Kropotkin's birthday, I really can't enthuse," she wrote to Joseph Cohen. "But I suppose that's what our dilettante have to have: birthdays, parties, concerts—anything lackadaisical and *safe*! I don't believe K. likes it much himself. He'd rather people were interested in some bigger thing than some individual's birthday."[55]

Similarly, when addressing a series of meetings in upstate New York in the autumn of 1910, she frowned upon the "respectable halls" in "respectable neighborhoods" filled with "respectable people," most of them middle class, with many liberals and Single Taxers but few genuine proletarians. As she wrote to Yanovsky, "I am disgusted with the 'respectability' of our 'movement,' and am glad that I shall not have to keep up this sort of thing more than a few weeks longer. It is

[53] Goldman, *Living My Life*, p. 56.

[54] Thomas H. Keell to Joseph Ishill, January 11, 1930, Ishill Collection.

[55] Voltairine de Cleyre to Joseph J. Cohen, March 28, 1912, Cohen Papers.

absolutely horrible, *horrible* to me to find that Anarchism has been made a 'fad' for 'intellectuals' to pat on the back. Ugh!" And in *Mother Earth* she declared: "I am more than ever convinced that our work should be with the workers, not with the bourgeoisie. . . . Comrades, we have gone upon a wrong road. Let us get back to the point that our work should be chiefly among the poor, the ignorant, the brutal, the disinherited, the men and women who do the hard and brutalizing work of the world."[56]

Taking this as an oblique personal attack, Emma Goldman denied having any craving for respectability and insisted that most of her work had been among the persecuted and deprived. Nevertheless, she maintained, "the pioneers of every new thought rarely come from the ranks of the workers" but "generally emanate from the so-called respectable classes." To limit one's activities to the masses was in any case "contrary to the spirit of anarchism," which builds "not on classes, but on men and women."[57]

"Emma was jealous of all the pretty women, all the attractive ones, including Voltairine, who came in her path," a friend remarked. "Yet she was big enough to love them none the less."[58] And in spite of their disagreements, which increased over the years, she treated Voltairine with respect. In 1907, when reporting on the American movement to the International Anarchist Congress in Amsterdam, she described her as "one of our few native revolutionary Anarchists, a brilliant woman of exceptional literary talent, whose untiring efforts in the cause of Anarchism deserve

[56] Voltairine de Cleyre to Saul Yanovsky, October 18, 1910, Ishill Collection; Voltairine de Cleyre, "Tour Impressions," *Mother Earth*, December 1910.

[57] Emma Goldman, "A Rejoinder," *Mother Earth*, December 1910.

[58] Interview with Jeanne Levey, Miami, Fla., December 19, 1972.

special mention." Twenty years later, in her portrait of Voltairine, which she considered "among the best things I have done" and which, despite some errors and distortions, is both informative and penetrating, she judged her the "most gifted and brilliant Anarchist woman America ever produced . . . a forceful personality, a brilliant mind, a fervent idealist, an unflinching fighter, a devoted and loyal comrade."[59]

On the other hand, said Emma, her life and work "have hardly left a trace" and "had little influence in America, which of course did not speak against her. It was due to her personality as it was hard for her to get out of her shell." And yet America needed anarchists of Voltairine's caliber. "The reason we have no movement in the States or in other countries outside of Spain," wrote Emma to Berkman in 1934, "is that we have no talents, not one able outstanding personality to make our ideas a living force. Whatever the reason, the fact remains that not since the death of Voltairine de Cleyre did one single native American of any consequence take up Anarchism as his or her life's goal."[60]

In 1935 Emma was extremely interested to hear from Joseph Ishill that he was in touch with Voltairine's sister, of whose existence she had not been aware. Emma apologized, moreover, for having dismissed Voltairine's son as a "one hundred per cent American," Ishill having informed her on the subject.[61] In the last years of her life, as her secretary testifies,

[59] Emma Goldman, "The Situation in America," *Mother Earth*, November 1907; Emma Goldman to Joseph Ishill, September 28 and December 29, 1927, Ishill Collection; Goldman, *Voltairine de Cleyre*, pp. 5-6. Cf. Goldman, "Was My Life Worth Living?" *Harper's Magazine*, December 1934.

[60] Emma Goldman to Alexander Berkman, February 20, 1929, Goldman Archive, and June 30, 1934, Berkman Archive. Cf. Emma Goldman to Rudolf and Milly Rocker, September 4, 1934, Rocker Archive, International Institute of Social History.

[61] Emma Goldman to Joseph Ishill, February 13, 1935, Ishill Collection.

Emma spoke often and with great affection of Voltairine. Roger Baldwin, too, recalls that Emma "was always talking to me about her, and she admired her greatly." When Emma died in 1940, Ben Reitman spoke at her funeral in the Waldheim Cemetery. "A great soul has returned to earth," he said, "and she rests where she wanted to rest, within fifty feet of Voltairine de Cleyre and the Chicago Anarchists who had inspired her."[62]

While lacking Emma's notoriety and dynamic vitality, Voltairine nevertheless emerged as one of the leading figures in the American anarchist movement between 1890 and 1910. In Philadelphia, she was active both among native-born libertarians and among Jewish immigrant revolutionists, serving as a vital link between them. She contributed a steady stream of articles and poems, sketches and stories to a variety of radical journals, of which *Lucifer*, *Free Society*, and *Mother Earth* were perhaps the most important.[63] No one worked more strenuously at her writings or revised more carefully and thoroughly. A friend has described her method of composing an essay or article: "Once a subject suggested itself to her mind, it anchored there well. Then she nursed it in her logical brain, fed it with

[62] Interview with Millie Desser Grobstein, Brooklyn, N.Y., April 20, 1975; interview with Roger N. Baldwin, New York City, January 29, 1974; Ben L. Reitman to Hutchins Hapgood, May 18, 1940, Abbott Papers.

[63] She also published in *The Open Court*, *Twentieth Century*, *Altruria*, *The Boston Investigator*, *The Liberal* (Chicago), *The Truth Seeker*, *Truth*, *Freethought*, *The Freethinkers' Magazine*, *The Pennsylvania Nationalist*, *The Independent*, *The Rights of Labor*, *The Labor Leader*, *The Magazine of Poetry*, *Liberty* (Boston), *Liberty* (London), *Freedom* (Chicago), *Freedom* (London), *Discontent*, *The Demonstrator*, *Solidarity*, *The Individualist*, *The Firebrand*, *The Beacon*, *The Rebel*, and other journals.

new suggestions, researched over it, added to it and deducted from it until she had it so complete in her mind that she could sit down and put it on paper as fast as if she were reading it. But still to her the work was not done yet. It had to be beautiful—improved, polished—she herself had to reflect on it, always trying to be better than life and circumstances permitted. Thus can be seen in the first copy of her manuscripts continuous changes of words and sentences—not for the sake of improving the thought, but for the sake of the sound or linguistic beauty. When she had improved the first copy to her satisfaction, then she made a second copy in her clear and beautiful handwriting, and the article or pamphlet was ready for print. But even then, if the manuscript did not go to the printer immediately, she kept on improving it, while time and conditions were suggesting new ideas to her, so that her work really never was done."[64]

In addition, she delivered innumerable lectures on anarchism and free thought in New York, Boston, and Chicago as well as in Philadelphia, "every word calculated to express the strongest possible idea."[65] During an engagement in New York in May 1894, she met Johann Most for the first time and heard him speak at a German gathering. "He is, or rather would be were it not for the goiter which spoils the right side of his face, ordinarily good looking; is rather courtly in his manners; and the personification of grace in his movements," she wrote to her mother. "His German is very musical, but he is too much of an actor to please me as an orator. . . . One can't help but admire the old man's courage and fortitude, though heaven knows I'd as lief have socialism by government as his communism. It is no wonder the press hates and caricatures and vilifies him, for his eloquence is so great that even German policemen against whom he thun-

[64] Kucera, "Voltairine de Cleyre," *Why?*, August 1913.
[65] Navro manuscript, Ishill Collection.

ders his anathemas, applaud him, using their clubs to pat the wall behind them so as not to be seen."[66]

Every March Voltairine would speak at meetings to commemorate the Commune of Paris, and every November to honor the martyrs of Chicago. The Haymarket affair remained forever in her thoughts. In 1893 she hailed the pardon of Fielden, Schwab, and Neebe by Governor Altgeld, "who thus sacrificed his political career to an act of justice." When Altgeld published his reasons for the pardon, Voltairine sent a copy to her mother: "Brave man! He has killed himself politically to save the poor workingmen! He deserves a wreath of laurels. And in the ages he'll get it too—as Paine is getting his now—after 100 years."[67]

In speech after powerful speech she paid moving tribute to her Haymarket comrades, "men who bowed at no shrine, acknowledged no God, believed in no hereafter, and yet went as proudly and triumphantly to the gallows as ever Christian martyr did of old." Nor had they died in vain, she said, addressing her words to the Illinois prosecutor, Julius Grinnell, "for every drop of blood you spilled on that November day you made an Anarchist. You sent their words on wings of flame in many tongues and many lands. . . . You struck a welding blow that beat the hearts of the working people of the world together. You lifted out of the obscurity of the common man five names, and set them as beacons upon a hill. You sent the word Anarchy ringing through every workshop. You gave us a manifold crucifixion, and dignified what had been a speculative theory with the sacrificial cast of a religion. In the heart of this black slag heap of grime and crime you have made a sacred place, for in it you lopped off an arm from the Cross and gave us the Gallows." Haymarket, she declared, was not the death knell of the anarchist

[66] Voltairine de Cleyre to Harriet De Claire, May 11, 1894, Labadie Collection.

[67] *Selected Works*, p. 56; Voltairine de Cleyre to Harriet De Claire, January 13, 1894, Labadie Collection.

movement. On the contrary, anarchism was growing. "Ay, it is growing, growing—your fear-word, our fire-word, *Anarchy.*"[68]

Voltairine's activities during these years were not limited to her lectures and writings. She involved herself also in the humdrum "Jimmie Higgins" tasks of arranging meetings, distributing literature, organizing groups and discussion clubs, performing, in short, all the day-to-day functions of the rank-and-file, without which "no movement could exist—no money for propaganda could be raised," and yet which "rarely are appreciated and never bring returns in the shape of name or fame."[69] With Dyer Lum and a British-born watchmaker named William Hanson, who wrote for Tucker's *Liberty* and who, like Lum himself, was to commit suicide a few years later, she started an anarchist study group during the early 1890s, whose twenty-odd members included Moses Dropkin, a Russian-Jewish immigrant, Thomas Earle White, a lawyer from a prominent Philadelphia family, and Margaret Perle McLeod, active also in the Ladies' Liberal League, a free thought and feminist group which Voltairine helped to found in 1892.

The Ladies' Liberal League, Voltairine tells us, was not a mere ladies' aid society or social club formed "to smile men into ticket-buying, and shame them into candy purchases, and wheedle them into ice-cream." Standing, rather, for "non-acquiescence to injustice," it provided a forum for lectures on a broad range of advanced topics, from sex, prohibition, and crime to socialism, anarchism, and revolution, for "there is forbidden fruit waiting to be gathered, the fruit of the tree of knowledge."[70] Around 1895, the Ladies' Liberal League joined forces with the Radical Library, estab-

[68] *The Rebel*, November 20, 1895; *Free Society*, November 26, 1899.

[69] *Why?*, August 1913.

[70] Voltairine de Cleyre, *The Past and Future of the Ladies' Liberal League*, Philadelphia, 1896.

lished by Voltairine and her friends to repair "a deficit
in our public libraries by furnishing radical works
upon all subjects at a slight expense to readers, and
being open at an hour when working men may avail
themselves of it."[71] Several years later, when the Ladies'
Liberal League disbanded, it left the books of the
Radical Library in the care of Natasha Notkin, a Rus-
sian-born anarchist, who passed them in 1905 to a
group of Jewish comrades headed by Joseph Cohen.
This group, setting up a club room at 424 Pine Street
and appropriating the name of Radical Library, began
a career in libertarian education and mutual assistance that continued for half a century.

Natasha Notkin, a pharmacist by profession, was
among the most dedicated activists in the Philadelphia
movement. From her drug store on East Lehigh Street
she collected funds for the Berkman Defense Association, arranged an annual tea party on behalf of imprisoned Russian revolutionaries, and distributed
Free Society and *Mother Earth*. Voltairine admired her
and saw in her the spirit of the Narodnik women, and
especially of Sophia Perovskaya, who went to the gallows for the assassination of Alexander II. According
to Abe Isaak, the editor of *Free Society*, Natasha Notkin was "married to the movement" and had no time
for ordinary love affairs. Emma Goldman calls her
"the true type of Russian woman revolutionist," completely devoted to the cause.[72]

Natasha Notkin and Perle McLeod were not Voltairine's only women associates in Philadelphia. Her
closest and truest friend was Mary Hansen, a Danish-
born anarchist, gentle and sympathetic, whose verse
appeared alongside Voltairine's in the columns of *Free
Society* and *Mother Earth*. "She had no mean qualities,"
noted Alexis Ferm, the libertarian educator, "no

[71] *Ibid.*
[72] *Free Society*, September 20, 1903; Goldman, *Living My
Life*, p. 123.

jealousies and so far as I could tell no hatreds. If the majority of people had her state of mind, there would be no wars, no jockeying for position, no 'grab while the grabbing is good.' "[73] Voltairine regularly had dinner with Mary and her companion, George Brown, and read and discussed literature with them. They found her to be "the best of good company," and she moved in with them when she left the Elliotts in 1894. She lived with them again after the turn of the century and paid occasional visits to their summer cottage in the Single Tax colony at Arden, Delaware, south of Philadelphia.[74]

Next to Voltairine herself, George Brown was the most popular anarchist orator in Philadelphia. A Yorkshireman by birth and a shoemaker by trade, he was of a type of artisan-preacher not unfamiliar in nineteenth-century radical movements. After five years in India teaching the natives his craft, he emigrated to the United States during the early 1880s, settled in Chicago, and organized a free thought debating club of which Albert Parsons was a member. Brown was present at the Haymarket meeting when the bomb was thrown. Taking up the cause of the condemned men, he was blacklisted by the shoe manufacturers of the city. He moved to Cincinnati and organized another debating society—he loved debating, in which he excelled—then went to Philadelphia in 1893, living there and at Arden until his death in 1915 of blood poisoning from a splinter in his hand.[75]

A fluent speaker with a strong taste for drink, Brown

[73] Alexis C. Ferm to Gladys Hourwich, March 31, 1952, Modern School Collection, Rutgers.

[74] *Mother Earth*, July 1912. In later years at Stelton, Mary Hansen spoke of Voltairine "all the time, glowingly, always with love." Interview with Sally Axelrod, Stelton, N.J., August 23, 1974.

[75] James B. Elliott, "George Brown," *Mother Earth*, April 1915. See also *Free Society*, November 16, 1902; and *Mother Earth*, November 1912.

often shared the platform with Voltairine, chairing
hundreds of meetings and lecturing to both native and
immigrant groups in Boston and New York as well as
Philadelphia. In 1894 he repaired the shoes of Jacob
Coxey's "industrial army" which passed through Philadelphia on its march to Washington to demand relief
for the unemployed. "He was an Anarchist of the type
that did not believe in remaining sober long," said
Alexis Ferm. "But he was also clever, so full of un-
answerable talk or argument that many people liked
him in spite of himself." Pugnacious and articulate, his
language in debates with rival reformers was tem-
pered only by a sardonic wit. "George never backed
water," wrote his friend Horace Traubel, the secretary
of Walt Whitman. "He was without apology."[76]

Combined with her teaching, Voltairine's labors for
the anarchist movement gradually depleted her
energies. Poverty further undermined her constitution,
so that Mary Hansen marveled at the "will strong
enough to force that frail body forward." "Who am
I?" Voltairine herself asked. "Only one of the com-
monest people, only a worked-out body, a shriveled and
withered soul."[77] Nor was she a sociable person, in
spite of her circle of friends. In her private life she
remained largely secluded, with cats and birds and fish
to keep her company. She had become, in her own
words, "a rather cold, self-reliant sort of an individual,
looking for help from nobody and given to biting my
lips a good deal." Even when addressing a meeting, her
voice, though clear and moving, seemed lonely to
some; and in her writings the gloom was only occasionally broken by a shaft of humor, as in "A Novel of

[76] Alexis C. Ferm to Gladys Hourwich, March 31, 1952,
Modern School Collection; *The Modern School*, April 1915.

[77] *Mother Earth*, July 1912; Voltairine de Cleyre, "Out of the
Darkness," *Selected Works*, pp. 47-48. Max Nettlau considered
this her finest poem. Nettlau to Joseph Ishill, November 20,
1924, Ishill Collection.

Color," a poem about three chipmunks and an elephant.[78]

Yet a formidable strength lay behind that loneliness and isolation. "My life has made me in a sterner mold than the original tendencies of childhood may have seemed to you to indicate," she wrote to her mother in 1897. ". . . I have my own principles, and should despise myself as a caitiff wretch did I not live in accordance with them."[79] Notwithstanding her weak health and precarious finances, she had found in Philadelphia the independence she had always craved; and, amid the many sorrows of her life, "she certainly had some good times" and some devoted friends to share them with, as Agnes Inglis observed. Although she did not love children and was impatient with ignorance and stupidity, she was kindness itself to the unfortunate and unsuccessful. "To me," writes George Brown, "she was the most intellectual woman I ever met; the most patient, brave, and loving comrade I have ever had. She spent her tortured life in the service of an obscure cause. Had she done the same work in some popular cause, she would have been famous and the world would have acclaimed her, as I believe her to have been, the greatest woman America has produced."[80]

[78] Voltairine de Cleyre to Harriet De Claire, June 26, 1897, Labadie Collection; *Selected Works*, pp. 64-65.

[79] Voltairine de Cleyre to Harriet De Claire, June 26, 1897, Labadie Collection.

[80] Agnes Inglis to Joseph Ishill, November 22, 1949, Ishill Collection; *Mother Earth*, July 1912.

4. England and Scotland

In the summer of 1894, an English anarchist named Charles Wilfred Mowbray arrived in the United States on a lecture tour. A self-educated tailor from the London slums who had served in the army as a youth, Mowbray was a big, athletic-looking man in his middle thirties, with black hair, blazing eyes, and a tempestuous eloquence that had stirred many an audience in Britain, where he had been a friend of William Morris and an active member of the Socialist League since its formation a decade before. A militant agitator of the Johann Most stamp, Mowbray had taken part in unemployment demonstrations and free-speech fights and in annual Paris Commune and Haymarket commemorations, sharing the rostrum with Peter Kropotkin, Errico Malatesta, Louise Michel, and Saul Yanovsky, who had come to London to edit *Der Arbeter Fraynd*, the Yiddish anarchist paper in Whitechapel. In November 1888 he had chaired a Haymarket meeting at which Lucy Parsons, on a lecture tour of the British Isles, spoke on the labor movement in America, followed by the singing of her husband's favorite song, "Annie Laurie," and of William Morris's "No Master."[1]

During the summer and fall of 1894, Mowbray lectured on anarchism in New York, Paterson, and other eastern cities with large immigrant and working-class populations. In the spirit of Bakunin and Most, he called for revolutionary action by all the disinherited elements of society, dismissing trade unionism of "the old sick benefit sort" as a failure. "We must denounce the brutal indifference of the employed to the sufferings of the unemployed—the criminals, the tramps, the casual laborers, the victims, in short, of the brutal system of class monopoly we are all suffering under,"

[1] *The Commonweal*, November 24, 1888.

he declared. In Paterson, according to a French anarchist paper in Pennsylvania, Mowbray's audience was held in thrall for an hour and a half by "the charm of his passionate and sincere voice, piling argument upon argument."[2]

On November 11, 1894, the seventh anniversary of the Haymarket executions, Mowbray addressed memorial meetings at the Thalia Theatre and Clarendon Hall in New York, followed by similar meetings in Hoboken, Paterson, and Newark. He then spoke in Pittsburgh and Baltimore before coming to Philadelphia in late December to address the Freiheit and Freie Wacht groups and the Ladies' Liberal League. So far, his tour had been "successful beyond my wildest hopes," he wrote. But on December 28th he received a setback. For when "the jolly comrade with the great head and greater heart," as Voltairine de Cleyre describes him, finished his lecture to the Ladies' Liberal League and was taking down names of persons who wished to form an anarchist group, he was arrested by detectives and charged with inciting to riot and sedition against the Commonwealth of Pennsylvania.[3]

Voltairine de Cleyre, who had welcomed Mowbray on behalf of the Ladies' Liberal League, immediately organized a defense fund, with herself as secretary and George Brown and Samuel Gordon among the members. Thanks to their efforts, Mowbray was quickly released and was able to proceed to Boston where, in early 1895, he settled down to practice his trade. It was not long, however, before he resumed his agitational work, addressing German, Bohemian, and

2 C. W. Mowbray, "Strikes, Organized Labor and the Militia," *Solidarity*, February 1, 1895; *L'Ami des ouvriers*, September 1894. See also *El Esclavo*, September 9, 1894.

3 "A letter from Comrade Mowbray," *Solidarity*, January 1, 1895; Voltairine de Cleyre, *Past and Future*, p. 6, and "Mowbray's Arrest," *Solidarity*, January 15, 1895; *L'Ami des ouvriers*, January 1895.

American groups throughout the northeast. In the summer of 1895 he embarked on an extended speaking tour which took him as far west as St. Louis and Chicago. The Chicago police, however, with memories of Haymarket still fresh, decided there would be no "anarchy nonsense" preached in their city. Accordingly, they interrupted a speech in which Mowbray favored "battling on Bunker Hill under the red flag, not the Stars and Stripes, but the glorious red flag of triumph." A riot nearly occurred, and only the bandmaster prevented disaster by striking up the "Marseillaise," which was "taken up by every man on the grounds until there was one great chorus."[4]

For the most part, however, Mowbray concentrated his propaganda on the east coast, and primarily in Boston. Among his ablest converts there was a twenty-four-year-old printer from Missouri named Harry Kelly, who, with Joseph Cohen and Leonard Abbott, was to become a key figure in the Modern School movement and a founder of the Stelton and Mohegan colonies which flourished in New Jersey and New York between the world wars. Kelly found Mowbray "a magnetic speaker" who was performing an "invaluable service" as an interpreter of anarchist theory to the working classes. To Emma Goldman, by contrast, Mowbray's lectures, for all their fiery rhetoric, were devoid of intellectual substance.[5]

Be that as it may, Kelly was presently the secretary of an Anarchist-Communist group in Boston created largely through Mowbray's efforts. Kelly and Mowbray, in addition, served as secretaries of the Union Cooperative Society of Printers and the Union Cooperative Society of Journeymen Tailors, both of which became

[4] *Solidarity*, April 1, 1895; *The Firebrand*, August 18, 1895; *The Rebel*, October 20, 1895; C. W. Mowbray to Josef Peukert, November 11, 1895, Peukert Archive, International Institute of Social History.

[5] Kelly, "Roll Back the Years," IV: 2.

affiliated with the Central Labor Union of Boston, imbuing it with an anarchist flavor. In the spring of 1895, at Mowbray's urging, Kelly traveled to London with a letter of introduction to John Turner, an active member of the Freedom Group and general secretary of the Shop Assistants' Union, which he had organized a few years earlier. Kelly remained in England more than three months, meeting Kropotkin, Malatesta, and other well-known figures and becoming the chief link between the Anarchist-Communist movements in Britain and the United States.

When Kelly returned to Boston, he was eager to start a journal to advance the ideas of the Anarchist-Communist school, a kind of American version of the London *Freedom*, founded in 1886 by Kropotkin and his associates. For this purpose, seventy dollars was raised by holding a raffle in which the prize was a tailor-made suit. Kelly and Mowbray peddled tickets among the Boston unions, in which they were now familiar figures, and bought material for the suit out of the funds collected. James Robb, another anarchist tailor, contributed the skills of his craft by sewing the prize suit.

So it was that *The Rebel*, "A Monthly Journal Devoted to the Exposition of Anarchist Communism," in the description on its masthead, was launched on September 20, 1895. Edited and printed by Kelly, Mowbray, and Robb, together with Henry A. Koch, a Boston hatter, and N. H. Berman, a Russian-Jewish immigrant who was to become Voltairine de Cleyre's lover four years later, it featured articles by Kropotkin and Louise Michel as well as by American anarchists who shared their economic convictions. Voltairine de Cleyre, though not an advocate of communal property, became a major contributor, with essays on the Chicago martyrs, the Ladies' Liberal League, and a streetcar strike in Philadelphia, published under her own signature or the pseudonym "X.Y.Z." In November

1895 she went up to Boston to speak at a Haymarket memorial in Caledonian Hall arranged by the Rebel Group. There was even talk of her editing the journal, but circumstances prevented her from taking up the post.[6]

Harry Kelly, with whom Voltairine shared the speaker's platform in Caledonian Hall, told her of his voyage to England and of all the fine comrades he had met; and after her return to Philadelphia she looked forward eagerly to the arrival of John Turner, a contributor to *The Rebel*, whom Kelly had invited to come on a lecture tour the following spring. It was the first of two trips that Turner would make to America: in a famous civil liberties case in 1903-1904, he became the first anarchist to be deported under the anti-anarchist law enacted after the assassination of President McKinley. Two years older than Voltairine de Cleyre, he too had been converted to anarchism as a result of the Haymarket tragedy. During his brief visit to Philadelphia, where he lectured on "The Anarchist Ideal" before the Ladies' Liberal League on April 22, 1896, he and Voltairine became such good friends that she was to stay at his house for more than two months when she journeyed to London the following year.

From Philadelphia, Turner went to Boston and was given a warm reception by Mowbray and Kelly when he addressed a May First celebration arranged by the Central Labor Union. Over the next six months he lectured in a dozen cities from New York to Denver, where he debated with Henry Cohen, a follower of Benjamin Tucker, on Anarchist-Communism versus Anarchist-Individualism, one of the principal issues dividing the movement at that time.[7] Compared to Mowbray, who had followed a similar route the

[6] *The Rebel*, September 20, 1895.

[7] An interesting account of the debate, by Lizzie M. Holmes, appeared in *The Firebrand*, May 2, 1897.

previous year, Turner was not an exciting speaker. But, in Emma Goldman's estimation, he was "the more cultivated and better informed of the two." Mowbray, in the meantime, continued his activities in Boston. In 1896 he and Johann Most were listed as speakers at a twenty-fifth-anniversary celebration of the Paris Commune, and with Harry Kelly he published a journal called *The Match*, which "sputtered for two numbers and went out."[8] A few years later, however, he moved to New York, and from there to Hoboken, where he opened a saloon and himself became a heavy drinker. Like John Turner, he was deported after the shooting of McKinley. Back in London, he was again addressing meetings alongside Malatesta and Kropotkin, as he had done so often in the past. But before long he abandoned anarchism to become a tariff reform lecturer. He died of heart failure in December 1910 at Bridlington, Yorkshire, in a hotel where he was staying.[9]

There were several reasons, in the spring of 1897, why Voltairine de Cleyre decided to go to England. She had wanted to travel to Europe ever since her childhood, yet she had never been outside the United States, except to study at the convent in Canada. Her health was in decline. She was worn out from her teaching and propaganda work and from her bitter quarrels with Gordon, who had been treating her with increasing neglect. A trip abroad would provide a much needed change from her enervating routine. In Philadelphia, her acquaintance with William Hanson, George Brown, and other anarchists of English birth had stimulated

[8] Goldman, *Living My Life*, p. 178; Harry Kelly, "An Anarchist in the Making," *Mother Earth*, April 1913.

[9] *The Star* (London), December 14, 1910. According to Harry Kelly, Mowbray drank himself to death. "Roll Back the Years," IV: 2.

her interest in their country, not to speak of her contacts with Kelly, Mowbray, and Turner. Nor was travel to England difficult in those days. Passage was cheap and restrictions were few. Apart from Harry Kelly, who had sailed to Liverpool for only ten dollars in 1895, Lucy Parsons and Emma Goldman had lectured in England and Scotland in 1888 and 1895. By the same token, more than a few British anarchists visited the United States during this period. Sam Mainwaring, Tom Cantwell, and Alfred Marsh all came over, besides Mowbray and Turner and such exiles in London as Stepniak, Kropotkin, and Malatesta.

And so, on June 13, 1897, Voltairine de Cleyre sailed for England. It was not a comfortable journey, what with "the terrible food, and the awful beds, and the disagreeable chattering lot of company," she wrote aboard ship. "I can't say that being 'rocked in the bosom of the deep' is the poetic thing altogether that it is alleged to be. . . ."[10] On June 19th she disembarked at Liverpool and a few days later proceeded by train to London, which Harry Kelly called "a Mecca for devout revolutionists of those days."[11] Her reputation as a writer and speaker had preceded her; and John Turner, who had been "deeply impressed" when he met her in Philadelphia, had sung her praise to his associates, who gave her a warm reception.[12]

Voltairine spent four months in Great Britain, from late June until late October, more than two of them in London as the guest of John and Mary Turner, who lived at 7 Lamb's Conduit Street and had a small grocery store on Red Lion Street. The Turners introduced her to the entire Freedom Group, of which they were both members. It was at their house that she met

[10] Voltairine de Cleyre to Harriet De Claire, June 18, 1897, Labadie Collection.

[11] Kelly, "Roll Back the Years," v: 1.

[12] *Freedom*, June-July 1897; interview with Marion Bell, Los Angeles, June 21, 1974.

the great anarchist historian, Max Nettlau, who found her "a friendly, quiet, charming young woman" and gave her a copy of his newly published *Bibliographie de l'Anarchie*.[13] She also met Abraham Frumkin, an editor of *Der Arbeter Fraynd*, who was to write one of the best essays about her in any language, and William Wess, who had served on a tailors' strike committee with Mowbray and Turner in 1889 and was the main liaison between the Yiddish and English speaking anarchists of the East End.

It was at Wess's flat in Whitechapel that Voltairine met Peter Kropotkin, whom she regarded as "the greatest man, save Tolstoy alone, that Russia has produced." Over tea, Kropotkin regaled her with the story of his dramatic escape from the St. Petersburg Military Hospital in 1876. For Voltairine it was a most memorable occasion: "We had our 'tea' in homely English fashion, with thin slices of buttered bread; and we talked of things nearest our hearts, which, whenever two or three Anarchists are gathered together, means present evidences of the growth of liberty and what our comrades are doing in all lands. And as what they do and say often leads them into prisons, the talk had naturally fallen upon Kropotkin's experience and his daring escape, for which the Russian government is chagrined to this day."[14]

Voltairine saw Kropotkin a second time, at his house in suburban Bromley, shortly before he himself departed for the first of two lecture tours in North

[13] Max Nettlau, untitled history of anarchism, manuscript, VII: 61, International Institute of Social History; *La Protesta*, March 31, 1928, p. 174.

[14] *Selected Works*, pp. 154-55. Kropotkin enjoyed telling the story of his escape and did so often. See, for example, Henry Seymour's account of his visit with Kropotkin in Harrow some years earlier, *Free Vistas*, II, 125. According to Stepniak, however, "he had been compelled to relate the particulars of his escape over and over again, until he was quite sick of the subject." *Underground Russia*, p. 162.

America. "It was so hot I wore no jacket," she wrote to
Will Wess, "and so caught a bad cold in my throat,
which is a nasty thing to go to Portsmouth with," where
she was to speak the following day. Voltairine came
away from her meetings with greater admiration than
ever for her comrade, "whose personality is felt more
than any other in the Anarchist movement—at once
the gentlest, the most kindly, and the most invincible
of men. Communist as well as Anarchist, his very
heart-beats are rhythmic with the great common
pulse of work and life."[15]

Present at Voltairine's first meeting with Kropotkin
were Mary Turner and her sister-in-law Elizabeth
Turner Bell, the wife of Thomas H. Bell, a young Scottish anarchist whom Voltairine thought very handsome, "with his gold hair and his white shadowy face."
Voltairine and Lizzie Bell at once became good friends
and were constant companions during her stay, completely "devoted to each other," as Tom Bell later recalled.[16] Thus when Voltairine lectured on anarchism
in Trafalgar Square and in Athenaeum Hall, Lizzie
Bell was at her side. After each address, it was Voltairine's practice to recite a poem, either one of her own
or else Freiligrath's "Revolution," a favorite of the
Chicago martyrs. Listening to one of her recitals in the
Whitechapel ghetto, Abraham Frumkin, despite his
poor command of English, hung on every word, moved
by her melodic tones and unable to take his eyes off
her. She reminded him of Louise Michel, who was also
in London at the time and whom Voltairine apparently
met, though we have no account of the occasion.[17]

[15] Voltairine de Cleyre to William Wess, n.d. [August 1897],
Wess Papers; *Selected Works*, p. 155.
[16] Voltairine de Cleyre to Elizabeth Turner Bell, n.d. [1898],
Bell Papers; Thomas H. Bell to Joseph Ishill, August 14, 1930,
in *The Oriole Press: A Bibliography*, Berkeley Heights, N.J.,
1953, pp. 257-58.
[17] Frumkin, *In friling fun yidishn sotsializm*, p. 225.

With Lizzie Bell, John Burns, and other comrades Voltairine saw the sights in London: Westminster Abbey and the Houses of Parliament, Tower Hill and the Crystal Palace, St. Paul's Cathedral and the Old Curiosity Shop. The Turner flat being close by, she went three times to the British Museum where, she wrote her mother, "I have seen your beloved Byron's own handwriting in a page of Childe Harold I think." (She later visited Byron's tomb and also the grave of George Eliot.) In addition, she was guided through the East End by Will Wess, who pointed out "interesting places in the history of reform meetings—obscure but delightful anecdotes, such as the spot where this or that rebel was arrested and why." One Sunday she went to Petticoat Lane and "bought a few things just to say I had." Nor did she miss the London theater, seeing *A Doll's House* by Ibsen and Sarah Bernhardt in *Camille*.[18]

One day she voyaged out to Stonehenge, which she describes with simple eloquence in a letter to her mother: "Oh! I dreamed about Stonehenge all my life, the powerful Druid ruin—the most gigantic stones standing upright in a circle with cross stones on their top. Old, so old the stones are eaten deep into with the gray moss—1000s of years they have stood there, and some have fallen flat, and some slant leaning on others, but 18 of them still standing, time defying. Right on top of the hill they stand in the centre of an immense plain with only groups of oaks, small groups, here and there. And while I stood picking moss from the stones a shepherd, with black cloak and wide black hat came driving his yellow sheep with black noses and legs, across the plain. And the dogs walked round keeping the herd together, and only the tinkle of the bells sounded over the plain. You would not have

[18] Voltairine de Cleyre to Harriet De Claire, August 3, 1897, Labadie Collection. Voltairine de Cleyre to Lillian Harman, April 1, 1898, Harman Papers.

thought there was so lonely a place in England."[19]

London, by contrast, she found "an abominably dirty place—that is the houses are black and ugly brown all over, though the streets are kept cleaner than the American city streets on the whole." And the air was "horribly smoky," making the days seem hotter than they actually were.[20] Nevertheless, in these new surroundings with pleasant friends and congenial work, Voltairine's health showed a dramatic improvement. It was a refreshing change from the hard life and grim routine of Philadelphia, and the weeks slipped quickly by. At one point, Lizzie Bell took her to a London studio to be photographed. In the picture, for which, says Marion Bell, "mother fixed her hair with a little curl,"[21] Voltairine, at thirty, looks young and happy. Her features had not yet assumed their later ascetic cast, for the spirit of youth and the joy of life had not yet evaporated.

Matters took a more somber turn with the arrival, at the beginning of August, of a group of Spanish exiles released from the Montjuich fortress in Barcelona. The previous year, following a bomb explosion in a religious procession, hundreds of anarchists had been arrested and subjected to savage tortures and mutilations, arousing a storm of protest in both Europe and America. Anarchists in New York, among them Emma Goldman and Harry Kelly, had organized a mass meeting at the Spanish consulate, while in Philadelphia Voltairine de Cleyre and her comrades had distributed 50,000 copies of *The Modern Inquisition in Spain*, an eight-page pamphlet documenting the atrocities, "the bare mention of which makes one shud-

[19] Voltairine de Cleyre to Harriet De Claire, October 26/27, 1897, Labadie Collection.
[20] Voltairine de Cleyre to Harriet De Claire, August 3, 1897, Labadie Collection.
[21] Interview with Marion Bell, June 21, 1974.

der," Voltairine remarked.[22] According to Nathan
Navro, Voltairine had "practically created the protest
movement in Philadelphia," writing to members of
Congress to press the Spanish authorities to end the
repressions. On May 29, 1897, two weeks before sailing
for England, she had written to William E. Chandler,
an influential Senator from New Hampshire, denounc-
ing "the crime committed by the Spanish government,
unparalleled even in Cuba itself. In my judgment this
crime demands *a protest from every civilized nation*,
to which end I beg you to use your influence in the
Senate."[23]

There were twenty-eight refugees in the first lot that
Voltairine and her comrades met at Euston Station one
early August afternoon, "homeless wanderers in the
whirlpool of London, released without trial after
months of imprisonment, and ordered to leave Spain
in forty-eight hours! They had left it, singing their
prison songs; and still across their dark and sorrowful
eyes one could see the eternal Maytime bloom."[24] Tom
Bell took them to a London doctor to treat the mutilations. A day or two later, a mass meeting was held at
which the tortured Spaniards were displayed before an
indignant crowd. "We stood upon the base of the Nelson monument in Trafalgar Square," Voltairine recalled. "Below were ten thousand people packed together with upturned faces. They had gathered to hear
and see men and women whose hands and limbs were
scarred all over with red-hot irons of the tortures in
the fortress of Montjuich. For the crime of an unknown
person these twenty-eight men and women, together
with four hundred others, had been cast into that terrible den and tortured with the infamies of the inquisition to make them reveal that of which they knew

[22] *Selected Works*, p. 160. Max Nettlau speculates that Voltairine herself was the author or editor of the pamphlet.

[23] Navro manuscript, Ishill Collection; Labadie Collection,
Vertical File.

[24] *Selected Works*, p. 161.

nothing." When one of the victims rose and "lifted his poor, scarred hands, the faces of those ten thousand people moved together like the leaves of a forest in the wind. They waved to and fro, they rose and fell; the visible moved in the breath of the invisible."[25]

Smaller gatherings took place in private homes, where the marks of the tortures, including crushed or mutilated sexual organs, were exhibited. "I have seen the scars on Francisco Gana's hands where they burned him with irons to make him accuse somebody," wrote Voltairine to her mother. "They tore out his toe-nails, put a gag in his mouth and pulled it back till his mouth was stretched to its utmost for hours. They drove him up and down the cell four days and nights without stopping. They crushed his head with a machine. At last they tore away his testicles. It is eleven months now since the torture but he has to go bandaged yet for that last wound."[26]

At one such meeting, in the Whitechapel apartment of Rudolf Rocker, a young Italian anarchist named Michele Angiolillo was so upset by what he saw and heard that he at once left for Spain on a mission of reprisal. On August 8, 1897, Angiolillo reached the summer resort of Santa Agueda where the Prime Minister, Antonio Cánovas del Castillo, was vacationing, and shot him to death. It was "one of those terrible acts of wild justice," said Tom Bell, who had known Angiolillo in London, "which, whether we approve of them or not, appear as inevitable as any natural phenomena."[27]

It is not known whether Voltairine de Cleyre herself

[25] *Ibid.*, pp. 201-202. See also Peter Kropotkin, "The Martyrs of Montjuich in London," *Free Society*, June 10, 1900, reprinted from *Les Temps Nouveaux*.

[26] Voltairine de Cleyre to Harriet De Claire, August 3, 1897, Labadie Collection.

[27] Interview with Fermin Rocker, New York City, February 17, 1972; Thomas H. Bell letter to *The Los Angeles Daily News*, March 17, 1937.

met Angiolillo before he set out to assassinate Cánovas. But she was deeply moved by his act ("His was the spirit that walked erect, and met the beast in its den. . . . His was the resolute hand that struck, steady and keen to its aim"). She wrote three separate poems to his memory, as well as a story, "The Heart of Angiolillo," describing his state of mind on the eve of his departure from London. Her poem "Germinal," Angiolillo's last word and the title of Zola's great novel, which had made a powerful impression on anarchists of her generation, reflects her feelings after Angiolillo's execution:

Germinal!–The Field of Mars is plowing,
And hard the steel that cuts, and hot the breath
Of the great Oxen, straining flanks and bowing
Beneath his goad, who guides the share of Death.

Germinal!–The Dragon's teeth are sowing,
And stern and white the sower flings the seed
He shall not gather, though full swift the growing;
Straight down Death's furrow treads, and does not
    heed.

Germinal!–The Helmet Heads are springing
Far up the Field of Mars in gleaming files;
With wild war notes the bursting earth is ringing.

Within his grave the sower sleeps, and smiles.[28]

The martyrdom of Angiolillo, by evoking the hangings in Chicago a decade before, inspired yet another poem, "Light Upon Waldheim." Written in London in October 1897, it depicts the Haymarket Monument as a kind of

[28] *Selected Works*, p. 65, written in London in October 1897, published in *Freedom*, January 1898, reprinted in *Free Society*, April 29, 1900. "Santa Agueda (In Memory of Angiolillo)" appeared in *Freedom*, August 1898, and "Angiolillo" in *Free Society*, October 7, 1900. Anarchists of this period named their groups, their journals, even their children "Germinal," and in the 1920s there was a Camp Germinal in Pennsylvania established by Joseph Cohen and the Radical Library Group.

anarchist Pietà, with its figure of a "warrior woman," the symbol of Revolution, placing a crown upon a fallen worker "with stone-caressing touch."[29]

Voltairine de Cleyre felt a strong bond of comradeship with the Spanish anarchists she met in London, foreshadowing her involvement with the Mexican anarchists in the final year of her life, when she began to study Spanish as she had earlier studied Yiddish in the Philadelphia ghetto. They were kindred spirits, these idealistic Spaniards, with their ascetic, quasi-religious character and their quest for natural justice. They strengthened her libertarian faith and provided a fresh source of inspiration in her work. Furthermore, they deepened her hatred of tyranny and her sympathy for those who sought to destroy by force the despotism capable of inflicting such monstrous tortures as had occurred in the dungeons of Montjuich.

The most impressive among them, as Voltairine wrote to her mother, was Fernando Tarrida del Mármol, who, along with Kropotkin and Nettlau, helped shape the development of her anarchist theories. A well-educated mathematician from one of Barcelona's leading families, the thirty-six-year-old Tarrida had evolved from the federalism and mutualism of Proudhon and Pi y Margall to the communist anarchism of Kropotkin and Ricardo Mella. In November 1889 he had attended an international gathering of anarchists in Barcelona to honor the Chicago martyrs and in September 1896 had been locked up in Montjuich after the Corpus Christi bombing, whose perpetrator, as in the Haymarket affair, was never discovered. Following his release, Tarrida, in Paris then in London, did more than anyone else to expose the barbarities of the Spanish government to which he himself had fallen victim. Voltairine de Cleyre considered him one of the finest personalities she had come to know within the inter-

[29] *Selected Works*, p. 66.

national anarchist movement, and we shall have more to say about him later.[30]

In London Voltairine de Cleyre also encountered a group of French anarchists, some of whom had been living in England since the suppression of the Paris Commune in 1871. At the home of one of these exiles she met Jean Grave, editor of *Les Temps Nouveaux*, the leading anarchist paper in France, and agreed to undertake a translation of his book, *La Société Mourante et l'Anarchie*, for which he had stood trial in 1894. In the middle of August she went across to Paris for a week, visiting the sights and calling on Sébastien Faure, editor of *Le Libertaire* and the foremost anarchist orator in France. The climax of her visit was a pilgrimage to the Père Lachaise Cemetery, the Waldheim of Paris, with its graves of famous revolutionaries and its Mur des Fédérés, where 147 Communards had been massacred in 1871. The leaves which Voltairine gathered there and sent to her mother remain preserved among her papers in the Labadie Collection.

Returning to London, Voltairine set forth on a month-long visit to Scotland, "my pet place of all the earth," she afterwards wrote to her hosts, Will and Maggie Duff of Glasgow. "If I could make my living in Scotland, I'd never care to come back to America to live," for Scotland is "the sharpest, ruggedest, wittiest place on earth—that's of the earth I've seen—(Scotch reservation). Oh, I love you all!"[31]

[30] See F. Tarrida del Mármol, *Les inquisiteurs d'Espagne*, Paris, 1897. Tarrida died in London on March 15, 1915, at the age of 54. See the obituary by Errico Malatesta, *Freedom*, April 1915.

[31] Voltairine de Cleyre to Will and Maggie Duff, May 28, 1898, and August 6, 1901, Ishill Collection. "O Scotland, bonnie, bonnie Scotland! I never loved a place so much as Scotland," she wrote to her mother on October 7, 1897.

A printer and craftsman of the William Morris type, Will Duff was a noteworthy figure in his own right and a good father and teacher—"indeed a *Man*," as his son described him to Joseph Ishill.[32] An admirer of Godwin and Shelley, Duff contributed to the London *Alarm* and to *Free Society* in America, of which he was the Glasgow distributor. He was a friend of Elisée Reclus, who had come to Scotland to lecture, and of Elisée's nephew Paul, who had lived for a time in Edinburgh and visited Glasgow often. Duff also knew Kropotkin; and in 1887, after the whole edition of Kropotkin's *In Russian and French Prisons* was bought up and destroyed by tsarist agents so that Kropotkin himself could not find a copy, it was Duff who sent him one.[33]

During her stay in Glasgow, Voltairine lived in the Duff home at 9 Carfin Street, Govanhill. On September 10th she sent her mother a sample of Scottish heather ("from Aberfoyle, Callanders, the country of Rob Roy MacGregor") and on September 25th a copy of *The Trossachs and Loch Lomond* with the inscription: "For my mother, from bonnie Scotland. Voltai. On the 2nd of Sept. I saw the snow upon Ben Ledi. Glasgow, Sept. 25, 1897."[34]

Meanwhile, she delivered a series of lectures in Glasgow, Edinburgh, Aberdeen, Paisley, and Dundee. Dundee, she was dismayed to find, was "no very bonnie the noo," but "black, smoky, disfigured by vomiting chimneys." In its once beautiful valley "wee children stand, for fifty-six long hours in the week, feeding the

[32] David Duff to Joseph Ishill, June 2, 1939, Ishill Collection. Duff named another son William Morris Duff.

[33] Will Duff to Joseph Ishill, August 31, 1930, Ishill Collection. Duff gave another copy to Emma Goldman when she lectured in Glasgow in 1895.

[34] Voltairine de Cleyre to Harriet De Claire, September 10, 1897, Labadie Collection. The heather is still preserved in the envelope, and the book is now in the possession of Renée de Cleyre Buckwalter.

deafening machines with jute, breathing a dust which
sets me coughing and choking, and living with un-
quenchable thirst."[35] In Glasgow alone she addressed
at least half a dozen meetings, some attended by more
than a thousand people. She appeared before the
Independent Labour Party and the Women's Labour
Party as well as before anarchist and rationalist groups.
As Will Duff reported, all her addresses were lucid and
scholarly, and "with her sincerity and originality of
thought she kept her vast audiences interested from
start to finish. Her lectures displayed the workings of a
great mind, a stimulating and clear intellect, every
point carrying with it a fund of pregnant thought." As
in London, she recited one of her poems at the close of
each lecture, "her voice and features portraying the
various emotions the words conveyed."[36]

Before Voltairine left Scotland, Will Duff presented
her with a copy of *Songs of the Army of the Night*, a
collection of poems by Francis Adams, an English
socialist whose verse appeared in *Free Society* and
other American periodicals of the 1890s. The following year Duff reissued Voltairine's long anti-religious
poem, "The Gods and the People," in pamphlet form.[37]
In 1903, as will be seen, she visited the Duffs again,
and they corresponded with each other until her death.
Will Duff survived her by twenty-seven years, dying in
Glasgow on the eve of the Second World War.

Leaving Glasgow on September 25, 1897, Voltairine
returned to London by way of Bradford, Leeds, and

[35] Voltairine de Cleyre to Harriet De Claire, October 7, 1897,
Labadie Collection; Voltairine de Cleyre, "Bonnie Dundee,"
The Herald of Revolt, September 1913, reprinted from *The
Boston Investigator*.

[36] Will Duff, "Voltairine de Cleyre's Tour in Scotland," *Freedom*, November 1897; Duff, "Voltairine de Cleyre," *The Herald
of Revolt*, September 1913.

[37] Solidarity Leaflet no. 1, Glasgow, 1898. Abe Isaak of *Free
Society* also published the poem in San Francisco. It originally
appeared in Lucy Parsons' *Freedom*, January 1, 1891.

Manchester, where she lectured to large and enthusiastic audiences. All told, she delivered some thirty lectures in England and Scotland on such subjects as
"The History of Anarchism in America," "The
Economic Phase of Anarchism," "The Woman Question," "The True Mental Attitude of a Freethinker,"
"Anarchism and the Labor Question," and "Why I am
an Anarchist." Once back in London, she concluded
her tour by addressing an assembly of Jewish anarchists at the South Place Institute on October 6th.[38]

Toward the end of October she sailed for the United
States. On her last night in England the London anarchists held a farewell party with music, singing, and
story-telling that went on until two in the morning. The
next day she left for Southampton. Her visit had been
an important and refreshing interlude in her life. She
had made new friends, among them such celebrated
figures as Peter Kropotkin and Louise Michel. She had
established ties with the international anarchist movement, French, Spanish, and Russian, as well as British.
Her trip had provided a badly needed respite from her
drudgery among the Philadelphia poor. At the same
time, it had broadened her view of anarchism by expos-
ing her to a variety of attitudes and theories regarding
property and organization, direct action and propaganda by the deed. This led her to develop a wide-
ranging libertarian philosophy—"anarchism without
adjectives," Tarrida del Mármol called it—which will be
analyzed in the succeeding chapters.

[38] The London *Freedom* afterwards commented (January
1898): "In 1896 John Turner visited the States arousing the
heartiest feelings of comradeship amongst American friends
and leaving a deep impression upon all the trade unions with
which he came into contact. This year the ties between the
revolutionary movements of the two countries have been
still further strengthened by the visit of Voltairine de Cleyre
to us and of Kropotkin to Canada and the States."

5. Pity and Vengeance

Voltairine de Cleyre returned to America with new ideas and contacts and with renewed strength, both physical and moral, to carry on her work. Landing in New York, she found her comrades "jubilant over the success of the Kropotkin meetings," which the Russian prince had been conducting on his first lecture tour of Canada and the United States.[1] Her own spirits were high; and her voyage stimulated a spate of poems and articles which appeared over the next few years in Abe Isaak's *Free Society*, in Moses Harman's *Lucifer*, and in the New York *Solidarity*, edited by John H. Edelmann, a former contributor to *The Rebel*.

In addition, she resumed her regular lectures for the anarchist cause, including her annual speeches at meetings to honor the Paris Commune and the Haymarket martyrs. Indeed, one of her first activities after returning to Philadelphia was to address a November Eleventh memorial at the Cigarmakers' Hall, where Emma Goldman had been arrested in 1893. She also continued her writing and speaking for the free thought movement. On March 15, 1901, for example, we find her lecturing on "The Gateway to Freedom" before the Liberal Convention at Topeka. By March 24th she had returned to Philadelphia to address a Paris Commune meeting alongside George Brown, Frank Stephens (a well-known Single Taxer and founder of the Arden Colony), and speakers in French, Italian, German, and Yiddish.[2]

But even this was not all. Immediately upon returning to America, she began to send reports to the London *Freedom*, under the heading "American Notes," which became a regular feature of the paper beginning in November 1897. At the same time, she set to work

[1] *Freedom*, February 1898.
[2] *Free Society*, March 24, 1901.

on her translation of Jean Grave's *Société Mourante et l'Anarchie*, a book, she said, whose main purpose lay in "furnishing an inclusive criticism of the institutions of our moribund society and the necessity of its speedy dissolution." She had originally agreed to the assignment at the prompting of her London comrades, who had promised to secure a British publisher, but "later developments" made it more expedient to get out an American edition, which was published by Abe Isaak in 1899.[3]

Of these later developments, as she tells us in her preface, the most pressing were the outbreak of the Spanish-American War and "the gigantic stride towards militarism which this country has taken during the past year." Before that, she had had second thoughts about having undertaken the assignment. "If ever one was well tortured for agreeing to translate a thing he had not read, it is I," she confided to Will and Maggie Duff. "The book is an *awful* jumble—and repetitious *ad nauseam*."[4] Furthermore, she had been doubtful about the "seditious" thirteenth chapter, for which Grave had been prosecuted and which, she had felt, was "likely to fall flat" on the unmilitary American public. "But now that we have entered upon the 'manifest destiny' of 'civilized nations'; now that our government has reverted to the same tactic of colonization, protection, subjugation, and conquest; now that our standing army has been increased fourfold and a military place-hunting is the ambition of the hour; now that our workingmen are seizing the opportunity to barter their 'free citizenship in the greatest country on earth' for the abject service of man-kill-

[3] Jean Grave, *Moribund Society and Anarchy*, translated with a preface by Voltairine de Cleyre, San Francisco, Free Society Library no. 2, 1899. The French edition appeared in Paris in 1893 with a preface by Octave Mirbeau.

[4] Voltairine de Cleyre to Will and Maggie Duff, March 28, 1898, Ishill Collection.

ing on foreign soil at the rate of $15.60 per month and keep, this proscribed Chapter XIII comes with its own note—a most discordant one indeed—into the war-chorus at present holding the public ear."[5]

"Yes," she had written the Duffs on her return to Philadelphia, "I am once more in the land of the patriot and the home of that proud bird which steals everything it can from smaller birds, and then sits gloating with its victorious eye fixed on a vacancy dreaming of what it will eat next." And yet, she could not condemn the war without qualification. For *"I remember Montjuich*, though I have not forgotten Chicago," she wrote in her "American Notes" for *Freedom*. "I recognize that we are still in an era of political organizations; that most people believe in them; and that at the present stage of the game there is no way to knock sixteenth-century Spanish torture on the head save through such a breaking up of its political authority as will either wipe it out entirely or force it to humanize itself at least to the not very difficult ideal of modern commercialism, people's beliefs being what they are it requires a government to do it."[6]

Presently, however, the heavy burden of work began to take its toll. In the months following her return, as she wrote to Lizzie Bell, she was already sick "an awful lot." Indeed, it was "the worst winter I've had for eight years, and to think I came home so well and strong. I could just cry remembering it."[7] To earn a living, moreover, she was compelled to resume her lessons among the immigrant poor, which further undermined her health. During the year 1900, when her

[5] Voltairine de Cleyre, Preface to *Moribund Society and Anarchy*, dated June 1899.

[6] Voltairine de Cleyre to Will and Maggie Duff, November 24, 1897, Ishill Collection; de Cleyre, "American Notes," *Freedom*, May 1898.

[7] Voltairine de Cleyre to Elizabeth Turner Bell, n.d. [1898], Bell Papers.

financial situation began to improve, she earned a total of $600 from her teaching, part of which she sent to her mother. Before that, according to Nathan Navro, her income was so meager that she often went without adequate food. Yet she insisted on making her own way, refusing to accept money from the movement as did Lucy Parsons and especially Emma Goldman, whom she doubtless had in mind when she wrote to Will and Maggie Duff, "There's one thing I absolutely decline to be—and that's a paid agitator making a *trade* of my beliefs."[8]

Threatened with physical collapse, Voltairine cut back on her writing and speaking, which had been overtaxing her limited energies. Accordingly, after the January 1899 issue of *Freedom* she gave up her "American Notes" column, in which she was succeeded by Harry Kelly, a writer of limited gifts who could not match his predecessor's standard, as he himself was the first to admit. "There is more than one comrade here, including myself," he wrote in 1900, while living near London, "who sadly miss those delightful 'American Notes' Voltairine de Cleyre used to write for *Freedom*. Cannot some one persuade her to take up her pen again?" Voltairine, however, was not up to the task. Kelly, she told the Duffs, has been "giving me several strong hints" to resume the column, "but I know my limitations. I am not strong enough to take up any more regular work than what I've got, so I keep quiet."[9]

In the summer of 1898, Voltairine's exhausting routine was interrupted by a welcome visit from her sister, who stayed for five weeks, from July 6th to August 12th. A photograph taken by Addie during this interval shows Voltai, in a plain white dress, seated

[8] Voltairine de Cleyre to Will and Maggie Duff, August 6, 1901, Ishill Collection.

[9] *Ibid.*; Harry Kelly, "American Notes," *Freedom*, November 1900.

⋮

at her desk reading a book. In another she is holding a stray cat which she had rescued from the street. Addie wrote on the back: "Taking a sunbath, in a back window, third storey roof, 620 N. 8th Street, Phil. This little waif-cat is one of many that Voltai rescued. She was always kind to animals, especially cats."

Of Voltai's acquaintances, Addie was most impressed by Nathan Navro and Mary Hansen ("a good friend to Voltai, and a good woman"). Her opinion was not shared by her mother, who visited the following year. Aside from Navro, Mrs. De Claire did not care much for any of her daughter's friends, not even the devoted Miss Hansen, whom Voltairine once called "a saint if there ever was one." Nor did she like the house where Voltairine was living, which was all infested with roaches. "It's a great shame the way she uses her money for others and neglects herself," Harriet De Claire protested to Addie. "The dress you made her was almost the only decent thing she had to wear."[10]

Voltairine, it is true, had begun to dress more plainly; and, before her mother's visit, she had cut off her hair, which had been falling out at an alarming rate, and it was now growing back "four or five shades darker than the old."[11] Yet she was still quite pretty and very interesting to look at, in her Japanese kimono and short dark hair, as a picture taken in 1901 reveals. Her health, however, remained fragile ("I feel as if it wouldn't take much to bury me," she wrote to her mother); and though she fled to Atlantic City for a three-day respite, she came back "more tired than I went." "I *hate* the city with an ever-increasing hatred,"

[10] Adelaide D. Thayer to Joseph Ishill, February 3, 1935, Ishill Collection; Voltairine de Cleyre to Adelaide D. Thayer, November 25, 1899, and August 15, 1911, Labadie Collection; Harriet De Claire to Adelaide D. Thayer, November 13, 1899, Ishill Collection.

[11] Voltairine de Cleyre to Will and Maggie Duff, July 24, 1900, Ishill Collection.

she declared. "I think of myself in heaven when I have a long fair day ahead of me and nobody to talk to me for ten hours solid."[12]

Only once during these years did she find the quiet that she craved. This was when she spent the summer of 1900 on a farm outside Philadelphia, in "a quaint old decaying wooden house" at Torresdale, Pennsylvania, owned by Sada Bailey Fowler, an elderly Quaker and spiritualist whom Voltairine had helped with her writing.[13] There, close to nature, she could gaze at the fields and hear "the low rippling of the wind along the corn," as she wrote to Addie. "I've had beautiful sunrise, and sunset, and moonlight, lots this summer. My bedroom faces the morning sun, and every day I could watch it rise, without the trouble of getting up—just watched many a time how the 'Gray Dawn' that Tyndall dreaded so, came creeping over the grass, and then the pale lighting of the lamp in the east, and the long, low glimmer across the sky and the whitening of the atmosphere, and then the rim of the great ball with its diamond spray shooting like a crown around it, and then the red ball itself, all round and fire, the underlining on the light clouds, and then—to lie down peacefully and sleep three hours more!"[14]

Such peaceful interludes, however, were all too brief. Before long she would be back in the crowded ghetto, tutoring her pupils, delivering her speeches, writing her articles and verse, or out on the road, addressing anarchist and secularist groups from Pennsylvania to Kansas, stopping occasionally at St. Johns

[12] Voltairine de Cleyre to Harriet De Claire, September 6, 1901, Ishill Collection.

[13] Voltairine de Cleyre to Will and Maggie Duff, July 24, 1900; Navro manuscript, Ishill Collection. For a review of Mrs. Fowler's novel *Irene: or, The Road to Freedom*, see *Liberty*, November 20, 1886.

[14] Voltairine de Cleyre to Adelaide D. Thayer, September 14, 1900, Ishill Collection.

to visit her mother and sister. The eleventh of November would usually find her in Chicago—she was there in 1899 and 1901 and nearly every year after 1905—for her annual Haymarket address. In 1901 she stayed with the Isaaks, who had moved there from San Francisco with their paper, *Free Society*. Mary, their teenage daughter, thought Voltairine "very beautiful," as did Mary's friend Sonia Edelstadt, a niece of the Jewish anarchist poet, whose impressions remained vivid more than seventy years later: "I have this cameo-like picture of her in my mind, as she was so striking, evidently, to a sixteen-year-old girl. She was tall, slender, attractive, with short hair and an air of intelligence and intellectuality."[15]

At one of these Chicago memorials, in November 1899, Voltairine encountered Nahum Berman, whom she had met four years earlier in Boston, where he was working on *The Rebel* with C. W. Mowbray and Harry Kelly. A native of Russia, where he had caught the fever of Populism in his youth, Berman had come to the United States in 1885, as he told Kelly, "to see the social revolution," which he had imagined to be looming on the horizon. Voltairine describes him as "a child of the twenty-fifth century." He despised commercialism "with a hatred amounting to passion" and was "one of those strange beings in whom the divine fire of self-immolation for a cause mingled with a veritable child's delight in life."[16]

Harry Kelly considered Berman "one of the best informed Anarchists I ever knew and one of the most idealistic." He was a scholar and dreamer with, as Voltairine de Cleyre puts it, "all the literature of Europe at his tongue's end." But he was also "the soul of

[15] Interview with Grace Umrath (Mary Isaak's daughter), New York City, September 24, 1974; Sonia Edelstadt Keene to Paul Avrich, January 20, 1975.

[16] Voltairine de Cleyre, "N. H. Burmin" [*sic*], *Free Society*, July 22, 1900; *Mother Earth*, April 1913.

modesty," so that his articles in *The Rebel* and *Free Society* appeared anonymously and his name was scarcely known outside a small circle of comrades. He threw himself into the thankless menial tasks of the movement—the mailing of papers, distribution of leaflets, arrangement of meetings, circulation of petitions, endless correspondence and running to and fro; and though Mowbray's name appeared as editor of *The Rebel*, Berman was in fact "the editor and compositor" as well as "writer, publisher and pressman" and, adds Harry Kelly, he passed on and "Englished" all copy, "notwithstanding that he was a Russian Jew. (What would we do without the Jews?)"[17]

A printer by trade, Berman had worked in New York for Johann Most's *Freiheit* and Dyer Lum's *Alarm* and Merlino and Edelmann's *Solidarity* before moving to Boston. It was there, in November 1895, that he first met Voltairine, who had come to address a Haymarket gathering in Caledonian Hall. A year or so later, Berman left Boston and rode the rails with Harry Kelly, ending up in Chicago where Voltairine discovered him in 1899. In his middle thirties, Berman was small, slightly built, and unimpressive to look at. But, as Kelly tells us, he was "a rare spirit, of a kind that one meets perhaps only once in a lifetime." Voltairine found him tender and affectionate, quite incapable of personal spite. For a brief time, until her return to Philadelphia, the two became lovers. But life for Berman had been hard. He had been often on the tramp and out of work. As with Dyer Lum, fifteen years of "cold, hunger, and privation" had worn him out; and not long after Voltairine's departure his mind and body both gave way. He died, insane, on July 1, 1900. "He was one of those strange characters who love life intensely, yet who can never adapt themselves to the condition of it," wrote Voltairine to Addie after his

[17] Kelly, "Roll Back the Years," vi: 1; *Revolt*, January 15, 1916; *Mother Earth*, April 1913.

death. "He was a born savage, a wild man, in his love
of nature—and life, life, in every manifestation of it."[18]

Inspired by Berman's dedication, Voltairine pledged
her efforts to the "continuation of his work."[19] Her first
step, in the fall of 1900, was to start a new anarchist
reading group, similar to the one which she and Dyer
Lum had belonged to in the early 1890s. Since that
time, her trip to Great Britain, and especially her conversations with Kropotkin, Tarrida, and Nettlau, had
made her acutely aware of the gaps in her own knowledge of anarchism, still more perhaps in that of her
associates. "Let us take up the work as quiet students,
not as disputatious wranglers," she declared in *Free
Society*, "and we shall get more solid information in a
short space of time, than by the unmethodical argument too often indulged in at our meetings. Let us
saturate ourselves with the facts concerning Anarchistic tendencies in society; then we may hope to convert others."[20]

At Voltairine's suggestion, C. L. James, a contributor
to *Free Society* whom she had met at an anarchist conference in Chicago in 1893 and considered "our most
learned and systematic thinker,"[21] drew up an outline
of subjects and a list of books to be read. The group,
in which Nathan Navro, George Brown, Mary Hansen,
Perle McLeod, and Natasha Notkin all took part, became known as the Social Science Club and met every

[18] Kelly, "Roll Back the Years," VII: 1; Voltairine de Cleyre
to Adelaide D. Thayer, September 14, 1900, Ishill Collection.
[19] Navro manuscript, Ishill Collection.
[20] *Free Society*, September 30, 1900.
[21] *Ibid.*, October 21, 1900. Cf. *Selected Works*, p. 98, and
her letter to Professor John B. Andrews, November 29, 1907,
Tamiment Collection. Benjamin Tucker, it might be mentioned,
did not share her esteem for James, whom he once called "the
champion humbug and mountebank of the Communist-
Anarchist movement." *Liberty*, December 19, 1891.

Sunday evening. Each member would give a talk on a particular thinker, whom they had all read during the week, and a discussion would follow. The Social Science Club also sponsored public lectures and issued anarchist literature, including Voltairine's "Crime and Punishment" and the first English edition of Kropotkin's *Modern Science and Anarchism*, translated from the Russian by a young Philadelphia doctor and anarchist named David A. Modell.[22] In the spring of 1901, Kropotkin himself came to America for his second lecture tour (he spoke in Boston, New York, and Chicago, but not in Philadelphia, which he had, however, visited in 1897), and Voltairine went to New York to see him.[23]

By the summer of 1901, the Social Science Club was firmly established as the leading anarchist group in Philadelphia. Earlier in the year, Voltairine had moved to 807 Fairmount Avenue, where she lived first with Perle McLeod, then with Mary Hansen and George Brown, who, together with Nathan Navro, remained her closest and dearest friends. "Nathan," she wrote in September 1901, "remains pure gold—in trouble or in joy always the same," where others (Gordon was uppermost in her mind) had proven themselves "brass, and badly tarnished brass at that."[24] She still saw "the MacGordon," she told the Duffs, but less and less frequently. After receiving his M.D. in 1898, he had drifted away from the movement, and by 1900 or 1901 they were no longer lovers. "I'm just the same friends with Gordon I always was," she wrote to her sister, "but he isn't satisfied with me because I won't agree to the

[22] Voltairine de Cleyre, *Crime and Punishment*, Philadelphia, 1903, a lecture to the Social Science Club, March 15, 1903; Peter Kropotkin, *Modern Science and Anarchism*, Philadelphia, 1903. Modell, a member of the Club, also contributed articles to *Free Society*.

[23] Voltairine de Cleyre to Lillian Harman, April 5, 1901, Harman Papers.

[24] Voltairine de Cleyre to Harriet De Claire, September 14, 1901, Ishill Collection.

regular program of married life (I don't mean the ceremony but the rest of it—exclusive possession, home, children, all that) so we don't see each other very often. I'm sorry, but I'll have to stand it. I've done the worst of my worrying over it, and have settled down to facts."[25]

Her time, in any event, was fully committed to the movement. During the spring of 1901, she and George Brown, with a small group of comrades, began a series of open-air meetings in different parts of the city, but especially at City Hall Plaza, in an effort to win new adherents. Voltairine threw all her energy into this work, "speaking in the open air, getting ready copy for leaflet, journeying to the printer, dodging the policemen while I distribute the leaflets under doors (there is a fool municipal regulation against it), collecting dues, writing postal cards to lazy workers, preparing an occasional in-door lecture—and house-work (I don't do that *properly* but still I must do some). I'm pretty near played out," she wrote to Moses Harman's daughter, Lillian.[26]

Before this campaign was launched, there were, by Voltairine's estimate, between 400 and 500 anarchists in Philadelphia, of whom 145 were active regulars. Seventy-five of these were Russian Jews, 40 were native Americans, 24 Germans, 3 Italians, 2 Cubans, and one Frenchman; 126 were men and 19 women; 124 were Anarchist-Communists, 12 Individualists, and 9 (including Voltairine) undefined. On November 11, 1900, the Haymarket commemoration was able to attract some 600 people, who heard speeches in English, Yiddish, German, French, and Italian, and music by Italian and Bohemian ensembles.

[25] Voltairine de Cleyre to Will and Maggie Duff, May 21, 1898; Voltairine de Cleyre to Adelaide D. Thayer, September 14, 1900, Ishill Collection.
[26] Voltairine de Cleyre to Lillian Harman, April 5, 1901, Harman Papers.

For the most part, these figures come from a report drafted by Voltairine de Cleyre for an International Anarchist Congress in Paris in 1900. As an "excellent" propagandist who was also fluent in French, Voltairine herself was suggested to represent American anarchists at the gathering,[27] but she declined, and Emma Goldman went instead, only to see the Congress suppressed by the police. Four sessions were held in secret, however, and the reports of Voltairine, Emma, and others were published as a special supplement to *Les Temps Nouveaux*, constituting a valuable source for the history and social composition of the anarchist movement.[28]

The following spring, the Philadelphia anarchists launched their open-air meetings around the city. The audiences, ranging from 200 to 600 in number, were handed anarchist leaflets and listened to speeches on economics, religion, ethics, education, sex, art, and literature. By the end of a typical session, some thirty to fifty would remain, a few of whom would return and eventually join the movement. "Not that anyone who attempts such propaganda need expect to convert crowds," remarked Voltairine de Cleyre, "but the very accustoming of the passer-by to the word 'Anarchism,' so that it is no longer a bugbear to him, so that he can hear it with the same equanimity that he hears 'Single Tax,' or 'Democrat,' is sufficient for the propagandist who knows that he is but one, and our whole labor is very great."[29] With the same objective, George Brown spoke on "The Spirit of Rebellion" before the Literary Culture Club, composed of high school and college students, while he and Voltairine distributed anarchist literature at union meetings, with particular success

[27] *Free Society*, May 13, 1900.

[28] *Les Temps Nouveaux*, supplement littéraire, 1900, pp. 190-92. See also Emma Goldman's account in *Free Society*, October 21 and 28, 1900.

[29] Voltairine de Cleyre, "A Report of the Movement in Philadelphia," *Free Society*, August 18, 1901.

among the cigarmakers, shoemakers, paperhangers, and garment workers, in spite of persistent harassment from the police. At the same time, their energetic Jewish comrade Hyman (Chaim) Weinberg, a lively speaker and veteran member of the Knights of Liberty Group, organized a Jewish Workers' Cooperative Association, which sponsored lectures, distributed literature, opened a cooperative shoe store and bakery, and succeeded in attracting nearly 900 members.

These activities, however, were sharply curtailed after the shooting of President McKinley by a self-proclaimed anarchist on September 6, 1901. The assassin, Leon Czolgosz, had acted on his own. He belonged to no anarchist group. But he had attended a lecture by Emma Goldman in Cleveland and afterwards called on her in Chicago at the home of the Isaaks, where his odd behavior aroused suspicion, so that five days before the assassination *Free Society* printed a warning that he was a spy. Nevertheless, the police tried to implicate the anarchists. On the night of the shooting, Abe Isaak, his wife, and their son and daughter were arrested without warrant along with some fifty other Chicago anarchists, including Hippolyte Havel and Jay Fox, charged with conspiracy to kill the President, and held without bail for seventeen days in the Cook County Jail, where their Haymarket comrades had awaited execution fourteen years before.

The attack on McKinley touched off a wild, savage rampage—a "stamping-out craze," a "Saint Bartholomew of the Anarchists," as C. L. James described it in *Free Society*.[30] Not only Chicago, but the whole of America was swept by a wave of hysteria worse than the one after Haymarket, as the assassin's victim was not a local policeman but the President of the United

[30] *Free Society*, October 27, 1901.

States. Across the country, from New York to Tacoma, anarchists were hunted, arrested, and persecuted. Homes and clubrooms were raided and papers and possessions confiscated. Denounced as satanic monsters, anarchists lost their jobs and lodgings and were subjected to violence and abuse. In New York City the ageing Johann Most was condemned to a year on Blackwell's Island, an ordeal which hastened his death, and the offices of the *Fraye Arbeter Shtime* on Henry Street were wrecked by an angry mob, although its editor, Yanovsky, who was afterwards cornered and beaten in a neighborhood restaurant, had repudiated the assassination. Bands of vigilantes invaded the mining and mill towns of western Pennsylvania and southern Illinois and drove out alleged anarchists and their families.

Over the next few weeks, men were tarred and feathered or threatened with lynching for expressing the least sympathy with Czolgosz. "Burn them in oil," "Hang them from the nearest lamppost," "Deport them to a desert island," were the stock phrases of the period. When Emma Goldman, like Albert Parsons before her, returned to Chicago and surrendered to the authorities, a policeman struck her in the face on the way to prison, knocking out one of her teeth. Once behind bars, "Beast Goldman" received a flood of unsigned hate letters accusing her of "the killing of our beloved president." "You damn bitch of an anarchist," one of them read. "I wish I could get at you. I would tear your heart out and feed it to my dog." "We will cut your tongue out, soak your carcass in oil, and burn you alive," declared another. Emma Goldman added: "The description by some of the anonymous writers of what they would do to me sexually offered studies in perversion that would have astounded authorities on the subject."[31]

Nor did Philadelphia escape the hysteria. The social atmosphere "is in such a tremolo," wrote Voltairine de

[31] *Ibid.*, October 6, 1901; Goldman, *Living My Life*, p. 301.

Cleyre to her mother on September 14th, "that one needs to be a rock not to feel the quivers. However, it's one of the whirlstorms that subside, like everything else, and when people get back to normal eating and drinking once more, we may be able to see where we are. I am sorry that McKinley didn't get well, for the sake of the others."[32] But the whirlstorm did not subside as quickly as she expected. A week later she wrote: "The whole general atmosphere is so surcharged with brutality—with the loosened savage—that one feels oneself in a den of wild beasts." Above all she was concerned with the fate of her *Free Society* comrades, fearing a repetition of Haymarket. For "they killed John Ball and they killed Wat Tyler, and they always want to kill somebody. And that gentle Jesus, they killed too, and I have no doubt the savages of that day were as anxious to tear him asunder as the savages of to-day are to tear those poor people in Chicago." Nor was Emma Goldman excluded from her sympathies: "I have never liked Emma Goldman or her speeches; I don't like fishwifery or billingsgate; but I never heard her say, nor any one of all I ever knew that heard her, that any one could do any good by killing: All she has ever said is 'If your rights are attacked by force you should resist, by force if necessary.'" The hysteria, Voltairine added, was making her sick, "so *sick* that I *wish they would deport us* to that island in the Sea, and let us live in peace far from anything that would ever remind me of America. I know I will get over it; but I feel so. I can't help it."[33]

Although Voltairine herself was not arrested, the Philadelphia anarchists were subjected to continual harassment by the police, who raided their clubs and broke up their open-air meetings. As a result, some of her comrades suspended their activities, while others

[32] Voltairine de Cleyre to Harriet De Claire, September 14, 1901, Ishill Collection.
[33] Voltairine de Cleyre to Harriet De Claire, September 22, 1901, Ishill Collection.

left the movement entirely, though Voltairine herself
remained "a rock."[34] For their annual November
Eleventh commemoration the anarchists were unable
to rent a hall, and so the stalwarts gathered in the home
of Natasha Notkin to pay homage to the Chicago
martyrs. Voltairine, however, went to Chicago to deliver her memorial address, in which she denounced
the recent repressions—"the cry of lynch, burn, shoot,
imprison, deport, and the Scarlet Letter A be branded
low down upon the forehead"—as a recapitulation of
1886-1887.[35]

Returning to Philadelphia, she continued her agitation in spite of the deepening reaction. In March 1902,
when Senator Joseph R. Hawley offered a thousand
dollars to have a shot at an anarchist (*The Nation*
magazine commented that if Hawley's hand was no
steadier than his mind an anarchist could pick up an
easy fortune), Voltairine offered herself as a target free
of charge. In "A Letter to Senator Hawley," published
in *Free Society*, she declared: "You may by merely pay-
ing your carfare to my home (address below) shoot at
me for nothing. I will not resist. I will stand straight
before you at any distance you wish me to, and you
may shoot, in the presence of witnesses. Does not your
American commercial instinct seize upon this as a
bargain? But if payment of the $1,000 is a necessary
part of your proposition, then when I have given you
the shot, I will give the money to the propaganda of the
idea of a free society in which there shall be neither
assassins nor presidents, beggars nor senators. Voltairine de Cleyre. 807 Fairmount Avenue, March 21,
1902."[36]

[34] Navro manuscript, Ishill Collection.

[35] *Selected Works*, p. 171.

[36] *Free Society*, April 13, 1902. Emma Goldman mistakenly
writes that Voltairine imposed the condition that Hawley
"permit her to explain to him the principles of anarchism before he fired." *Living My Life*, p. 332.

1. Voltairine de Cleyre, Philadelphia, Christmas 1891

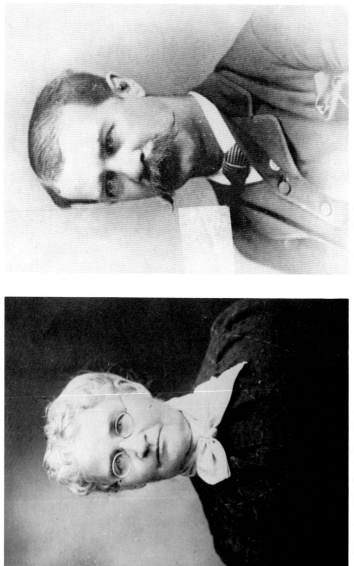

2. Harriet Elizabeth De Claire

3. Dyer D. Lum

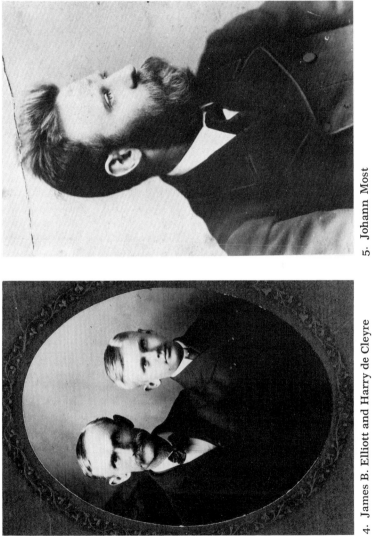

4. James B. Elliott and Harry de Cleyre

5. Johann Most

6. Harriet Elizabeth De Claire, St. Johns, Michigan

7. The Haymarket Martyrs

8. Lucy Parsons

9. The Haymarket Monument

10. Benjamin R. Tucker, Boston, c. 1887

11. Voltairine de Cleyre, London, 1897

12. Peter Kropotkin

13. Thomas H. Bell, 1888

14. Voltairine de Cleyre, Philadelphia, August 1898

15. Voltairine de Cleyre, Philadelphia, 1901

16. Leon Czolgosz, Buffalo, 1901

17. Alexander Berkman, 1892

18. Emma Goldman, St. Louis, 1912

No. 517 N. Randolph St.
Aug 7, 1906

My dear Alex:—

Do you really want to
go to Russia? Cash need not stand in your
way. But I don't want you to go to
Russia. I don't see why. I think Russia
is fighting for something we can have no
part in. I know you are thinking, "in
what have I a part?" Has I too, I have
no part in things, in the last analysis.
In the last analysis it is life itself I hate —
not a fat bourgeois. Life, life this fiendish
thing which brings millions of little creatures
forth mercilessly, only to hunger, pain, madness
There is not a day when the sufferings
of the little waif animals in the street, does
not create in one a bitter rage against
life. And this thing called indifferently
"broadness" and "tolerance", is the refuge
we take from too much feeling: it is a
voluntary stunning of the nerves as an
escape from the terrible tension: I can't, I
can't, I simply can't endure the agony of

19. Letter of Voltairine de Cleyre to Alexander Berkman, August 7, 1906

20. Saul Yanovsky, New York, c. 1910

21. Yiddish manuscript by Voltairine de Cleyre

22. The Execution of Francisco Ferrer, Barcelona, October 13, 1909

THE
MODERN SCHOOL
By FRANCISCO FERRER

Ferrer

MOTHER EARTH PUBLISHING ASSOCIATION
210 East 13th Street, New York

23. *The Modern School* by Francisco Ferrer, translated by Voltairine de Cleyre in 1909

24. The Philadelphia Modern School, Radical Library, 1910 or 1911:
Mary Hansen (center, holding girl's arms), George Brown (right,
holding boy), Joseph Cohen (next to Brown, with daughter Emma
in front)

25. Harry Kelly, 1922

26. Leonard Abbott, New York, c. 1905

27. Ricardo and Enrique Flores Magón

28. Voltairine de Cleyre, Chicago, 1910

VOLTAIRINE DE CLEYRE

NOTED LECTURER AND WRITER
: : DIED, JUNE 20th 11 a. m. : :

A Public Meeting

TO HONOR HER MEMORY

WILL BE HELD ON

SUNDAY, JUNE 23rd, 8 p. m.

Labor Lyceum

SIXTH AND BROWN STREETS

Geo. Brown, J. C. Hannon, H. Wineberg
and many other prominent speakers .

Arranged by the RADICAL LIBRARY

Branch 273 Workmen's Circle

DOOR OPEN AT 7 p. m.

United Printing Co.   76 264 South 5th Street

29. Voltairine de Cleyre Memorial, Radical Library, Philadelphia, June 23, 1912

In the meantime, Emma Goldman and the Isaaks had been released from prison, and *Free Society* had retracted its accusations against Czolgosz, who died in the electric chair on October 29, 1901. The killing of McKinley, the journal maintained, was "the price of empire" and of capitalist injustice,[37] a view which Voltairine de Cleyre shared. Before the assassination she had sharply criticized McKinley's administration for its expansionist policies in the Pacific and the Caribbean. "Yes," she had written to Addie in September 1900, "this Chinese affair [the Boxer Rebellion] is abominable; same as the Philippines and Porto Rico and Cuba and the rest of it. But when the American and European capitalists make up their minds to have markets, they'll pull the North Pole out before they stop. I really don't know what they'll do by the time they have 'civilized' Asia and Africa, and got them on the same business basis as themselves, i.e., producing a great deal more than they consume and hunting a place to sell the surplus (while their own folks starve and half-starve)."[38] And while she regretted Czolgosz's action, it was mainly because of the repressions that would inevitable follow. "The boys outside are crying the Extras over McKinley's assassination," she wrote her mother on the day of the attack. "It's rather a pity—not so much for him, at least no more than for the old lady cut to pieces on Brown Street yesterday —but for the scale of the reactionary sentiments it creates for a time. However, it's all in the play, as Humbert said the first time his life was attempted: 'It's one of the risks of the king business.' "[39]

Her real sympathies lay, rather, with Czolgosz, "a child of the great darkness, a spectre out of the abyss,"

[37] *Free Society*, October 13, 1901.

[38] Voltairine de Cleyre to Adelaide D. Thayer, September 14, 1900, Ishill Collection.

[39] Voltairine de Cleyre to Harriet De Claire, September 6, 1901, Ishill Collection.

for whom, whatever his mental or emotional confusion, McKinley had stood as the symbol of capitalist exploitation and of American plutocracy and imperialism. Not anarchism, she insisted, *"but the state of society which creates men of power and greed and the victims of power and greed,* is responsible for the death of both McKinley and Czolgosz." Upon McKinley's hand "was the 'damned spot' of official murder, the blood of the Filipinos, whom he, in pursuance of the capitalist policy of Imperialism, had sentenced to death. Upon his head falls the curse of all the workers against whom, time and again, he threw the strength of his official power." The wonder, therefore, is not that there should be some who strike back, but that there are not more. *"The hells of capitalism create the desperate; the desperate act—desperately!"*[40]

Voltairine de Cleyre's defense of Czolgosz represented a distinct shift in her attitude toward violence. As Emma Goldman observed: "Voltairine began her public career as a pacifist, and for many years she sternly set her face against revolutionary methods. But greater familiarity with European developments, the Russian Revolution of 1905, the rapid growth of capitalism in her own country, with all its resultant violence and injustice, and particularly the Mexican Revolution, subsequently changed her attitude."[41] Though somewhat oversimplified, this is a reasonably accurate summary of Voltairine's metamorphosis with regard to social revolution and propaganda by the deed. In her early years as an anarchist, she had been an

[40] Voltairine de Cleyre, "McKinley's Assassination from the Anarchist Standpoint," *Mother Earth*, October 1907. In a letter to her mother, October 15, 1901, Voltairine struck a somewhat different note: "I'm glad that electrocution will soon be over, and that poor boy at peace. How terribly unhappy and weary of his life he must have been to do such a thing!" Labadie Collection.

[41] Goldman, *Living My Life*, p. 505.

advocate of nonresistance to evil. To admit resistance, she had argued, "is at once to admit—the State";[42] and Dyer Lum, it will be recalled, addressed her as "Moraline" and "Gusherine" because of her Tolstoyan sympathies. In place of violence she had stressed peaceful propaganda as the proper function of the anarchist movement. "Let our friends be patient," she said after Mowbray's arrest in Philadelphia. "There will be opportunity enough for going to jail, to the scaffold, for our ideals. Our present duty is the more prosaic task of education."[43]

At the same time, however, she had sympathized with those (like the Haymarket martyrs) who called for a social revolution. Given the character of government and its power-hungry custodians, she herself regarded revolution as a natural phenomenon, like cyclones or tornadoes, beyond the powers of anyone to prevent. "The rulers of the earth are sowing a fearful wind, to reap a most terrible whirlwind," she warned. As early as 1889, in "The Drama of the Nineteenth Century," she forecast a social upheaval in America, "when an omnivorous rumble prefaces the waking of terrific underground thunder, when the earth shakes in a frightful ague fit, when from out the parched throats of the people a burning cry will come like lava from a crater, 'Bread, bread, bread! No more preachers, no more politicians, no more lawyers, no more gods, no more heavens, no more promises! Bread!' And then, when you hear a terrible leaden groan, know that at last, here in your free America, beneath the floating banner of the stars and stripes, more than fifty million human hearts will have burst! A dynamite bomb that will shock the continent to its foundations and knock the sea back from its shores!"[44]

[42] Voltairine de Cleyre, "Resistance," *The Individualist*, August 26, 1890.
[43] *Solidarity*, January 15, 1895.
[44] *Liberty*, February 15, 1890; *Selected Works*, p. 406.

As the years passed, and especially after her journey to England, she drew closer and closer to the position of Dyer Lum. "I have gradually worked my way to the conviction that, while I cannot see the logic of forcible physical resistance (entailing perpetual retaliations until one of the offended finally refuses to retaliate), there are others who have reached the opposite conclusions, who will act according to their convictions, and who are quite as much part and parcel of the movement towards human liberty as those who preach peace at all costs," she wrote in 1907.[45] Indeed there were times, she had come to believe, when acts of violence were the only means of opposing exploitation and tyranny. Like Kropotkin, she refused to sit in judgment over the lonely assassins who were driven by despair or by a passion for retribution to retaliate against the authors of popular misery. She understood the impulse which pushed these young men to commit such extreme acts, their horror at the suffering and injustice around them, at the organized violence of the state and the rapacious brutality of capitalism. "It is not the business of Anarchists to preach wild or foolish acts— acts of violence," she wrote in 1908 after a bomb incident in Union Square. "For, truly, Anarchism has nothing in common with violence, and can never come about save through the conquest of men's minds. But when some desperate and life-denied victim of the present system does strike back at it, by violence, it is not our business to heap infamies upon his name, but to explain him as we explain others, whether our enemies or our friends, as the fated fruit of the existing 'order.' "[46]

We must not preach violence, she was saying, but we must not condemn the perpetrators either. While she did not approve of terrorism in theory, she never-

[45] *Mother Earth*, January 1907.
[46] Voltairine de Cleyre, "Our Present Attitude," *Mother Earth*, April 1908.

theless defended it in practice by shifting the ultimate blame onto the state and governing classes. "These creatures," she wrote with indignation, "who drill men in the science of killing, who put guns and clubs in hands they train to shoot and strike, who hail with delight the latest inventions in explosives, who exult in the machine that can kill the most with the least expenditure of energy, who declare a war of extermination upon people who do not want their civilization, who ravish, and burn, and garrote and guillotine, and hang, and electrocute, they have the impertinence to talk about the unrighteousness of force!"[47]

For this reason, she upheld the attack of Berkman against Frick, of Angiolillo against Cánovas, of Bresci against Umberto, and, finally, of Czolgosz against McKinley. Such deeds were inevitable replies to the much greater violence—war, execution, torture—perpetrated by the state against the people. The greatest bombthrowers and murderers have not been the isolated individuals driven to desperation, but the military machine of every government—the soldiers, militia, police, firing squads, hangmen. Such was her position. "How would your new husband stand an anarchist in his house?" she asked Addie after the assassination of Umberto in 1900. "A party that thinks that so long as starving people are shot, as in the streets of Milan, or caged up in a state of siege, as in Sicily, for parading in the streets and crying for bread, so long will the king under whose orders they are shot get no worse than he deserves if *he* gets a bullet through him? That's what I think, and your folks mightn't like me around."[48]

Even more, her emotions were deeply stirred by the

---

[47] *Selected Works*, p. 170.

[48] Voltairine de Cleyre to Adelaide D. Thayer, September 14, 1900, Ishill Collection. Voltairine accepted Bresci's act "without reserve" and "in silent acknowledgment of the strength of the man." *Selected Works*, p. 116.

self-sacrificing gestures of the assassins. That an Angiolillo or a Bresci, a Vaillant or a Caserio, gentle in their daily lives, lofty in their ideals, could be driven to commit acts of vengeance in the name of oppressed humanity was neither appalling nor reprehensible. On the contrary, she was moved by their noble intentions and by their terrible fate. She felt their sacrifice as her sacrifice, their death as the death of part of herself. She suffered and grieved over their loss with the mournful love of a sister. In the end, they came to exert an almost morbid fascination, and she was haunted by their memory for the rest of her life. Within her austere and expiatory nature, so similar to their own, they evoked a cry of pain, a cry of compassion, a feeling of shared martyrdom, expressed again and again in the most intensely felt poems she ever wrote, with their volcanoes and hurricanes and rivers of blood.[49]

Repelled by expanding capitalism, with its rampant cruelty and injustice, she threw her support behind the tactics of "direct action," which, as she wrote in an essay of that title, may be "the extreme of violence" or "as peaceful as the waters of the Brook of Siloa that go softly."[50] Both forms were necessary, each in its time and place. Toward the end of her life she pinned her greatest hopes on the Mexican Revolution, to which she devoted her waning energies. Not that she had

---

[49] Some of these poems, including "The Feast of Vultures," "The Hurricane," "Light Upon Waldheim," "Germinal," and "Santa Agueda," were collected under the title of *The Worm Turns*, Philadelphia, 1900. See also "Marsh-Bloom (To Gaetano Bresci)," *Free Society*, July 28, 1901, reprinted in *Selected Works*, p. 74; and "A Song of the Night," *The Herald of Revolt*, September 1913, which reads in part: "Vengeance and death will come to you, and come like a thief in the night/ For the Law of Justice yet rules the earth, and it will avenge the right!" Her last lover, Joseph Kucera, found it "only natural that sentimental natures hate their social antagonists as much as they love their own class." *Why?*, August 1913.

[50] *Selected Works*, p. 223.

abandoned her preference for nonviolent means of
resistance. First and foremost, she still believed, there
had to be a revolution within the individual, a fundamental revaluation of values, if the goal of a free
society was to be reached. She was encouraged by the
popularity of Tolstoy's writings, "an evidence that
many receive the idea that it is easier to conquer war
with peace." From peaceful experiment alone can come
a lasting solution, she concluded. "But let no one mistake this for servile submission or meek abnegation;
my right shall be asserted no matter at what cost to
me, and none shall trench upon it without my
protest."[51]

[51] *Ibid.*, pp. 162-63.

6. Anarchism without Adjectives

The shift in Voltairine de Cleyre's attitude toward violence was part of the general evolution of her anarchist philosophy toward a more flexible and ecumenical position. Thus a parallel shift took place in her attitude toward property. At first, as has been seen, the doctrines of Benjamin Tucker exerted a strong influence on her thinking. In 1888 she began to read his journal *Liberty* and soon considered herself an adherent of the Individualist school of which he was the foremost exponent. In early 1890, when she delivered her first lecture in Boston, under the auspices of the American Secular Union, she made it a point to call on Tucker, who found her "bright, agreeable, and interesting," and printed her address, "The Economic Tendency of Freethought," in his magazine.[1]

At that time, Voltairine de Cleyre sharply distinguished her economic position from that of Emma Goldman: "Miss Goldman is a Communist; I am an Individualist. She wishes to destroy the right of property; I wish to assert it. I make my war upon privilege and authority, whereby the right of property, the true right in that which is proper to the individual, is annihilated. She believes that co-operation would entirely supplant competition; I hold that competition in one form or another will always exist, and that it is highly desirable it should."[2]

By the middle of the 1890s, however, she had discarded her Tuckerite individualism for the mutualism of Dyer Lum, which, based on the teachings of Proudhon, hovered between individualism and socialism and allowed scope for cooperative effort without accepting

[1] Benjamin R. Tucker to Joseph Ishill, November 25, 1934, Ishill Collection, reprinted (with some errors) in *The Oriole Press: A Bibliography*, pp. 381-82; *Liberty*, February 15, 1890.
[2] *Selected Works*, p. 217.

governmental control. Living in the Philadelphia ghetto, Voltairine, like Lum, felt greater sympathy than Tucker for the immigrant, the worker, the poor. Tucker, she had come to believe, was "very able and very strong, but very narrow and hard." As a champion of unity within the movement, she was repelled by his scathing attacks upon fellow anarchists, "sending his fine hard shafts among foes and friends with icy impartiality, hitting swift and cutting keen—and ever ready to nail a traitor."[3] She respected his intelligence and literary ability, but he was too cold, aloof, and wanting in human compassion to suit her taste. "I think it has been the great mistake of our people, especially of our American Anarchists represented by Benjamin R. Tucker, to disclaim sentiment," she declared. For her own part, it was "the possession of a very large proportion of sentiment" that had moved her to join the anarchist movement in the first place. "It is to men and women of feeling that I speak," she had written in 1889, "men and women of the millions, men and women in the hurrying current! Not to the shallow egotist who holds himself apart and with the phariseeism of intellectuality exclaims, 'I am more just than thou'; but to those whose every fiber of being is vibrating with emotion as aspen leaves quiver in the breath of Storm! To those whose hearts swell with a great pity at the pitiful toil of women, the weariness of young children, the handcuffed helplessness of strong men!"[4]

For Tucker, by contrast, sentiment got in the way of reason, disrupting the dispassionate analysis required for the solution of social and economic problems. It led, he felt, to inconsistency and ambivalence,

---

[3] Voltairine de Cleyre to Benjamin R. Tucker, April 6, 1907, Tucker Papers, New York Public Library; *Selected Works*, pp. 115-16.

[4] Voltairine de Cleyre, "Why I Am an Anarchist," *Mother Earth*, March 1908; *Selected Works*, p. 382.

as demonstrated by Voltairine de Cleyre herself. "Miss de Cleyre believes in non-resistance," he wrote in 1894, "and at the same time urges the people to resistance."[5] On practical grounds, moreover, he criticized her opposition to prisons, which she expressed in *Liberty* in 1890. She was appalled by the brutalizing punishments and immense human suffering caused by prison life. Far from reforming the offender, it only hardened him in his criminal ways. "We know what prisons mean—they mean broken down body and spirit, degradation, consumption, insanity," she declared. "The law makes ten criminals where it restrains one."[6]

At least in part, this attitude stemmed from what she regarded as her own incarceration in the convent, which she often compared to a prison, of the soul as well as the body. Anarchism, she insisted, must eliminate coercive institutions of every type and inaugurate a society "without officials, police, military, bayonets, prisons, and the thousand and one other symbols of force which mark our present development." To Tucker this was not anarchism but rather "the Christian millennium." Anarchism would not allow crimes to go unpunished and "does not exclude prisons, officials, military, or other symbols of force. It merely demands that non-invasive men shall not be made the victims of such symbols of force. Anarchism is not the reign of love, but the reign of justice. It does not signify the abolition of force-symbols but the application of force to real invaders."[7]

After their meeting in 1890, Tucker saw Voltairine only one more time, in Philadelphia many years later. By then his estimation of her talents had further deteriorated. "Towards the end," he wrote to Joseph Ishill, "she seemed to me not entirely sane—probably

[5] *Liberty*, March 10, 1894.

[6] Voltairine de Cleyre, "On Liberty," *Mother Earth*, July 1909; *Liberty*, February 15, 1890.

[7] *Liberty*, October 10, 1891.

as the result of misfortune or hardship. We were so different temperamentally that we could hardly be considered kindred spirits. But she commanded my respect." Ishill replied: "Yes, you are right when you say that later on when you met her she seemed quite a pathetic person! True she suffered from severe headaches, which malady dates from her early childhood, but she was *never* insane."[8]

Although she early abandoned her individualism, Voltairine de Cleyre did not, as Rudolf Rocker writes in his *Pioneers of American Freedom*, turn to "the ideas of Peter Kropotkin and communist anarchism." Emma Goldman made the same error when reporting to the Amsterdam Congress of 1907 that Voltairine had become "one of the staunchest and most uncompromising workers in the cause of Anarchist Communism."[9] Voltairine, it is true, lived and worked chiefly among anarchists of the Kropotkinite and Mostian persuasion. With the passage of time, moreover, she drew closer to their social revolutionary viewpoint. Yet, despite Kropotkin's growing influence on her thinking, especially after their meeting in 1897, she was at pains to deny ever holding communistic views. "I am not now, and never have been at any time, a Communist," she declared in 1907 in reply to Emma Goldman's statement. She had not altered her conviction, expressed a decade before, that "the amount of administration required by Economic Communism would practically be a meddlesome government, denying equal freedom." And if extreme individualism was "vicious and liberty destroying," as she now believed, then com-

[8] Benjamin R. Tucker to Joseph Ishill, November 25, 1934, Ishill Collection; Ishill to Tucker, December 30, 1934, Tucker Papers.

[9] Rocker, *Pioneers of American Freedom*, p. 143; *Mother Earth*, November 1907. The error is repeated by Eunice M. Schuster in *Native American Anarchism*, Northampton, Mass., 1932, p. 160; and by Henry J. Silverman in *American Radical Thought*, p. 154.

munism, in fact collectivism in general, was even more so, resting ultimately upon authority and subjecting the individual "to the decisions of a mass of managers, to regulations and regimentations without end."[10]

As the offspring of small-town America, Voltairine de Cleyre remained distinctly more individualistic in her outlook than the immigrant Kropotkinites among whom she lived. And as she craved independence and privacy in her own life, she prescribed them for society as a whole. "Must we be licensed, protected, regulated, labeled, taxed, confiscated, spied upon, and generally meddled with, in order that correct statistics may be obtained and a 'quantity prescribed'?" she asked in 1892, while still in her individualist phase. ". . . For my part, sooner than have a meddlesome bureaucracy sniffing around in my kitchen, my laundry, my dining-room, my study, to find out what I eat, what I wear, how my table is set, how many times I wash myself, how many books I have, whether my pictures are 'moral' or 'immoral,' what I waste, etc., *ad nauseam*, after the manner of ancient Peru and Egypt, I had rather a few cabbages should rot, even if they happen to be my cabbages."[11]

Nor did her fears evaporate as the years progressed. Like Benjamin Tucker himself, she continued to maintain that supervision and interference were inevitable features of communism, even of the professedly stateless variety. "My old objection to communistic economy remains," she declared in 1900, "and *no system of economy* so far proposed is. . . entirely compatible with freedom."[12] To this conviction she adhered until the end of her life. Neither individualism nor collectivism,

[10] *The Firebrand*, July 11, 1897; *Mother Earth*, December 1907, March 1908.

[11] Voltairine de Cleyre, "A Glance at Communism," *Twentieth Century*, September 1892.

[12] Voltairine de Cleyre, "A Suggestion and an Explanation," *Free Society*, June 3, 1900.

nor even the middle ground of mutualism, was entirely satisfactory. For "Socialism and Communism both demand a degree of joint effort and administration which would beget more regulation than is consistent with ideal Anarchism," while "Individualism and Mutualism, resting upon property, involve a development of the private policeman not at all compatible with my notions of freedom."[13] Which system, then, was preferable? If collectivism contained the seeds of authority, was it not at odds with anarchist fundamentals? Was communism at all compatible with individual autonomy? Voltairine provided no answer. Toward property, as toward violence, she arrived at no fixed position. "I am an Anarchist, simply," she told Emma Goldman, "without economic labels attached."[14]

This notion of an unhyphenated anarchism, of an anarchism without labels or adjectives, had been developed in the late nineteenth century by the two most respected theorists of the Spanish anarchist movement, Ricardo Mella and Fernando Tarrida del Mármol, the same Tarrida who in 1897 made such a strong impression on Voltairine de Cleyre during her visit to London. Mella and Tarrida, troubled by the bitter debates between mutualists, collectivists, and communists in the 1880s, worked out a new theory, summarized in the formula "anarchism without adjectives," which called for greater tolerance within the movement regarding economic questions. "Among the various revolutionary theories which claim to guarantee complete social emancipation," Tarrida told a Haymarket meeting in Barcelona in November 1889, "that which most closely conforms to Nature, Science, and Justice is the one which rejects all dogmas, political, social, economic,

[13] *Selected Works*, p. 112.
[14] *Mother Earth*, December 1907.

and religious—namely, Anarchy without adjectives."[15]
A year later, Tarrida repeated this message in a letter
to the French anarchist journal *La Révolte*: "We are
anarchists, and we proclaim anarchy without adjectives. Anarchy is an axiom; the economic question is
secondary."[16] The rejection of dogma and of rigid systematic theory, argued Tarrida, was the very essence
of the libertarian attitude. Whatever their differences,
he added, Proudhon, Bakunin, and Kropotkin all agreed
on the negation of the state and put forward ideas
which for the most part were complementary rather
than contradictory.

During the next few years, Errico Malatesta adopted
a similar position, as did Elisée Reclus, Max Nettlau,
and other prominent European anarchists. "Unique
solutions will never do," said Nettlau, who called for a
"non-sectarian conception of anarchism." Individualism and communism were both important. "All human
life vibrates between these two poles in endless
varieties and oscillations." Furthermore, economic preferences will vary according to climate, customs,
natural resources, and individual taste, so that no
single person or group can possess the one correct solution. Anarchists, therefore, must "never permit themselves to become fossilized upholders of a given system," for "neither Communism nor Individualism, if it
became the sole form, would realize freedom, which
always demands a choice of ways, a plurality of possibilities."[17]

[15] F. Tarrida del Mármol, "La teoría revolucionaria," quoted
in V. Muñoz, ed., *Antología ácrata española*, Barcelona, 1974,
p. 31. See also Ricardo Mella, "La Anarquía no admite
adjetivos," *La Solidaridad* (Seville), January 12, 1889.
[16] Tarrida, "Anarquismo sin adjetivo," *La Révolte*, September
6 and 13, 1890, in Muñoz, ed., *Antología*, pp. 29-39. An English
translation, "Anarchism Without an Adjective," appeared in
Free Society, May 29, 1904.
[17] Max Nettlau, "Anarchism: Communist or Individualist—
Both," *Freedom*, March 1914, and *Mother Earth*, July 1914;

This ecumenical position represented an important tendency in the history of anarchist thought, anticipating the doctrines of "united anarchism" (*edinyi anarkhizm*) and "synthetic anarchism" (*la synthèse anarchiste*) evolved by Vsevolod Volin and Sébastien Faure after the First World War. In America, too, the idea that economic differences must be subordinated to the common struggle against the state had a long pedigree. Ever since the 1880s, as Rudolf Rocker noted, there were those who, in contrast to Benjamin Tucker, "believed that mutualism, collectivism, and communism represent only different methods of economy, the practical possibilities of which have yet to be tested, and that the first objective is to secure the personal and social freedom of men no matter upon which economic basis this is to be accomplished."[18]

To this group belonged Dyer Lum, who wrote in *The Alarm* in 1886: "Anarchy, or the total cessation of force government, is the fundamental principle upon which all our arguments are based. Communism is a question of administration in the future, and hence must be subordinated to and in accord with the principles of Anarchy and all of its logical deduc-

---

Nettlau, "My Social Credo," manuscript, October 7, 1931, Sunrise Colony Archives. In the 1920s, Nettlau criticized the title of the American anarchist journal *The Road to Freedom*, insisting that there were many roads to freedom, not just one. Compare Errico Malatesta in *Il Risveglio* (Geneva), November 1929: "One may prefer communism or individualism or any other system, and work by example and propaganda for the achievement of one's personal preferences; but one must beware, at the risk of certain disaster, of supposing that one's own system is the only and infallible one, good for all men everywhere and at all times, and that its success must be insured at all costs by means other than those which depend on persuasion, which spring from the evidence of facts. What is important and indispensable, the point of departure, is to insure for everybody the means to be free."

[18] Rocker, *Pioneers of American Freedom*, pp. 160-61.

tions."[19] In 1893 an international anarchist conference in Chicago, organized by William T. Holmes, a close friend of Lum and Parsons, sought to hammer out a common program that would be acceptable to all anarchist groups. Holmes and his wife Lizzie were among the delegates, as were Voltairine de Cleyre, Lucy Parsons, C. L. James, Honoré Jaxon, and W. H. Van Ornum. But both Tucker and Most refused to attend, each regarding the other's views on property as being incompatible with anarchist principles.

Throughout the 1890s, Holmes and his wife, along with Van Ornum, Ross Winn, and others, continued to press for a reconciliation among the quarreling factions and even proposed a united front with socialists, nationalists, and Single Taxers to achieve a cooperative commonwealth "free from the blighting effects of authority." Let us shed our divisive labels, proclaimed Van Ornum, for "we are frittering away our strength in mutual destruction instead of mutual and helpful construction."[20] In a similar spirit, the Jewish anarchist physician, Dr. J. A. Maryson, came out in 1895 for a "pure and simple" anarchism without prefixes or suffixes, allowing for freedom of choice in economic as well as other matters. Mankind, he argued, is too diverse to be squeezed into any preconceived mold; and diversity is essential to the evolution of freedom.[21]

[19] Dyer D. Lum, "Communal Anarchy," *The Alarm*, March 6, 1886.

[20] Ross Winn, "Let Us Unite," *Twentieth Century*, January 18, 1894; W. H. Van Ornum, *Fundamentals of Reform*, Columbus Junction, Iowa, 1896, pp. 2-7. See also William Holmes, *The Historical, Philosophical and Economical Bases of Anarchy*, Columbus Junction, Iowa, 1896; and the articles by Lizzie M. Holmes in *The Individualist*, September 7, 1889, and *Freedom* (Chicago), February 1, 1891.

[21] F. A. Frank [Dr. J. A. Maryson], "Anarchy Pure and Simple," *Solidarity*, April 1, 1895; Maryson, "Nur Anarkhizm," *Di Fraye Gezelshaft*, October 15, 1895. See also his letter in *Liberty*, June 13, 1896.

And so, quite apart from Voltairine de Cleyre, a number of American anarchists had been pushing for a unification of the different anarchist schools and for a flexibility that would accommodate a variety of attitudes and viewpoints. By the turn of the century, however, Voltairine had emerged as the leading apostle of tolerance within the anarchist movement, pleading for cooperation among all who sought the removal of authority, regardless of their economic preferences. Tuckerites and Mostians, Kropotkinites and Tolstoyans must suspend their factional bickering and close ranks in the common quest for a free society. Such was the central theme of her writings during the final decade of her life.

Not that she was blind to the difficulties involved. For the movement, she acknowledged in her fullest statement of the problem, had its "fanatical adherents of either collectivism or individualism" who believe that "no Anarchism is possible without that particular economic system as its guarantee." But, she hastened to add, "this old narrowness is yielding to the broader, kindlier and far more reasonable idea that all these economic conceptions may be experimented with, and there is nothing un-Anarchistic about any of them until the element of compulsion enters and obliges unwilling persons to remain in a community whose economic arrangements they do not agree to." If this standpoint is accepted, she said, we shall be "rid of those outrageous excommunications which belong properly to the Church of Rome, and which serve no purpose but to bring us into deserved contempt with outsiders."[22]

To Voltairine de Cleyre a whole range of economic systems—individualistic, mutualistic, communistic—might be "advantageously tried in different localities. I would see the instincts and habits of the people ex-

[22] Voltairine de Cleyre, "Anarchism," *Free Society*, October 13, 1901; reprinted in *Selected Works*, pp. 96-117.

press themselves in a free choice in every community; and I am sure that distinct environments would call out distinct adaptations." "Liberty and experiment alone can determine the best forms of society," she wrote on another occasion. "Therefore I no longer label myself otherwise than 'Anarchist' simply."[23]

What was essential, however, was that there be "*no compulsion*" and no predetermined blueprints. Pragmatic and skeptical by nature, Voltairine was repelled by stringent dogmas and arid theoretical schemes. "She had little use for people of high-sounding theories," a friend remarked. "It was activity she was seeking in preference to theories." She was an intellectual, yet without "assuming the air of intellectuality in order to make others feel inferior in her presence." Moreover, unlike so many intellectuals, she preferred to associate "with simple people, with active comrades, whose hearts are still beating for the Anarchist idea."[24] Nor did she boast of any clearly defined notion of the future society, which must be free to make its own arrangements. For individuals not only differ from each other, but they never cease growing and changing, and their development must be given full scope.

Like most anarchists, therefore, she refused to force the natural evolution of society into any preconceived framework. Her own impulsive character, her restless spirit and unrestrained yearning for freedom in all areas of life, prevented her from accepting labels or systems that might set limits upon one's thoughts or activities. "The ideal society without government allures us all," she wrote. "We believe in its possibility, and that makes us anarchists. But since its realization is in the future, and since the future holds unknown factors, it is nearly certain that the free society of the

[23] *Selected Works*, pp. 113, 158. "I am not an individualist nor a communist, not an egoist nor an altruist, but I am an anarchist," she wrote in *Altruria*, February 1907.

[24] Kucera, "Voltairine de Cleyre," *Why?*, August 1913.

unborn will realize itself according to no man's present forecast, whether individualist, communist, mutualist, collectivist, or what-not." The unknown is "always a misty thing." For the present, all experiments involving greater liberty "are *good*, as tentative effort in the right direction."[25]

Voltairine de Cleyre, then, cannot be fitted into any single anarchist category or pinned with any specific anarchist label. She herself maintained that no anarchist faction was free of shortcomings or enjoyed a monopoly of truth. Thus her chief intellectual effort over a period of fifteen years was to preach a mutual accommodation among the disputing groups and to synthesize the best elements of each into a pragmatic and flexible philosophy. Contributing to diverse anarchist periodicals and speaking to groups of every persuasion, she drew upon all the libertarian schools, individualist and collectivist, native and immigrant. Among those who inspired her were such varied thinkers as Tolstoy and Bakunin, Godwin and Kropotkin, Tucker and Most; and while she rejected the extreme individualism of Max Stirner, she could write, not unsympathetically, of this "scintillant rhetorician, the pride of Young Germany, who would have the individual acknowledge nothing, neither science, nor logic, nor any other creation of his thought, as having authority over him, its creator."[26]

In evolving her wide-ranging philosophy, Voltairine de Cleyre nourished herself upon American as well as European sources. Like Dyer Lum and Benjamin Tucker, she was fully alive to the libertarian strand in the American radical tradition represented by such figures as Paine and Jefferson, Emerson and Thoreau. Anarchists, Tucker once remarked, are "simply unterrified Jeffersonian Democrats. They believe that 'the

[25] *Mother Earth*, January 1907; *Free Society*, June 3, 1900.
[26] *Selected Works*, p. 152. Among her possessions when she died was a copy of Godwin's *Political Justice*.

best government is that which governs least,' and that
that which governs least is no government at all."[27]
Pursuing this theme in "Anarchism and American
Traditions," Voltairine de Cleyre helps dispel the illu-
sion that anarchism is solely the product of alien
ideologies. She traces the principles of anarchism—a
doctrine which most Americans regarded, in Hippolyte
Havel's phrase, as a "foreign poison imported into the
States from decadent Europe by criminal paranoiacs"
—to its indigenous origins, showing that many of the
ideas most typical of the anarchist philosophy are
rooted deeply in native soil, "begotten of religious rebellion, small self-sustaining communities, isolated conditions, and hard pioneer life."[28] Protestantism itself,
she writes, echoing Stephen Pearl Andrews' *Science of
Society*, a book she greatly admired, "in asserting the
supremacy of individual conscience, fired the long train
of thought which inevitably leads to the explosion
of all forms of authority." The political writers of the
eighteenth century, in asserting the right of self-gov-
ernment, carried the line of advance a step further,
while the American Revolution itself was fought on
essentially "the same social ground from which the
modern Anarchist derives the no-government theory;
viz., that equal liberty is the political ideal."

In many respects, therefore, Voltairine saw a "fundamental likeness between the Revolutionary Repub-
licans and the Anarchists," both of whom upheld
individual conscience, local self-rule, and the decen-
tralization of power. "Government at best is a necessary
evil," she quotes Thomas Jefferson, "at worst an intolerable one." But the Revolution did not go far
enough. For the Constitution was designed chiefly to

[27] Benjamin R. Tucker, "State Socialism and Anarchism,"
Liberty, March 10, 1888.
[28] Voltairine de Cleyre, "Anarchism and American Traditions," *Mother Earth*, December 1908 and January 1909; reprinted in *Selected Works*, pp. 118-35.

satisfy "the demands of commerce," and, as Jefferson had warned, the absorption in "mere money-making" has led us "down hill from the Revolution." The desire for material acquisition, the lust for power and possession, "long ago vanquished the spirit of '76," she writes, so that today "the commercial interests of America are seeking a world-empire." But the chief sin of our fathers was that "they did not trust liberty wholly. They thought it possible to compromise between liberty and government, believing the latter to be a 'necessary evil.'" And the moment that compromise was made, "the whole misbegotten monster of our present tyranny began to grow." With Thoreau and Tucker, Voltairine de Cleyre insisted on carrying the principle of Jeffersonian democracy to its logical conclusion: "NO GOVERNMENT WHATEVER."[29]

Such were the origins of Voltairine de Cleyre's brand of anarchism, without hyphens or qualifying labels attached. From these diverse sources, in the words of Max Nettlau, she arrived at "a conception of anarchist thought that, in its tolerance, breadth of outlook, high seriousness, close reasoning, and clear definition, had its equal, so far as we know, only in Elisée Reclus." Sharing her wide perspective, Nettlau considered her the "finest flower" sprung from the American soil, "the broadest mind of all."[30] Yet, however flexible in economic doctrine, she adhered with unyielding tenacity to her overall anarchist ideal, which, while variable in detail, must not be compromised in its fundamentals. An area of particular concern to her was that of sexual equality. The sex question, she told her sisters of the Ladies' Liberal League in 1895, is "more intensely important to us than any other, because of the

[29] *Selected Works*, p. 127.
[30] Nettlau, *La anarquía a través de los tiempos*, pp. 243-44; Nettlau to Benjamin R. Tucker, March 22, 1937, Tucker Papers.

interdict which generally rests upon it, because of its
immediate bearing upon our daily life, because of the
stupendous mystery of it and the awful consequences
of ignorance of it."[31]

At that time, the law in most American states treated
a wife as the chattel of her husband, sanctioning his
use of violence against her, denying her the disposal
of her own property, and refusing to recognize her
rights as a parent. Voltairine de Cleyre's whole life was
a revolt against this system of male domination which,
like every other form of tyranny and exploitation, ran
contrary to her anarchistic spirit. "Let every woman
ask herself," she declared, " 'Why am I the slave of
Man? Why is my brain said not to be the equal of his
brain? Why is my work not paid equally with his?
Why must my body be controlled by my husband? Why
may he take my labor in the household, giving me in
exchange what he deems fit? Why may he take my
children from me? Will them away while yet unborn?'
Let every woman ask."[32]

These words were spoken in 1890. As the years
passed, Voltairine tells us, she became "even more interested in the special work of arousing in women the
desire and will to be industrially independent, thus win-
ning the only basis for a true solution to the sexual
problem."[33] Over the next two decades she wrote and
lectured on such subjects as "Sex Slavery," "Love in
Freedom," "Those Who Marry Do Ill," and "The Case
of Woman vs. Orthodoxy." About her favorite feminist
heroine, Mary Wollstonecraft, she wrote a number of
essays and poems and spoke in Chicago and Boston
as well as in Philadelphia and New York. In 1895 she
called for "the recognition, by an annual commemoration, of the life and service of Mary Wollstonecraft, the
great pioneer of the woman's equality movement

[31] Voltairine de Cleyre, *Past and Future*, p. 9.
[32] *Selected Works*, pp. 348-49.
[33] Voltairine de Cleyre, autobiographical sketch, Wess Papers.

among English speaking people. It is to the discredit of our freethinking world that while they have set apart a day to recognize the service of Thomas Paine, the friend of Mary Wollstonecraft, they have not thought of giving to this, or any other woman, such recognition. It shows that their pretended equality belief is largely on their lips alone." In 1903 she returned to the subject: "I do not disparage Thomas Paine's efforts nor works, but if we must have hero worship, let us have a little she-ro worship to even things up a wee bit!"[34]

In language that seems equally up to date, she attacked the stereotyped roles assigned to the sexes from early childhood: "Little girls must not be tomboyish, must not go barefoot, must not climb trees, must not learn to swim, must not do anything they desire to do which Madame Grundy has decreed 'improper.' Little boys are laughed at as effeminate, silly girl-boys if they want to make patchwork or play with a doll. Then when they grow up, 'Oh! Men don't care for home or children as women do!' Why should they, when the deliberate effort of your life has been to crush that nature out of them. 'Women can't rough it like men.' Train any animal, or any plant, as you train your girls, and it won't be able to rough it either. Now *will* somebody tell me why either sex should hold a corner on athletic sports? Why any child should not have free use of his limbs?"[35]

In the same vein, she chafed at the restrictions placed on women because of their sex, the "subordinate cramped circle, prescribed for women in daily life, whether in the field of material production, or in domestic arrangement, or in educational work." She felt a "bitter, passionate sense of personal injustice in this respect; an anger at the institutions set up by

[34] Voltairine de Cleyre, *Past and Future*, pp. 11-12; *Lucifer*, February 12, 1903, under the pseudonym of "Flora W. Fox."
[35] *Selected Works*, p. 355.

men, ostensibly to preserve female purity, really working out to make her a baby, an irresponsible doll of a
creature not to be trusted outside her 'doll's house.' A
sense of burning disgust that a mere legal form should
be considered as the sanction for all manner of bestial-
ities; that a woman should have no right to escape
from the coarseness of a husband, or conversely, without calling down the attention, the scandal, the scorn
of society. That in spite of all the hardship and torture
of existence men and women should go on obeying the
old Israelite command, 'Increase and multiply,' merely
because they have society's permission to do so, without regard to the slaveries to be inflicted upon the unfortunate creatures of their passions."[36]

Much of this outrage was plainly rooted in Voltairine's own experience, in her treatment by most of
the men in her life—Garside, Elliott, Gordon—as a sex
object, breeder, and domestic servant. She regarded
the married woman as "a bonded slave, who takes her
master's name, her master's bread, her master's commands, and serves her master's passions; who passes
through the ordeal of pregnancy and the throes of
travail at *his* dictation—not at her desire; who can control no property, not even her own body, without his
consent." Men, she told a Scottish audience in 1897,
may not mean to be tyrants when they marry, but
"they frequently grow to be such. It is insufficient to
dispense with the priest or the registrar. The spirit of
marriage makes for slavery." Thinking back to her
relationship with Gordon, she advised "every woman
contemplating sexual union of any kind, never to live
together with the man you love, in the sense of renting
a house or rooms, and becoming his housekeeper."[37]
After her return to America, she herself was never

[36] *Mother Earth*, March 1908.
[37] *Selected Works*, p. 344; Voltairine de Cleyre, "The Woman
Question," *The Herald of Revolt*, September 1913.

again to enter into any monogamic union, much less formal marriage.

Again and again she returned to this theme. "Every individual should have a room or rooms *for himself exclusively*," she wrote to her mother, "never subject to the intrusive familiarities of our present 'family life.' A 'closet' where each could 'pray in secret,' without some persons who love him assuming the right to walk in and do as they please. And do you know how I was pleased beyond measure the other day to find that William Godwin, the great English philosopher, and Mary Wollstonecraft, mother of Mrs. Shelley, taught and as far as possible *practiced* the same thing just 100 years ago." Asserting her independence as a person, as the possessor of her own body and mind, she rejected the traditional role of mother and household drudge, subject to the dictates of a husband. True love was natural and free, she said, while marriage, with or without official sanction, was artificial and confining, an instrument of bondage and exploitation that suppressed a woman's individuality, talents, and intellect. "To me," she told her mother, "any dependence, any thing which destroys the complete selfhood of the individual, is in the line of slavery and destroys the pure spontaneity of love."[38]

Apart from her militant feminism, another matter on which Voltairine de Cleyre refused to compromise was the use of the term "anarchist," which a number of her colleagues wished to discard for "libertarian" or some weaker euphemism, on the grounds that "anarchist," with its connotations of violence and destruction, frightened away prospective adherents and alienated the general public. For such proposals she had lit-

[38] Voltairine de Cleyre to Harriet De Claire, January 13, 1894, Labadie Collection.

tle sympathy. On the contrary, she shared the sentiments of Carrard Auban in John Henry Mackay's novel
The Anarchists: "The word Anarchy describes precisely
what we want. It would be cowardly and imprudent
to drop it on account of the weaklings."[39] The "trium-
phant word of Anarchism," she declared, alone has the
power "to stir the moral pulses of the world." It is the
only word which "can animate the dreamer, poet,
sculptor, painter, musician, artist of chisel or pen, with
power to fashion forth his dream. . . ."[40]

Anarchism, in short, was Voltairine's "Dominant
Idea," to borrow the title of one of her most important
essays, a work which Leonard Abbott called a "radical
classic."[41] Every age, she maintained, has a dominant
idea to which the majority of people adhere. The
dominant idea of the modern era is material possession, the acquisition of money and power, "the shame-
less, merciless driving and over-driving, wasting and
draining of the last bit of energy, only to produce heaps
and heaps of things—things ugly, things harmful,
things useless, and at the best largely unnecessary."
Not everyone shares this idea, however. There are a
few "restless, active, rebel souls" (Voltairine herself
among them) who recoil from the Mammon of accumulation, the "moral bankruptcy of Thing-Worship."

They recoil, too, from the "so-called Materialist
Conception of History," the notion that "ideas are but

[39] John Henry Mackay, *The Anarchists*, Boston, 1891, p. 148.

[40] *Mother Earth*, March 1908; *Selected Works*, pp. 137-38.
The debate over the label "Anarchist"—the only label that Voltairine de Cleyre would accept—has recurred periodically in the
movement throughout its history. When Harry Kelly proposed
"libertarian socialist" as a substitute and formed a Libertarian
Socialist League in 1938, Hippolyte Havel denounced its members as "ersatz Anarchist" (*Man!*, December 1938). For a
similar controversy in France, see Jean Maitron, *Le mouvement
anarchiste en France*, 2 vols., Paris, 1975, I, 16.

[41] *The American Freeman*, July 1949.

attendant phenomena, impotent to determine the actions or relations of life." Against this notion, which Voltairine considered "a great and lamentable error," she asserted the principle of free will and individual moral responsibility. In place of the Marxian and Owenite formula, "Men are what circumstances make them," she substituted the opposing declaration, "Circumstances are what men make them." Not that material factors are unimportant. But mind and matter, man and environment interact upon one another. "In other words, my conception of mind, or character, is not that it is a powerless reflection of a momentary condition of stuff and form, but an active modifying agent, reacting on its environment and transforming circumstances, sometimes greatly, sometimes, though not often, entirely."[42]

We must not, then, underestimate the "power and role of the Idea." For the state itself—"the creator and defender of privilege, the organization of oppression and revenge"—is not founded on economics alone, but "has its root far down in the religious development of human nature, and will not fall apart merely through the abolition of classes and property." Thus anarchism means something more fundamental than a replacement of the economic and political system. It means a moral revolution, "freedom to the soul as to the body —in every aspiration, every growth."[43] As Alexander Berkman once put it, "the idea is the thing." To prepare men and women for a freer life, it is necessary to eliminate their authoritarian presuppositions, to alter their attitudes toward the sanctity of privilege and power, to nourish a new idea, a spirit of freedom and mutual aid which will enable them to live as brothers and sisters in harmony and peace.

The moral revolution envisioned by Voltairine de

[42] Voltairine de Cleyre, "The Dominant Idea," *Mother Earth*, May 1910; *Selected Works*, pp. 79-95.
[43] *Selected Works*, pp. 110, 115, 170.

Cleyre required the abandonment of "Thing-Worship" and the return to a more austere mode of existence, such as she herself practiced. Anarchism "pleads with men to renounce the worthless luxuries which enslave them," she wrote, using the language of Thoreau. It beckons them to replace "the rush and jangle of the chase for wealth" with "the silence, the solitude, the simplicity of the free life."[44] Faced with the growing concentration of economic and political power, with its dehumanizing effects and its encroachments on individual liberty, Voltairine de Cleyre looked back to a world as yet undefiled by the intrusion of large-scale industry and the bureaucratic state. Her ideal society was predominantly rural, composed of independent farmers and craftsmen. Throughout her writings runs a nostalgia for a simpler past before centralized government and industry began to transform men and women into an army of faceless robots. In "Anarchism and American Traditions," for example, she portrays a young, uncorrupted America pervaded with Jeffersonian liberties and with the vanished agrarian virtues of the antebellum age.

Voltairine herself came from a small Michigan village, and her image of the good society was rooted in the values of the midwestern countryside where she was reared. Exalting nature over artifice, she felt a Thoreauvian or Tolstoyan hostility for nearly every aspect of urban life. She herself had chosen to live in the city only because that was where anarchists and freethinkers congregated and where she could do the kind of work for which she felt suited. But she was repelled by the decadence of the great metropolises, centers of commercialism and corruption, of poverty and crime, of physical and moral pollution. She complained that "the buying and selling of the land has driven the people off the healthy earth and

[44] Voltairine de Cleyre, "Anarchism in Literature," *Selected Works*, pp. 145-46.

away from the clean air into these rot-heaps of humanity called cities, where every filthy thing is done, and
filthy labor breeds filthy bodies and filthy souls."[45] Like
Thoreau, she lamented the growing rift between man
and nature. She yearned for the resurrection of a simple preindustrial world where one might "watch things
grow and blossom, and feel again the joy of life and
the sweet kinship with all living things—learn the forgotten lore of the savage who knew all the colors of
the leaves, and the shapes of them, and the way they
turn to the sun, and the peculiar instrument that played
in the throat of every bird, and the promises of weather
that boded in the sky, and saw every night a full clear
unbroken view of the great arch with all its stars, not a
blue patch cut into angles with roofs, fouled with
smoke, seen out of the cellar of existence."[46]

Such a vision implied an almost total rejection of
the forms of economic and social organization which
emerged in America after the Civil War and which
came to dominate much of the world in the twentieth
century. Her emphasis on the natural and spontaneous,
on the individual and personal, set her against the
whole centralized, hierarchical, and bureaucratic structure of modern industrial society. Hers was a romantic,
backward-looking vision of an idealized rural past
inhabited by sturdy artisans and homesteaders who
lived in harmony with nature, joined by the ties of
voluntary cooperation. It was a simplified world in
which the natural social unit was the village, the
tribe, or the "affinity group," rather than the artificial
city or state. The future society, she hoped, would get
back to the roots of life, recapture the direct human
relations of the past, and restore a healthy balance
between man and his environment. In such a society
"natural friendships will soon produce what a thousand

[45] *Selected Works*, pp. 168-69.
[46] Voltairine de Cleyre, "Our Martyred Comrades," *Free
Society*, December 16, 1900.

years of artificial attempt could not create, an organization, spontaneous, free, solid with the solidity of personal affection," in which human beings would co-
operate "as the leaf cooperates with the sun, as the
moon with the tide, as lover with lover, asking no rules
since none are needed."[47]

Such, said Voltairine, had been the life of the American Indian, "that much maligned and race-crushed
people whose ideals were trodden by the Anglo-Saxon
race, until with many of us they are but a tradition.
Let us learn so much from the vanished spirits—to go
back 'near to nature's heart.'"[48] She felt a deep and
abiding compassion for all the primitive folk—American Indians, Mexican peons, Filipino tribesmen—who
had fallen victim to modern "civilization," a word she
often used with contempt. For theirs was the vanished
world that she cherished, uncontaminated by the spirit
of Mammon, the Dominant Idea of the age. American
Indians and Mexican peons, Andalusian peasants and
East European artisans, Scottish highlanders and
Stonehenge shepherds—such were the inhabitants of
her ideal world. Her favorite song, characteristically,
was an Hawaiian folk melody. Perhaps, with her
ascetic nature, rural background, and cult of the primitive, which elevated crafts over industry, village over
city, the natural and aesthetic over the artificial and
material things of life, she was closer in spirit to the
Russian, Spanish, and Italian anarchists than to many
of her American comrades, especially the unsenti-
mental rationalists of the Tuckerite persuasion. Nor,
in her view, was science, any more than material accumulation, a sufficient guide to happiness and self-

[47] *Lucifer*, late 1894 (date obliterated).
[48] *Ibid.* She accused the American government of having
"murdered the aboriginal people, that you might seize the land
in the name of the white race" (*Selected Works*, p. 167). In
all this, she was strongly influenced by her friend Honoré
Jaxon, a Chicago anarchist of French and Indian descent.

understanding. As she wrote to her mother, "Science has delved, and dug, and pounded, and exploded, and gone to the stars, and chased out hell and heaven, and yet we know no more than did the ancient Greek who held the world to be a lotus-leaf floating on water. To those that come after us our wisdom will be as foolish, our facts as mythical, as the Mosaic cosmogeny is to us, and after all, *who can ever get outside of himself* to know whether the universe is the dream of his consciousness or a fact outside of him?"[49]

Not that she was averse to scientific and technological progress. For all her romantic yearnings, she welcomed new inventions that would relieve men of tedious labor and allow time for cultural and intellectual pursuits. Yet she wished to preserve the advantages of machinery within the context of a small society. What disturbed her most about modern technology was its excessive centralization and division of labor, with their corrosive effects on the human spirit. Minute specialization, she argued, benefited only the employer, while promoting boredom and frustration among the workers, accentuating the master-slave relationship, and reinforcing the invidious distinction between manual and intellectual work.

Like Kropotkin and William Morris, she was the natural enemy of an economic system that reduced labor to sheer drudgery while starving the workers, housing them in crowded ghettos (such as the one in which she herself lived), stunting the minds and bodies of their children, and befouling the land and the air. She condemned the ravages of a profit-driven technology, wantonly destroying the traditions and crafts of a thousand years. Before the factory system was introduced, she said, the workshop was a place where owner and employee worked together, knew no class feeling, and relied on friendship and common interests to pre-

[49] Voltairine de Cleyre to Harriet De Claire, February 25, 1894, Labadie Collection.

serve a harmonious relationship. What was more, "the individuality of the workman was a plainly recognized quantity." With the emergence of large-scale industry, however, the employer has become "a man apart, having interests hostile to those of his employees, living in another circle altogether, knowing nothing of them but as so many units of power, to be reckoned with as he does his machines, for the most part despising them, at his very best regarding them as dependents whom he is bound in some respects to care for, as a humane man cares for an old horse he cannot use."

The time had come, therefore, for "the spirit of Dare" to reverse the trend toward centralization, to alter the relations between master and man, and to inaugurate a system "which will preserve the benefits of the new production and at the same time restore the individual dignity of the worker—give back the bold independence of the old master of his trade, together with such added freedoms as may properly accrue to him as his special advantage from society's material developments." The anarchist, she declared, "looks with fierce suspicion upon an arithmetic with men for units, a society running in slots and grooves" and smelling "of machine oil."[50]

Thus the division of labor, which "makes of one man a Brain and of another a Hand," must be eliminated and production carried out in small workshops where labor would be varied and agreeable. Voltairine was deeply impressed by Kropotkin's *Fields, Factories and Workshops*, in which these ideas are set forth. Under such an arrangement, the worker, without sacrificing the gains of modern technology, would regain the dignity of being his own master and no longer be treated as a chattel or a marketable commodity.

Yet, despite her acceptance of technical innovation, Voltairine's basic assumptions and outlook ran

[50] *Selected Works*, pp. 100-102, 139-40.

contrary to mass production and consumption, however decentralized in structure. They ran contrary to the ethos not only of modern America but of Western society as a whole. An ascetic to the core, she would have been no friend of the "affluent society" and continually expanding economy of recent times. In her ideal world, rather, men and women would live, as she herself lived, in simplicity and frugality, their lives rich not in material abundance but in freedom and self-rewarding work. Her anarchist commonwealth would be a free society "where there are neither kings, presidents, landlords, national bankers, stock-brokers, railroad magnates, patent-right monopolists, or tax and tithe collectors; where there are no overstocked markets or hungry children, idle counters and naked creatures, splendor and misery, waste and need," as she described it in 1890. She looked forward to "a day when there shall be neither kings nor Americans—only Men; over the whole earth, MEN."[51]

To Voltairine, however, "the Anarchist ideal was something more than a dream of the future," as the London *Freedom* noted after her death. "It was a guide for everyday life, and not to be compromised with."[52] For the millennium, she realized, would not be attained overnight. Indeed, freedom and justice may never be fully realized, let alone in our lifetime. "It requires courage to struggle for any ideal," remarked Harry Kelly, "even when it seems close at hand; it requires far more courage and greater devotion to struggle for the ideal in itself, regardless of when it shall be realized. The latter was the case with Voltairine."[53] As she saw it, men and women of conscience had no choice but to fight—if need be to suffer—for their principles. "It is the old story," she wrote in "The Dominant Idea." " 'Aim at the stars, and you may hit the top of the gatepost;

[51] *Liberty*, February 15, 1890; *Selected Works*, p. 135.
[52] *Freedom*, August 1912.
[53] *Mother Earth*, July 1912.

but aim at the ground, and you will hit the ground.' "
As her friend Rudolf Rocker summed it up: "Social
ideas are not something only to dream about for the
future. If they are to mean anything at all they must be
translated into our daily life, here and now; they must
shape our relations with our fellow-man."[54]

[54] Rudolf Rocker, *The London Years*, London, 1956, p. 56.

7. Herman Helcher

On the afternoon of December 19, 1902, Voltairine de Cleyre was on her way to give a lesson when she was accosted by a former pupil named Herman Helcher. She was stepping onto a streetcar at the corner of Fourth and Green Streets when Helcher pulled her sleeve. As she turned toward him, he raised a pistol and fired point blank. The bullet struck her in the chest, above the heart. As she whirled about under its impact, Helcher fired three more times, one bullet missing, the others lodging in her back. In spite of her wounds, she managed to run half a block before collapsing on a doorstep. Another of her pupils, a doctor who lived close by, rushed to her aid. He immediately called for an ambulance, and she was taken to Hahnemann Hospital, where her wounds were pronounced fatal.

Hahnemann was a homeopathic hospital, and no operation was performed. The bullets were left in her body and were never removed. For several days she hovered between life and death, and it was thought that she would not recover. Quite suddenly, however, she began to improve. Before long she was pronounced out of danger. "Ah, dearest Maggie," she later wrote to her Scottish friend, "I can imagine how it went to your soft heart when you heard about that horrible shooting. In fact I believe that outside of the actual physical pain of the first three days, my friends suffered more than I did. I don't know what kind of a curious constitution I am blessed with, but some way I settled down to the coldest kind of mental attitude in which the chief characteristic was unshakable determination not to die."[1]

[1] Voltairine de Cleyre to Will and Maggie Duff, July 13, 1903, Ishill Collection. Ed Brady, Emma Goldman's companion, went to Philadelphia and reported that the two bullets in her

Who was Herman Helcher? Why had he committed
his act? A twenty-four-year-old cigarmaker of Russian-
Jewish origin, Helcher had taken English lessons from
Voltairine a few years earlier. As a fellow anarchist, he
was keenly interested in her work. According to Nathan
Navro, he came to worship her and her then companion
Gordon. When Voltairine and Gordon had their falling-
out, Helcher was greatly upset, and he took it upon himself to bring about a reconciliation, "for the good of the
cause," as he put it.[2] His desire to reunite the couple
soon became an obsession. But when he approached
Voltairine about it she refused to listen. And so his
agitation increased. He became sullen and morose. He
began to see Voltairine as an enemy who had thwarted
his well-meaning intentions. The idea preyed on his
mind. In the end, it drove him to act.

Previously, Helcher's character had been mild and
gentle. "He was a little foolish, but very sincere in his
anarchism," says Navro. But long before the shooting
he had exhibited abnormal behavior and harbored
strange ideas. Wherever he went he used to carry a
sandwich in his pocket; and he once asked Chaim
Weinberg for the address of John Wanamaker, the
wealthy Philadelphia merchant, so he could steal into
his house at night and cut off his daughter's hair.[3]
Medical examination afterwards revealed that he had
been suffering from "paranoia, or progressive insanity"
since childhood, caused by an accumulation of uric

---

back had been extracted but that the third could not be touched
because it was embedded too close to the heart. (Goldman, *Living My Life*, p. 333.) All other sources, however, say that none
of the bullets were removed and that she carried them in her
body for the rest of her life.

[2] Navro manuscript, Ishill Collection.

[3] *Ibid.*; Voltairine de Cleyre to Lillian Harman, December
31, 1902, Harman Papers; Chaim Weinberg, *Fertsig yor in
kamf far sotsialer bafrayung*, Los Angeles and Philadelphia,
1952, p. 72.

acid in the bloodstream, which ultimately affected his brain.[4]

In time, his irritation with Voltairine developed into a full-blown persecution mania. He imagined that she had got him blacklisted by the Social Science Club and also fired from his job, when in fact he was still employed (at the Oppenheim cigar factory) and had not been discharged. He even came to believe that she was anti-Semitic, which was idiotic, as Emma Goldman noted, since Voltairine "had devoted most of her life to the education of Jews."[5] Not least, he fancied himself in love with Voltairine and brooded on his unrequited passion, though he never once hinted to her of his feelings. The detective who questioned him, according to Voltairine, said he "declared he loved me, that I had broken his heart, and he had made up his mind two months before that I deserved to die."[6]

One day Helcher bought a revolver and, donning a false mustache, hid himself in a building that Voltairine normally passed on her way to her lessons. As she approached, he saw that Mary Hansen (with whom she was then living) was with her, so his plan was momentarily spoiled. A few days later, however, she came by alone and he succeeded in carrying out the attack. After the shooting he did not try to escape but stood quite still until arrested. An hour later, Mary Hansen came to the station house. Confronting Helcher, she said: "Why, Herman, why ever did you do this?" He answered: "I don't know; I had to." Mary Hansen: "But if anything was the matter, why did you never come and tell us anything? Miss de Cleyre did not even know you were in the city." Helcher: "Well, why didn't she know? She ought to have known. No-

[4] *Free Society*, March 8, 1903; Navro manuscript, Ishill Collection; Frumkin, *In friling fun yidishn sotsializm*, pp. 252-54.

[5] Goldman, *Voltairine de Cleyre*, p. 20.

[6] Voltairine de Cleyre, "Facts and Theories," *Free Society*, March 8, 1903.

body cared about me. I had nothing to eat for three days, and fourteen cents in my pocket."[7]

What tragic irony that Voltairine de Cleyre, with her great compassion for the lonely assassins of those years, should herself become the target of an anarchist's bullets. And how remarkable was the consistency of principle with which she reacted to this attack upon her own person, displaying the same sympathetic understanding that she had shown toward Angiolillo and Bresci and Czolgosz. In accordance with the teachings of Tolstoy, the doctrine of returning good for evil, she refused to identify Helcher as her assailant or to press charges against him. When he was taken to her bedside for identification the day after the incident, she said that she knew him as a comrade and former pupil but that she could not recognize him as the man who had shot her. Two days later she dictated the following statement to the Philadelphia *North American*:

> The boy who, they say, shot me is crazy. Lack of proper food and healthy labor made him so. He ought to be put into an asylum. It would be an outrage against civilization if he were sent to jail for an act which was the product of a diseased brain.
>
> Shortly before I was shot the young man sent me a letter which was pitiful—nothing to eat, no place to sleep, no work. Before that I had not heard from him for two years.
>
> These things discouraged the crazed mind of the boy. He did not know what he was doing. He was simply a lunatic, acting as a man with a fever. I had not seen him for two years. Suddenly, when I was not thinking about him, he appeared in front of me, and, I am told, shot me. I did not recognize him at the time.

[7] *Ibid.*

I have no resentment towards the man. If society were so constituted as to allow every man, woman and child to lead a normal life there would be no violence in this world. It fills me with horror to think of the brutal acts done in the name of government. Every act of violence finds its echo in another act of violence. The policeman's club breeds criminals.

Contrary to public understanding, Anarchism means "Peace on earth, good will to men." Acts of violence done in the name of Anarchy are caused by men and women who forget to be philosophers— teachers of the people—because their physical and mental sufferings drive them to desperation.[8]

In her behavior toward Helcher, Voltairine de Cleyre was following the example of Errico Malatesta and Louise Michel, who had earlier been victims of shootings and refused to press charges against their assailants. Malatesta, while speaking in West Hoboken, New Jersey, in 1899, was shot in the leg by a member of a rival anarchist faction, who was disarmed by none other than Gaetano Bresci, the future assassin of Umberto; and in 1888 Louise Michel was shot behind the ear by a deranged individual named Pierre Lucas after addressing a meeting in Le Havre. While her head was being bandaged she said to reporters: "You understand, my dears, he has a wife and children, that man Lucas! What will the judges do if you fall on him? And what will the mother and kids do if the judges send him to jail?" Emma Goldman describes Louise's courage as the doctors probed for the bullet: "The operation, though very painful, called forth no complaint from her. Instead she lamented her poor animals left alone in her rooms and the inconvenience the delay would cause her woman friend who was waiting for her

---

[8] The Philadelphia *North American*, December 24, 1902; re-printed in *Free Society*, January 11, 1903.

in the next town." After her recovery she wrote a letter
of sympathy to Lucas's wife, secured a lawyer for his
defense, and herself delivered a plea for acquittal, so
that he was sent to a mental institution from which,
after repeated demands by his victim, he was shortly
released.[9]

In a similar manner, Voltairine de Cleyre did all in
her power to shield Herman Helcher from punishment. While recovering from her wounds, she invoked
the biblical injunction, "Judge not, that ye be not
judged," as an argument against law courts and
prisons. She refused to appear as a witness against
Helcher and, when she had regained sufficient
strength, worked actively for his release from confinement, deliberately returning good for evil while at the
same time living up to her belief that crimes are caused
by illness and social abuse and that prisons only make
matters worse. In a letter to *Free Society* she asked her
associates to show forgiveness toward the disturbed
young man by raising a fund for his defense:

Dear Comrades,
    I write to appeal to you on behalf of the un-
fortunate child (for in intellect he has never been
more than a child) who made the assault upon me.

[9] *Free Society*, May 10, 1904; Goldman, *Living My Life*, p.
167. See also Edith Thomas, *Louise Michel*, Paris, 1971, pp.
315-29; and *Liberty*, February 11, 1888. Peter Kropotkin later
referred to these episodes in a letter to Lenin condemning the
Bolshevik practice of taking hostages during the Russian Civil
War: "And revolutionaries in court—Louise Michel, for instance—undertake to defend their own would-be assassins, or
they refuse, as did Malatesta and Voltairine de Cleyre, to press
charges against them. Even kings and popes have rejected
such barbarous means of defense as the taking of hostages.
So how can the advocates of a new life and the builders of a
new society resort to such a weapon of defense against their
enemies?" Kropotkin to Lenin, December 21, 1920, in Paul
Avrich, ed., *The Anarchists in the Russian Revolution*, Ithaca,
N.Y., 1973, pp. 148-49.

He is friendless, he is in prison, he is sick—had he not been sick in brain he would never have done this thing.

Nothing can be done to relieve him until a lawyer is secured, and for that money is needed. I know it is hard to ask, for our comrades are always giving more than they can afford. But I think this is a case where all Anarchists are concerned that the world may learn our ideas concerning the treatment of so-called "criminals," and that they will therefore be willing to make even unusual sacrifices.

What this poor half-crazed boy needs is not the silence and cruelty of a prison, but the kindness, care and sympathy which heal.

These have all been given to me, in unstinted quantity. I can never express the heart of my gratitude for it all. Be as ready now to help the other who is perhaps the greater sufferer.

>With love to all,
>Voltairine de Cleyre
>Philadelphia, 807 Fairmount Avenue.[10]

Meanwhile, Voltairine continued her appeals to the authorities for clemency. But they fell on deaf ears. Helcher was made to stand trial and, found guilty of attempted murder, was sentenced to six years and nine months in prison. Soon afterwards, however, he was transferred to the insane asylum at Norristown, from which he was released in the custody of his parents. At home he grew more and more uncontrollable, so that he had to be recommitted. He died of his illness a few years later.

As for Voltairine de Cleyre, given the gravity of her wounds and her generally frail constitution, she made

---

[10] *Free Society*, January 11, 1903. In this same issue, the editors of *Free Society* took Yanovsky to task for condemning Helcher in the *Fraye Arbeter Shtime*.

a surprisingly rapid recovery. On January 2, 1903, after two weeks in the hospital, she was able to come home, where she steadily regained her strength. Before long she was up and about and resumed playing the piano.[11] On March 15th she was even able to return to the lecture platform. At Odd Fellows' Temple she spoke before the Social Science Club on "Crime and Punishment," with George Brown in the chair. The audience of 1,200 gave her a magnificent reception. After a recitation by James Williams, an iron molder, she was introduced by the Single Tax leader Frank Stephens, as a detective sat nearby on the platform. She wore a white shirtwaist and black silk skirt, "the plainness of her attire being relieved with a corsage bouquet of red roses and ferns," a reporter noted. Considering her recent ordeal, "Miss de Cleyre looked remarkably well, and spoke in clear, forcible tones that could be heard all over the hall."[12]

Herman Helcher dominated Voltairine's thoughts as she delivered her address, in which she denounced the prison system. The greatest crimes are committed by the state itself, she declared, yet "this chiefest of murderers, the Government, its own hands red with the blood of hundreds of thousands, assumes to correct the individual offender, enacting miles of laws to define the varying degrees of his offense and punishment, and putting beautiful building stones to very hideous purposes for the sake of cageing and tormenting him therein." "We have punished and punished for untold thousands of years, and we have not gotten rid of crime, we have not diminished it," she went on. She contemptuously dismissed the much-discussed theories of Cesare Lombroso ("that learned donkey," Alexander Berkman called him) regarding the criminal type: "I

[11] See the letters of J. A. Wilson in *Lucifer*, January 15, 1903; and George Brown in *Freedom*, March 1903.

[12] Unidentified newspaper clipping in the possession of Renée de Cleyre Buckwalter.

am inclined to doubt a great deal that is said about the born criminal. Prof. Lombroso gives us very exhaustive reports of the measurements of their skulls and their ears and their noses and their thumbs and their toes, etc. But I suspect that if a good many respectable, decent, never-did-a-wrong-thing-in-their-lives people were to go up for measurement, malformed ears and disproportionately long thumbs would be equally found among them if they took the precaution to represent themselves as criminals first."

Thinking of Helcher, however, she admitted that there are some who "through some malformation or deficiency or excess of certain portions of the brain are constantly impelled to violent deeds. Well, there are some born idiots and some born cripples. Do you punish them for their idiocy or for their unfortunate physical condition? On the contrary, you pity them, you realize that life is a long infliction to them, and your best and tenderest sympathies go out to them. Why not to the other, equally a helpless victim of an evil inheritance? Granting for the moment that you have the right to punish the mentally responsible, surely you will not claim the right to punish the mentally irresponsible! Even the law does not hold the insane man guilty. And the born criminal is irresponsible; he is a sick man, sick with the most pitiable chronic disease; his treatment is for the medical world to decide, and the best of them—not for the prosecutor, the judge, and the warden."

Prisons in any case do not reform. Their story is the story of "the lash, the iron, the chain and every torture that the fiendish ingenuity of *the non-criminal class can devise by way of teaching criminals to be good!*[13] To teach men to be good, they are kept in airless cells, made to sleep on narrow planks, to look at the sky

[13] One of Voltairine de Cleyre's most powerful stories is "The Chain Gang," *Mother Earth*, October 1907; reprinted in *Selected Works*, pp. 414-19.

through iron grates, to eat food that revolts their
palates, and destroys their stomachs—battered and
broken down in body and soul; and this is what they
call reforming men!" "Do you think," she asked in conclusion, that "people come out of a place like that
better? With more respect for society? With more
regard for the rights of their fellow men? I don't. I
think they come out of there with their hearts full of
bitterness, much harder than when they went in." So
let us have done with "this savage idea of punishment,
which is without wisdom. Let us work for the freedom
of man from the oppressions which make criminals,
and for the enlightened treatment of the sick."[14]

Voltairine de Cleyre's speech was widely covered in
the Philadelphia press. For her shooting by Helcher,
still more her refusal to press charges against him, had
aroused a good deal of publicity and made her something of a celebrity. Local newspapers, which had for
years been filled with invective against the anarchists,
softened their attitude because of Voltairine's behavior
throughout the affair. One reporter even wrote that
"anarchism is really the doctrine of the Nazarene, the
gospel of forgiveness."[15] At the same time, commercial
publishers began to solicit her poems and articles. Her
reply, noted Will Duff, was characteristic: "She said
that her works were dedicated to Humanity, and that
she wished them to be published through the love of her
comrades."[16]

Little by little, meanwhile, she resumed her labors
for the anarchist movement. In May 1903, for example,
she and George Brown and Mary Hansen addressed a
series of open-air meetings in support of striking textile
workers in neighboring Germantown, Pennsylvania.
These activities, however, left her exhausted, and her

[14] Voltairine de Cleyre, "Crime and Punishment," *Selected
Works*, pp. 173-204. See also Mary Hansen's report of the lecture in *Free Society*, March 29, 1903.
[15] Goldman, *Living My Life*, p. 334.
[16] *The Herald of Revolt*, September 1913.

doctors advised complete rest. Accordingly, she decided to go to Norway, the country of Ibsen, for a prolonged recuperation amid the fjords and forests.

On June 22nd she went to New York, spending two days with Perle McLeod, who had moved there from Philadelphia. She sailed on June 24th on the steamship *United States* bound for Christiania (now Oslo). At that time, Kaiser Wilhelm of Germany was visiting Norway, and the Christiania press reported that the anarchists had dispatched a "good looking young American lady" to assassinate him. Because of this ridiculous charge, she was watched by detectives aboard ship and questioned when she docked in Christiania. From the moment she disembarked on Norwegian soil, her movements were observed and recorded, her mail was intercepted, and reports were filed with the police.[17]

In Christiania, where she stayed for several days, she was conducted around town and through the local art galleries by Kristofer Hansteen, a leading Norwegian anarchist, the translator of Most and Kropotkin and editor of *Til Frihet* and *Anarkisten*, to whom she wrote a fine tribute in *Mother Earth* when he died three years later.[18] After this, she went up-country to stay at Nes, in the Hallingdal district, with an old comrade, a construction engineer named Olav Anderson, who had lived in America and was working on a new railroad linking Christiania with Bergen. At Hallingdal, where she remained for five weeks, she hiked over the hills and breathed pure air, and her "city nerves" were soothed by "the music of a shadowy waterfall."[19] On the

[17] Voltairine de Cleyre, "Ven an anarkhist fergint zikh a veykeyshon," *Di Fraye Gezelshaft*, July 1910; Olav Koringen, manuscript on Voltairine in Oslo, Ishill Collection.

[18] Voltairine de Cleyre, "Kristofer Hansteen," *Mother Earth*, May 1906.

[19] *Di Fraye Gezelshaft*, July 1910, p. 605. See also her beautiful description of Hallingdal in a letter to her mother, July 16, 1903, Labadie Collection.

whole, however, she found Norway disappointing and
was anxious to proceed to Glasgow and her dear friends
the Duffs, "if you have a corner left for me yet, which
I am sure you have if you have one for yourselves,"
she wrote them. "I cursed myself for a fool when we
were passing Scotland that I had not gone there instead at first. This place is decidedly 'chilly' both as
to climate and people. I wonder when I look at them
how the human race ever gets propagated."[20]

On August 16th she left Hallingdal for Christiania.
There, on the 18th, the Norwegian Labor Party held
a mass meeting in the Arbeidersamfund, the hall of
the Socialist Youth League, where a crowd of 800 heard
her speak on "The Anarchist Ideal." Olav Koringen,
editor of the daily *Social-Demokraten*, a "big, kindly
Norseman" whom she had met in the United States and
who had defended her against the rumor that she had
come to murder the Kaiser, printed the lecture in his
newspaper.[21]

Three days later Voltairine set sail on the *Scotland*,
arriving in Glasgow on August 24th. With Will and
Maggie Duff, who now lived at 91 Aitkenhead Road,
she spent nearly three delightful weeks. And though
she had fled Philadelphia "to recover from too much
talking,"[22] she agreed to repeat her lecture "Crime and
Punishment" before the Progressive Union at Pollok-
shaws. In advance of the meeting she asked the chairman, William McGill, to make his introduction brief
and avoid complimentary remarks, as she wished no
adulation for her recent conduct in Philadelphia,

[20] Voltairine de Cleyre to Will and Maggie Duff, May 27 and
July 13, 1903, Ishill Collection. See also her letter to Harriet
De Claire, July 17, 1903, Labadie Collection.

[21] Voltairine de Cleyre, *Det Anarkistiske Ideal*, Christiania,
1903. Koringen, who had edited a socialist paper in Minnesota,
thought Voltairine "one of the best and most charming women
I have met."

[22] Voltairine de Cleyre to Will and Maggie Duff, July 13,
1903, Ishill Collection.

which, she felt, simply accorded with her philosophy. As Jay Fox observed, "she knew the baneful effect of hero worship and despised it. She would be nobody's god." McGill therefore made the following announcement: "Comrade Voltairine de Cleyre will deliver a lecture on 'Crime and Punishment.' Voltairine will now speak for herself." This, she said, was an ideal chairman's speech.[23]

How she loved being in Glasgow again with the Duffs and their friends! No sooner had she departed for England (on September 12th) than she began to miss them, for "my heart is always more in Scotland than London."[24] At the station in London she was met by Harry Kelly, who conducted her to a welcoming tea party attended by sixty-five comrades, among them Errico Malatesta, Nicholas Chaikovsky, V. N. Cherkezov, and Sophie Kropotkin. Peter Kropotkin was away but sent his greetings, as did Louise Michel from Paris. For the next week or so Voltairine stayed with Harry Kelly and his Russian-Jewish companion Mary Krimont at their house in Cambridge Road, Anerly, a suburb southeast of the city. There she was visited by Rudolf Rocker, editor of *Der Arbeter Fraynd* and *Germinal*, the Yiddish anarchist weekly and monthly published in London. Her friends in Philadelphia had told her about this young German gentile who, like herself, lived among the Jews and had taken the trouble to learn their language. It was to be their only meeting, however, for when Rocker voyaged to America in 1913 she had been dead nearly a year, and he visited her grave in the Waldheim Cemetery by the tomb of the Chicago martyrs.[25]

[23] *The Agitator*, July 15, 1912; *The Herald of Revolt*, September 1913.

[24] Voltairine de Cleyre to Will and Maggie Duff, September 14, 1903, Ishill Collection. She once said that "one inch of Scotland is worth all England put together." Voltairine de Cleyre to Lillian Harman, April 1, 1898, Harman Papers.

[25] Rocker, *The London Years*, p. 182.

On September 17th Voltairine again delivered her lecture "Crime and Punishment," this time before a big London audience at the South Place Institute, with Harry Kelly (duly forewarned to "cut the heroine business") in the chair.[26] Nellie Ploschansky, the ten-year-old daughter of Jewish immigrants, remembers her as a tall, slender figure dressed in odd but interesting clothes. Sam Dreen, a young Jewish tailor, thought her "very nice-looking—not like Emma—and a good speaker. She was highly regarded by all the comrades."[27]

So ended Voltairine de Cleyre's second sojourn in Europe. When she returned to the United States her health and spirits were markedly improved, as after her first trip in 1897. But her recovery was short-lived. Once back in Philadelphia, we learn from Nathan Navro, she experienced a sudden and "terrible decline." This was caused not so much by the effects of Helcher's bullets (though they continued to give her pain) as by the recurrent inflammation of the sinuses from which she had suffered since early childhood. The illness was diagnosed as a progressive "atrophy of the tissues of the roof of the mouth," resulting from a "chronic catarrh of the nose." It ultimately reached the middle ear and infected her entire head, so that in early 1904 she suffered from temporary deafness, and for the rest of her life she was afflicted with a continual pounding in her ears that was "louder than the noise of the locomotives stationed within a few yards from her house."[28]

[26] *Freedom*, October 1903; *Mother Earth*, July 1912 and June 1913.

[27] Interviews with Nellie Ploschansky Dick, Miami, Fla., December 17, 1972, and Oyster Bay, N.Y., September 16, 1974; interview with Sam Dreen, Tom's River, N.J., August 17, 1974. On May 1, 1910, Nellie Ploschansky recited a poem by Voltairine de Cleyre at the anarchist club in Jubilee Street, Whitechapel.

[28] Navro manuscript, Ishill Collection.

So severe was the infection that Voltairine was compelled to stop working and devote herself to complete rest. The pain in her head and throat prevented her from lecturing and even from raising her voice. Unable to concentrate, she would abandon her writings in mid-course. It was a time, she later recalled, when "Disease laid its hand on me, and all my MSS ended in a dash."[29] Once a week, however, from November 1903 to March 1904, she wrote to John Turner, who was being held for deportation on Ellis Island, the first to be evicted under the anarchist exclusion law enacted after the assassination of McKinley. "She wrote me regularly every Monday from Philadelphia," Turner told Joseph Ishill, "in that extraordinarily clear handwriting of hers, letters which made me feel glad to be there and receive them."[30]

In July 1904 Voltairine spent a month in the Jewish Hospital without improvement. In August and September she sought refuge on a farm in Torresdale, still, however, without relief, and when she returned to the city she entered the Medico-Chirurgical Hospital where she remained until January 1905, suffering from daily convulsions and not expecting to survive. By October 1904 her condition had sunk so low that Moses Harman's *Lucifer* printed a premature obituary and devoted an issue to her life's work.[31]

To help her through her illness, her Philadelphia comrades, headed by Natasha Notkin, formed the "Friends of Voltairine de Cleyre," which made an appeal for money in the anarchist press.[32] A telegram

[29] *Mother Earth*, May 1906.

[30] John Turner to Joseph Ishill, June 18, 1930, Ishill Collection. The letters, unfortunately, were discarded.

[31] "No champion of the faith in the three big cities, New York, Chicago or Philadelphia, made so many converts as she," the journal declared. *Lucifer*, October 27, 1904.

[32] *Ibid.*, November 10, 1904. The appeal read in part: "Devoting herself unceasingly to the uplifting and enlightening of the human family without hope or thought of reward except that feeling of exhilaration that comes to the soldier of progress,

was sent to Emma Goldman, who agreed to become
secretary of the fund, although she had scarcely seen
Voltairine since 1894, when they had fallen out over
Gordon. "On my last visit to Philadelphia," Emma
recalled, "I had been told that she was having a severe
struggle to make a living teaching English to Jewish
immigrants and giving music lessons, while at the
same time keeping up her activities in the movement.
I admired her energy and industry, but I was hurt and
repelled by what seemed to me her unreasonable and
small attitude toward me. I could not seek her out,
nor had she communicated with me in all these years.
Her fearless stand during the McKinley hysteria had
helped much to increase my respect for her, and her
letter in *Free Society* to Senator Hawley, who said he
would give a thousand dollars to have a shot at an
anarchist, had made a lasting impression on me."[33]

With Voltairine now in the hospital, her life in immediate danger, Emma responded handsomely to the
call. Thrusting personal antagonisms aside, she
plunged into the chores of raising money, assisted by
her lover, Ed Brady.[34] A friend, Dr. Hillel Solotaroff,
suggested that Samuel Gordon be approached, as he
was now a successful physician and well able to help
his former benefactress and companion. Solotaroff
himself volunteered to speak to Gordon and went to
Philadelphia to see him. But Gordon, according to
Emma Goldman, declined to aid Voltairine. "The latter had drudged for years to help him through college,"
commented Emma, who had always disliked Gordon,
"and now that she was ill, he had not even a kind word
for her. My intuition about him had been correct."[35]

---

it was inevitable that now in the hour of physical disability,
she should find herself penniless and helpless."

[33] Goldman, *Living My Life*, p. 332.

[34] See her appeal for funds in *Lucifer*, December 9, 1904,
and *Freiheit*, December 10, 1904.

[35] Goldman, *Living My Life*, p. 334.

On Christmas Day of 1904, in spite of her feeble condition, Voltairine left her bed in the Medico-Chirurgical Hospital and walked through the snow to attend a mass meeting for Catherine Breshkovskaya, the celebrated Socialist Revolutionary, who was in America on a fund-raising tour amid growing revolutionary ferment in Russia. Like all anarchists of this period, and especially the immigrants with whom she lived, Voltairine was enamored of the Russian Populists of Breshkovskaya's stamp, with their faith in the common people and their self-sacrificing dedication to freedom. Indeed, Voltairine herself, as Emma Goldman remarked, was an American version of these "Russian heroes and heroines."[36]

In Voltairine's mind the Populist martyrs of Siberia were linked with the anarchist martyrs of Chicago. As early as 1889 she had used the phrase "the People's Will" in a poem about Haymarket, and in February 1890 she addressed another poem "To the Czar, on a woman, a political prisoner, being flogged to death in Siberia."[37] Furthermore, she revered Tolstoy and Kropotkin, hailed Maxim Gorky as the "Spokesman of the Tramp, Visionary of the Despised," and took an active part in the yearly Russian Tea Party arranged by Natasha Notkin to support the Russian revolutionary movement.[38] Sick as she was, therefore, she

[36] *Ibid.*, p. 155.

[37] Voltairine de Cleyre, "Ut Sementem Feceris, Ita Metes," *Selected Works*, p. 36. The title was not Voltairine's but was inserted by Paul Carus, editor of *The Open Court*, where it was originally published. "I did not know and don't know to this day what that d–d Latin means; for all of me it might be Choctaw," she wrote to Joseph A. Labadie, May 28, 1906, Labadie Collection. It means, "As ye sow, so ye shall reap."

[38] *Selected Works*, p. 151. In 1906, however, she scolded Gorky, who had come to America on a fund-raising tour, for staying in Philadelphia's posh Bellevue-Stratford Hotel, "surrounded by the vulgar gaud of modern riches, paid for—by whom? By those who are down in the depths where you once

dragged herself to hear Breshkovskaya. Afterwards, she herself delivered an extemporaneous address in the midst of which "my throat filled with stuff that I couldn't spit, and choked me," so that she was "forced by her friends to return to the hospital in a carriage."[39]

The following month Voltairine left the hospital and went to live at 815 North Eighth Street, where her mother came from Michigan to take care of her. Her health did not improve. She was poised, as she wrote to Moses Harman, "on a see-saw between life and death," with an "incessant pumping engine in my head." Desperately ill, unable to work, and without any means of support, she felt, says Leonard Abbott, "a strong inclination to give up the battle altogether."[40] Several years before, she and Gordon had attempted suicide, and since that time, as her writings reveal, she frequently brooded on "that on-creeping of Universal Death," "the roses of Early Death." Now, more than ever, suicide haunted her thoughts. Her life, says Nathan Navro, who rented a room in the same house, had become a "continuous torture."[41]

After her mother returned to St. Johns, Navro himself would sit at her beside till the late hours of the night, trying to nurse her back to health. But his efforts had little effect; and one night, when he was away, she took an overdose of morphine. She left a note willing her body to the Hahnemann Medical College to be used for scientific research. "I want no ceremonies nor speeches over it," she wrote. "I die, as I have lived, a free spirit, an Anarchist, owing no

---

were!" Voltairine de Cleyre, "An Open Letter," Philadelphia, August 1906, *Mother Earth*, September 1906.

[39] Voltairine de Cleyre to Alexander Berkman, August 24, 1906, Berkman Archive; *The New York Times*, December 26, 1904.

[40] *Lucifer*, August 3, 1905; *Mother Earth*, October 1914.

[41] Voltairine de Cleyre, "A Rocket of Iron," *Free Society*, January 5, 1902; Navro manuscript, Ishill Collection.

allegiance to rulers, heavenly or earthly. Though I sorrow for the work I wished to do, which time and loss of health prevented, I am glad I lived no useless life (save this one last year) and hope that the work I did will live and grow with my pupils' lives and by them be passed on to others, even as I passed on what I had received."[42]

The morphine, however, "failed to bring the desired result." Under the care of Nathan Navro and of an anarchist doctor named Gartman, she made a gradual recovery. The pain was never to leave her, nor the "maddening, ever-present din" in her ears.[43] For the rest of her life her weeks and months were plagued by illness. By the spring of 1906, however, she was back on her feet. Her last Philadelphia period had begun.

[42] Navro manuscript, Ishill Collection; Goldman, *Voltairine de Cleyre*, pp. 21-22.

[43] Navro manuscript, Ishill Collection. Dr. Gartman was a member of the Social Science Club and lectured at its forums.

8. The Broad Street Riot

The decline of Voltairine de Cleyre's health coincided with a decline of the anarchist movement itself in the wake of McKinley's assassination. In all parts of the United States anarchist groups curtailed their activities, while individual adherents left the movement or were driven underground. In 1903 the anti-anarchist law prevented foreign anarchists from entering the country, and in 1904 *Free Society*, the principal revolutionary anarchist journal in America, ceased publication, leaving the English-speaking movement without a regular organ.[1] An additional blow came with the death of Johann Most on March 17, 1906, while lecturing in Cincinnati.

After this, however, a turnabout began and matters improved rapidly. The same month, March 1906, *Mother Earth* was launched by Emma Goldman in New York, filling the gap left by the demise of *Free Society* and inheriting many of its subscribers and contributors, including George Brown, Mary Hansen, and Voltairine de Cleyre herself. (Natasha Notkin became *Mother Earth*'s Philadelphia agent, as she had been for *Free Society*.) On May 18, 1906, Alexander Berkman was released from prison, providing *Mother Earth* and the movement as a whole with much-needed organizational and literary talent. In addition, the Russian Revolution of 1905-1906, and the visits to America of Catherine Breshkovskaya and Nicholas Chaikovsky, gave the anarchists a further impetus to revive their dormant activities.

The year 1906 likewise opened a new phase of activity in the life of Voltairine de Cleyre. For the

---

[1] Benjamin Tucker's *Liberty*, the leading nonrevolutionary and individualist magazine, survived until 1908, when it was wiped out by a fire, after which Tucker moved to Europe where he remained until his death in 1939.

previous three years, owing to her severe illness, it had been virtually impossible for her to do any work, either for the movement or her personal support. As late as October 1905, as the London *Freedom* reported, she remained "an invalid, making but little if any progress towards better health."[2] The next few months, however, saw a dramatic improvement in her physical and moral condition. By the spring of 1906, under the attentive care of Nathan Navro and Dr. Gartman, she had regained sufficient strength to resume her accustomed routine. Leaving her sickbed on North Eighth Street, she moved to new quarters at 517 North Randolph Street and, shortly afterwards, to 929 Wallace Street, where she returned to her teaching and writing. On March 18th, the day after Johann Most's death, she felt strong enough to take part in a Paris Commune commemoration sponsored by the Radical Library and the Social Science Club, sharing the speaker's platform with George Brown, Frank Stephens, and Chaim Weinberg, as well as with French, German, and Italian anarchists. It was her first public appearance since the Breshkovskaya meeting in December 1904, and the police, who were in evidence, did not interfere.

Two months later, on May 27, 1906, Voltairine's father, Hector De Claire, died in his seventy-first year at the Soldiers' Home in Milwaukee. "Poor old man!" wrote Addie, who had not seen him in two decades. Voltairine too was affected ("He hadn't much out of his life either, had he?" she wrote to her mother), but her recovery was not interrupted.[3] As her strength returned, she plunged again into agitational work. In October 1906 she helped to organize the fall lecture series of the Social Science Club and was herself among

[2] *Freedom*, October 1905.
[3] Adelaide D. Thayer to Joseph Ishill, February 3, 1935; Voltairine de Cleyre to Harriet De Claire, May 27, 1907, Ishill Collection.

the speakers, along with Alexander Berkman from New York and Lizzie Holmes from Denver. The following month she was in Chicago to address the annual meeting in honor of the Haymarket martyrs, speaking alongside Lucy Parsons in Brand's Hall, where her "tender and loving tribute to their memory deeply touched the immense assembly."[4] The next evening she addressed Chicago's Social Science League on the subject "Anarchism in Literature," and three days later she spoke at another Haymarket meeting in Detroit.

With the exception of 1907, when she appeared before the twentieth anniversary memorial in New York with Emma Goldman, Alexander Berkman, and Harry Kelly, Voltairine went to Chicago every November for the rest of her life to deliver her yearly Haymarket oration. Driven by a compulsion to spread her ideas, a missionary urge that would not let her rest, she also resumed her periodic lectures for the free thought movement in New York, Chicago, and Philadelphia, not to mention smaller cities in between. For instance, on October 5, 1906, she and Saul Yanovsky were among the speakers at a free thought gathering in Cooper Union, and on April 28, 1907, she addressed the Radical Liberal League of Philadelphia on the question of marriage.[5]

On her trips to New York during these years, she would call on her old London friends, Lizzie and Tom Bell, who had lately immigrated to America. Their daughter, Marion Bell, remembers how much her parents looked forward to her visits. "We all did, in fact, because she was interested in us as children. And she gave us cookies!"[6] She would also, on rarer occasions,

[4] *Lucifer*, November 22, 1906. The speech was printed in *The Demonstrator*, December 5, 1906.

[5] *Fraye Arbeter Shtime*, September 29, 1906; Voltairine de Cleyre, "They Who Marry Do Ill," *Mother Earth*, January 1908.

[6] Interview with Marion Bell, June 21, 1974.

call on Emma Goldman in her apartment at 210 East
13th Street, where *Mother Earth* was edited and published. Although Emma and Voltairine were never to
become intimate friends, their relations improved
markedly after Emma, to her credit, came to Voltairine's assistance during the worst period of her illness. Having mended their differences, at least in part,
they now shared the rostrum at anarchist gatherings
and spoke and wrote to each other for the first time
in a dozen years.

In 1907, when Emma went on her annual lecture
tour to raise money for *Mother Earth*, she sent reports
to Voltairine about the health of the movement, in
Canada as well as the United States. "I was more than
tickled with the newspaper clippings you sent me,"
Voltairine replied. "What a splendid growth it shows
—there in Winnipeg especially! . . . I had seen Weinberg at the Russian Tea Party and he had spoken to me
of Winnipeg, and tried to urge touring on me. If only
I had the health I had at 20. But you see, I have to be
where I can properly attend to my nose and throat; if
not I suffer tortures within 48 hours of the neglect. And
you know that's impossible on the road. Besides I dare
not break up my work here. You see how it is: at a
trade one can work in any city, but in work like this
you have to create your own job and stick to it. And yet,
how I would like to get out on 'the open road.' One of
the dearest dreams up till this sickness gripped me
was to go on foot to the Pacific, talking in little towns
along the road, and distributing literature. I'll never
be able to realize it now." By 1909, at a public meeting
in New York, Voltairine was able again to call Emma
"my friend and my comrade";[7] and in 1911, with Alexander Berkman, Harry Kelly, and Leonard Abbott,
among others, she signed a protest to the London

[7] Voltairine de Cleyre to Emma Goldman, May 16, 1907, in
possession of Renée de Cleyre Buckwalter; *Mother Earth*, July
1909.

socialist paper *Justice*, which had charged (quite absurdly) that Emma was a paid agent of the tsarist police.

In the meantime, Voltairine became a regular contributor to *Mother Earth*. Over a six-year period, from its establishment in 1906 until her death in 1912, the magazine was the principal outlet for her literary work. Between 1903 and 1906 she had scarcely written a line, but now she made up for it, producing a steady flow of articles, stories, and verse, as well as letters and reviews. In these works she grappled with the central problems which plagued and divided the anarchist movement at the beginning of the century and which continue to plague it to this day, above all the problems of individualism versus collectivism and of violence versus pacifism. As before, in spite of her puritanical fervor, her position was flexible and conciliatory rather than dogmatic and unyielding. Her first contribution to *Mother Earth* was an unsigned translation of I. L. Peretz's "Hofenung un Shrek" (Hope and Fear) in the April 1906 number. In addition, the Mother Earth Publishing Association reprinted her most important essays—"Anarchism and American Traditions," "Direct Action," "The Dominant Idea"—in pamphlet form for sale at the frequent lectures and entertainments arranged for the magazine's benefit.

It was through her association with *Mother Earth* that Voltairine formed her close friendship with Alexander Berkman, who served as editor beginning in 1907. "I'm so glad you have done well for M. E.," wrote Voltairine to Emma Goldman in May of that year. "And yes, Alex makes an excellent editor; but he's desperate to work for, I'd a heap sight rather work for you. He wants copy, copy, copy—and he wants it all at once, and he wants to lay it away for three, four, six, an indefinite number of months. He wants impossibilities; he wants a thorough international review and he wants it in 3 or at the outside 4 pages. He wants me to put in,

in a month's review, what others put in in a week; and
take no more place. Now Emma, you know the thing
can't be done."[8] Later in the year, Voltairine signed an
appeal for funds to start a new anarchist weekly, working class in orientation and edited by Berkman, to
supplement the "theoretical, literary, and educational"
function of the monthly *Mother Earth*,[9] a project that
went unrealized until 1916, when Berkman launched
The Blast in San Francisco.

The initial contact between Voltairine de Cleyre and
Alexander Berkman had occurred in 1893, a year after
Berkman's attack on Frick, when Voltairine began writing to him in prison. "Here and there the gloom is rent:
an unknown sympathizer, or comrade, sends a greet-
ing," noted Berkman on the arrival of her first letter.
"I pore eagerly over the chirography, and from the
clear, decisive signature, 'Voltairine de Cleyre,' strive
to mold the character and shape the features of the
writer."[10] A few months earlier, Dyer Lum had committed suicide without smuggling poison to Berkman
as he had intended. Now Voltairine considered herself
"the heir of his purpose," determined to see "that you
got his *gift*." But she kept putting it off and finally
abandoned the idea, sending him messages of encour-
agement instead, though her attitude toward his act
was ambivalent. "It isn't my business to pass judgments
on what you did," she wrote. "I don't, in the large, know
whether it was good or bad. But I know you did what
you willed to do, and that appeals to me."[11]

Over the next dozen years the arrival of Voltairine's
letters, with their "great charm and rebellious thought,"
took on vital importance for Berkman, lending "color

[8] Voltairine de Cleyre to Emma Goldman, May 16, 1907.

[9] *Mother Earth*, September 1907.

[10] Alexander Berkman, *Prison Memoirs of an Anarchist*, New
York, 1912, p. 331.

[11] Voltairine de Cleyre to Alexander Berkman, July 10, 1906,
Berkman Archive.

to my existence," he remarked. His replies, by the same
token, helped Voltairine herself at moments when she
was in particular need of sympathy and encourage-
ment. "Your letters from prison (especially the con-
traband ones) were a relief to me in my agony," she
told him in 1906. "They pulled me up towards the light
and air for a little while, when I was like one gasping
under dark, cold water."[12] During the late 1890s,
Voltairine joined Harry Kelly and others in the campaign for Berkman's release, drafting an eloquent
appeal on his behalf. But their efforts were unavailing.
For fourteen years (he went in at twenty-one and came
out at thirty-five) Berkman remained in the Western
Penitentiary of Pennsylvania, an experience haunting-
ly described in his *Prison Memoirs of an Anarchist*,
which Voltairine encouraged him to write. Although
his survival of prison, with its long stretches of solitary
confinement, bears witness to his indomitable spirit,
Berkman emerged on the edge of collapse. Tormented
by nightmares of the past, assailed by doubts of the future, he struggled to readjust to life. After a period of
deep inner turmoil, verging at times on suicide, his
spirits at last began to revive. "I feel like one recovering
from a long illness," he said, "very weak, but with
a touch of joy in life."[13]

In this "resurrection," as Berkman called it, Voltairine played a critical role. At the moment of his
greatest need, she provided the kind of support of
which Emma Goldman, who had never felt such crushing despair, was incapable, notwithstanding all her efforts on Berkman's behalf. For Voltairine herself had
gone through similar agonies and, having twice attempted suicide, could write him letters full of sympathetic understanding of what was tormenting his
innermost spirit:

[12] Berkman, *Prison Memoirs*, p. 350; Voltairine de Cleyre to
Alexander Berkman, August 7, 1906, Berkman Archive.
[13] Berkman, *Prison Memoirs*, p. 415.

I was between the living and the dead so long—
and with only that one idea for two years. . . .
'No—don't commit suicide, and don't go to Russia.'
I might urge you in the usual way, tell you life holds
much for you etc.; but you would know that was a
lie. I don't think it holds much for any of us. But
I do believe that this present phase of yours is largely
incidental and transitory. It is due to your being
thrust from the grave into the world. It may take
a year to pass; it has nothing to do with insanity;
it is a very logical conclusion from the peculiar
mental condition which has been thrust upon
you. . . .

You are too cold-headed a reasoner not to know
that this sudden transformation *must* produce some
sort of curious psychological reflex. And do you know
every one recognizes in you the strong soul? Even
those who aforetime thought you must be weakly
enthusiastic! You don't care for that, I know; but
it is good to conquer.

And you have conquered Alex; you won out
against Death in a slow fight. Don't surrender. Your
capacities are all there, living, intense—only
stunned. The peace of death is sure—you can wait
for it.

Will it be of any use to say I am one of those few
who would suffer if you did it? Certainly there are
those who have known and loved you longer and
better; their regard has a deeper claim on you than
mine; but I would feel—black. . . .

But I do not like to urge this on you: when I was
ill and people said to me 'Live for my sake,' I thought
it selfish of them to want me to suffer so; though
I knew they were only lovingly trying to appeal to
any motive at all to rouse the desire for life, yet it
seemed selfish. And so I don't like to say 'Stay in
life and be a torture to yourself because I will feel
bad if you die.' It is only that I am sure you will out-

wear it, that makes me try to persuade you: if I knew all your life would be so, I would say 'Do it.' . . .

Touch hands across the gulf, Alex; *we are not alone*. There is comradeship in the depths. Let the lamps burn a while yet. To what indefinite end, let us not trouble.

I salute you. And write soon again—write your soul out as gloomy as you feel it. I am listening and feeling.[14]

During the summer of 1906, Berkman came to Philadelphia and visited Voltairine. Making his acquaintance, she said, was a "memorable and vivid" occasion, and she remained his friend for the rest of her life. "I like you as a spirit akin," she wrote, "without any consciousness that you are a man and I am a woman; I like you because you are strong, and because you are troubled with weakness; because you are not cock sure; because you have lost the power to be narrow—as I have."[15]

An admirer of Voltairine's writing, Berkman asked her advice regarding the composition of his prison memoirs. She urged him to "strike out an indepedent line. On no account write like anybody else." Although he followed her counsel, he had difficulty working out his ideas and putting them to paper, a problem that Voltairine herself confronted more and more often. "Now let the book idea drop for the present," she suggested, "and if what you feel most like doing is lying on the grass and watching the ants, do it. Let the sun burn into you, and the water run over you; do it day after day, and if you can get where you *don't think* about anything but the bugs etc. and insects so much the better. Don't worry about constructing the book,

[14] Voltairine de Cleyre to Alexander Berkman, August 7, 1906, Berkman Archive.

[15] Navro manuscript, Ishill Collection; Voltairine de Cleyre to Alexander Berkman, August 24, 1906, Berkman Archive.

till the thoughts fill you again. I think that such a book written from an anarchist viewpoint would be a great addition to the serious bibliography of anarchism." "Don't try to *force* the book," she repeated. "But *do* try to force the solitude longing away. Have you tried the relief of long walks? Just the physical exertion is a help to rid yourself of thoughts while you are at it. I don't mean it will drive them out: nothing will do that: but it sort of quiets them." "You are a writer of some skill," she reassured him. "When the time comes for things to be said you will say them. You leave a forceful impress on people—that is the real transmigration of the soul. All there is in life for any man is still open to you; be assured your forces will return—will awaken rather. Let them sleep awhile, and do not worry about it in the least."[16]

During the five years that it took Berkman to complete the book, Voltairine de Cleyre could always be relied on for assistance. She read the manuscript at every stage and corrected the proofs when it was finished, answering Berkman's queries regarding style and usage and helping him to master written English. "I don't think you are able to handle the novel style," she remarked, correctly, at one point, "though I may be wrong in my estimate. I guess the best will be to make it a combination of sketch and biography. As to further suggestions, only one—*Dare*: write things which others have been afraid to write."[17]

Writing the *Prison Memoirs* was an emotional catharsis for Berkman, purging him of the phantoms of Allegheny City and enabling him to come to grips with life. Once completed, it was hailed, as Voltairine had predicted, as a masterpiece of anarchist literature,

[16] Voltairine de Cleyre to Alexander Berkman, July 10 and August 7, 1906, Berkman Archive.

[17] Voltairine de Cleyre to Alexander Berkman, June 24, 1910. Her comments and corrections, always careful and to the point, are preserved in the Berkman Archive.

the most powerful description of prison life from the
libertarian viewpoint. For this Voltairine must receive at least a small part of the credit. Tragically, she
did not live to see the book's appearance, which came
a few weeks after her death. In token of appreciation,
Berkman was to edit a selection of her own writings,
brought out under the Mother Earth imprint in 1914.

During the winter of 1907-1908, the United States
lay in the grip of a severe economic depression. The
cause, declared Berkman in *Mother Earth*, was "our
fallacious economic system." Millions were out of work,
and there were unemployment demonstrations in many
cities, including Chicago, New York, and Philadelphia.
On the afternoon of February 20, 1908, the Jewish and
Italian anarchists of Philadelphia called a mass meeting in the New Auditorium Hall on South Third Street.
Some 2,000 workers attended, many of them idle and
impoverished, to hear speeches by Voltairine de Cleyre,
George Brown, and Yiddish, Italian, and Russian speaking radicals. In her short address, Voltairine lashed out
at the capitalist system as the breeder of exploitation
and misery. Upholding the right of the workers to the
instruments of production, she called for "direct universal expropriation," urging her listeners to "take the
land, the mines, the factories as your own."[18]

Chaim Weinberg came next with a blistering oration in Yiddish. When George Brown mounted the platform, following an Italian speaker, the audience was
already aroused and, stirred to action by his passionate
rhetoric, surged out of the hall to demand jobs, despite
appeals by the speakers to remain and listen. Emma
Cohen, then four years old, remembers being picked

[18] The Philadelphia *Public Ledger*, February 21, 1908. She
was not necessarily advocating communal ownership; the
individualists and mutualists believed in free access to raw
materials and in land tenure based on "occupation and use."

up from a pile of coats and handed through a window.[19] The demonstrators marched toward City Hall, but when they reached Broad Street, Philadelphia's chief north-south thoroughfare, their way was blocked by police, who charged forward in an effort to disperse them. The demonstration was suddenly transformed into a bloody riot. One marcher was so enraged that he drew a pistol and fired two shots, but no one was hit. The police now began to make arrests. Four Italians, Michael Costello, Dominick Donelli, Angelo Troi, and Francesco Piszicallo, were charged with inciting to riot and with assault and battery with intent to kill. Later that day, Chaim Weinberg and Voltairine de Cleyre were arrested and held under $1,500 bail each, charged with inciting to riot, while two young members of the Radical Library Group were detained merely for renting the hall and distributing circulars.[20]

It was the only time Voltairine was ever arrested. The two detectives who came to her apartment were surprised to find that she did not at all resemble the typical anarchist depicted in the newspapers. "Them's orders," they apologized, as they placed her in custody. Searching through her papers, one of them came upon a copy of *The Worm Turns*, her booklet of revolutionary poems. "What's this?" he asked. His partner took a look and threw it aside: "Hell, it's only about worms!"[21]

Voltairine and Weinberg were tried on June 18th. When the prosecution's only witness failed to appear and no other evidence was produced, the judge directed a verdict of not guilty.[22] Meanwhile, the four Italians

[19] Emma Cohen Gilbert to Paul Avrich, April 20, 1975.

[20] Voltairine de Cleyre, "The Case in Philadelphia," *Mother Earth*, March 1908.

[21] *Mother Earth*, July 1909; Goldman, *Voltairine de Cleyre*, p. 38.

[22] Voltairine de Cleyre, "The Philadelphia Farce," *Mother Earth*, June 1908. According to Voltairine's son, Weinberg had

had been convicted in a separate proceeding and sentenced to long prison terms. Donelli, who apparently fired the shots and was the only anarchist among them, received five years at hard labor. According to Nathan Navro, the police had bribed witnesses to perjure themselves against the defendants, who, for their own part, were unable to find a single "quiet-looking, respectable-appearing" individual willing to testify in their behalf.[23]

Voltairine threw herself into the struggle for their release. A defense committee was organized, and funds were raised through *Mother Earth*, the *Fraye Arbeter Shtime*, and other publications for an appeal to the Pennsylvania Board of Pardons.[24] A number of groups and individuals contributed (including Voltairine's son Harry), and by the end of the year nearly $400 was collected, part of which went to the prisoners' families. Donelli, meanwhile, had been beaten and Costello put in solitary for striking a trustee who had been victimizing him. Recalling the unsuccessful campaign for Berkman during the 1890s, Voltairine began to despair of securing clemency. "I know that the only way prisoners will ever be delivered," she told Joseph Cohen, will be when the people "storm the prison." Yet

---

bribed the witness to stay away from the trial. Harry de Cleyre to Agnes Inglis, February 15, 1948, Labadie Collection. I have found no evidence to support this allegation.

[23] Navro manuscript, Ishill Collection; Henry J. Nelson to Voltairine de Cleyre, November 6, 1908, Cohen Papers. Nelson, the defense attorney, was a Philadelphia socialist.

[24] Voltairine de Cleyre, "The Case of the Imprisoned Italians in Philadelphia," *Mother Earth*, October 1908. A leaflet issued by the committee, "The True History of the Broad Street Riot," is to be found in the Labadie Collection and is reproduced in Cohen, *Di yidish-anarkhistishe bavegung*, p. 222. Cohen was secretary of the committee. Its members included George Brown and Mary Hansen, but Cohen, according to Voltairine, was "the only person who outside of myself has worked hard for these fellows." Voltairine de Cleyre to Alexander Berkman, October 28, 1908, Berkman Archive.

she persisted in her efforts, which were rewarded with Costello's release in May 1909, followed by Troi's a few months later.[25]

The Broad Street Riot was one of a series of unemployment and free-speech struggles in which American anarchists were engaged in the years preceding the war. Another incident occurred on May 23, 1909, when a lecture by Emma Goldman, "Henrik Ibsen as the Pioneer of the Modern Drama," was broken up by the New York City police. Outraged by this suppression of fundamental liberties, Alden Freeman, a well-to-do liberal, hired a hall for Emma in his home town of East Orange, New Jersey. At the last minute, the owner of the hall, under pressure from the authorities, refused to open up, whereupon Freeman brought Emma to his own estate, where she spoke to an overflow crowd.

To protest the mounting violations of free speech, a mass meeting was held in Cooper Union on June 30, 1909, organized by the National Free Speech Committee. Voltairine de Cleyre, Perle McLeod, Tom Bell, Leonard Abbott, and Harry Kelly were among the anarchist members, along with Alden Freeman and such prominent socialists and liberals as Eugene V. Debs, William English Walling, Clarence Darrow, and Jack London. Voltairine took part in the meeting, delivering what Freeman called "a most stirring oration." Freedom of speech, she declared, means nothing "if it does not mean the freedom for that to be said which we do not like." "There is but one way that free speech can ever be secured," she went on, "and that is by persistent speaking. It is of no use to write things down on paper, and put them away in a store-

[25] Voltairine de Cleyre to Joseph J. Cohen, November 2, 1908, and n.d. [November 1908], and April 22, 1909, and May 20, 1909; Voltairine de Cleyre, "The Release of Michael Costello," *Mother Earth*, June 1909. Piszicallo served less than a year; Donelli was released in 1911 and returned to Italy.

room, even if that store-room happens to be the Library
at Washington, and the thing written is that 'Congress
shall make no law abridging the freedom of speech.'
That's like anything else put away on a shelf and forgotten. *Speak, speak, speak*, and remember that whenever any one's liberty to speak is denied, your liberty
is denied also, and your place is there where the attack
is."[26]

For the rest of the year protest meetings alternated
with continued police interference. Thus when Emma
Goldman was prevented from speaking in Philadelphia
on September 28th, a public rally followed at which
Voltairine de Cleyre denounced "Our Police Censorship" ("It doesn't matter who Emma Goldman is, nor
where she comes from, nor what she has to say.
Lawyers and judges may quibble and define use and
abuse, and liberty and license, and rigmarole and
rigmarig. But I will stand for the whole thing—nothing
less.").[27] On October 17th Emma Goldman was again
barred from the platform in Philadelphia, this time
at a meeting to protest the execution of the Spanish
educator Francisco Ferrer, and Voltairine once again
objected.

[26] Voltairine de Cleyre, "On Liberty," *Mother Earth*, July
1909. Cf. her "Anarchism and American Traditions," *Selected
Works*, p. 132: "Anarchism says, Make no laws whatever concerning speech, and speech will be free; so soon as you make a
declaration on paper that speech shall be free, you will have
a hundred lawyers proving that 'freedom does not mean abuse,
nor liberty license'; and they will define and define freedom
out of existence. Let the guarantee of free speech be every
man's determination to use it, and we shall have no need of
paper declarations. On the other hand, so long as people do
not care to exercise their freedom, those who wish to tyran-
nize will do so; for tyrants are active and ardent, and will
devote themselves in the name of any number of gods,
religious or otherwise, to put shackles upon sleeping men."
[27] Voltairine de Cleyre, "The Free Speech Fight in Philadelphia," *Mother Earth*, October 1909, and "Our Censorship,"
ibid., November 1909.

And so it went from week to week. Given Voltairine's limited stamina, it is a wonder that she was able to maintain such a rigorous schedule. For, beyond her free-speech appearances, she continued to teach in the evenings, to write for *Mother Earth* and the *Fraye Arbeter Shtime*, and to lecture in New York, Chicago, and Philadelphia before anarchist and rationalist audiences. On November 11, 1908, she addressed more than a thousand people at a Haymarket memorial in Chicago. In the afternoon she had hoped to visit Wald-heim Cemetery, "but it is raw and cold," she wrote Joseph Cohen, "and I must save my throat."[28] On March 26, 1909, she lectured on "Anarchism and American Traditions" before the Harlem Liberal Alliance in New York; and in Philadelphia she spoke repeatedly at meetings of the Social Science Club and the Radical Library, which in 1909 became a branch of the Workmen's Circle, the Jewish mutual-aid society, with Voltairine as a member. Young Zalman Deanin, who heard her lecture in New York, thought her "a wonderful, charming woman. We all liked Emma Goldman too, a good speaker and writer, though a different type from Voltairine." To Morris Gamberg, another New York anarchist, she was "a beautiful personality who left a strong impression." According to Shaindel Ostroff, a teenage member of the Radical Library, "the human qualities were just shining out of her eyes," although she seemed ethereal and remote and "you could not get too close to her." "Some kind of glow came from her," recalled Boris Yelensky, another member of the Radical Library. And Chaim Weinberg, who attributed her spiritual nature to the legacy of the convent, called her the "poetic soul" of the Philadelphia movement.[29]

[28] Voltairine de Cleyre to Joseph J. Cohen, November 11, 1908, Cohen Papers. The date is underlined four times.
[29] Interviews with Zalman Deanin, Farmingdale, N.Y., September 18, 1974; Shaindel Ostroff, the Bronx, N.Y., Septem-

By 1908 Voltairine was earning enough from her lessons to move to a comfortable three-room flat, for ten dollars a month, at 531 North Marshall Street, where she remained until her move to Chicago. Yet, in spite of her various activities, she was an unhappy, tormented figure, subject to long spells of brooding melancholy. In part this was due to her persistent illness, the inflammation of her nose and throat. "No, my head isn't so bad that I have to stand up, nor give up any of my teaching," she told her mother, "but it always hurts, even in its best days." To Alexander Berkman she wrote: "I can't, I can't, I simply can't endure the agony of letting the pain of life go thro' me. It twists my throat up like an iron hand."[30]

Small wonder that her constant physical tortures should have "cast a gloom over her spirit."[31] She saw in life nothing but a "vast scheme of mutual murder, with no justice anywhere, and no God in the soul or out of it." In the last analysis, she wrote to Berkman, "it is life itself I hate—not a fat bourgeois. Life, life, this fiendish thing which brings millions of little creatures forth mercilessly, only to hunger, pain, madness. There is not a day when the suffering of the little waif animals in the street, does not create in me a bitter rage against life."[32] For all the devotion of her friends, she remained essentially alone; and much as she cherished her privacy, she felt isolated and depressed. At one point, her former lover Gordon came to visit

ber 28, 1973; and Boris Yelensky, Brooklyn, N.Y., August 12, 1972; Weinberg, *Fertsig yor in kamf far sotsialer bafrayung*, p. 70.

[30] Voltairine de Cleyre to Harriet De Claire, May 27, 1907, Ishill Collection; Voltairine de Cleyre to Alexander Berkman, August 7, 1906, Berkman Archive. In a letter to Berkman of June 24, 1910, she again complains of her "murderous throat."

[31] Navro manuscript, Ishill Collection.

[32] *Selected Works*, p. 42; Voltairine de Cleyre to Alexander Berkman, August 7, 1906, Berkman Archive.

her, but she refused his hand, as though she did not know him. "What, don't you recognize me?" he asked. "No," came the curt reply. Gordon pointed to an old picture of himself still hanging on her wall: "And that man—don't you know him?" "Yes," she answered. "But he was a different person then."[33]

In her illness and isolation Voltairine became increasingly ingrown and self-absorbed, imbued with a sense of the tragedy which had haunted her life. From her physical and psychological torment there seemed no escape. And the consciousness of her misfortune bred a growing indulgence in the poisonous emotion of self-pity. "No use my seeking joy, Mother," she wrote in February 1909. "It doesn't appeal to me. I have seen everything I ever believed in (or rather every person) as a different thing from what I thought. And I believe in nobody, except with a question mark. That poisons everything and always will. Things that are joy and comfort to others might as well be displayed to a stone as to me, for all the satisfaction they give me. Very likely it is my own fault in much. I do not doubt it is; but fault or not, it is so."[34]

At times the moral anguish and physical pain could plummet her into total despair. "I feel myself going down deeper and deeper, and more hopelessly all the time," she wrote to Joseph Cohen in May 1909, "and I really see no end to it, except that end that will finish everything. It is a miserable thing to be both dead and alive at once!" And again: "I don't know what kind of state I am getting into, but I have no will or energy to do anything that I ought. I feel like the coal of a dying fire, getting ashy at the edges."[35]

---

[33] Frumkin, *In friling fun yidishn sotsializm*, p. 258. Gordon died in 1921 at the age of fifty.

[34] Voltairine de Cleyre to Harriet De Claire, February 11, 1909, Labadie Collection.

[35] Voltairine de Cleyre to Joseph J. Cohen, May 5 and 28, 1909, Cohen Papers.

Lonely and despondent, Voltairine decided to spend a few weeks with her mother at the family home in St. Johns. In July 1909 she wrote to Addie that she was coming in the fall, after her Haymarket appearance in Chicago. Mother, however, should not expect much help around the house. "I've never got over hating cookery, and suppose I never shall; but I like to sweep and dust and scrub and souse and arrange, if I have time; and I suppose I'd have time there."[36]

Following her Haymarket address, Voltairine left Chicago for St. Johns, stopping in Detroit to visit a cousin, then going up to Port Huron and Sarnia, which she had not seen since her graduation from the convent. Both towns had decayed over the years, she thought, just as she herself had decayed. Her visit was brief, but it stirred deep-seated emotions as she was moved to recall her unhappy adolescence. In a poignant letter to Mary Hansen she describes her reaction:

> Port Huron must have stopped when I left it, 26 years ago, and gone backward slowly ever since. Where once the busy sawmill chewed up logs and spit them out, no trace of life is seen; the mill is gone; discouraged piles of lumber stand leaning here and there, and rank weeds grow up to the rotting backwater. Heaps of ruin where life was. Only one ferry wharf where two were once; the other not only dismantled but completely removed. This is on the Black River, in the heart of the city. By the *great* river wharf—the first place from which I ever saw live water—the blue St. Clair, which is just *really* as blue as it has been all these years in my dreams—only lonesome, darkened buildings stood. Rotting piles stand by the ivy-covered water works,

[36] Voltairine de Cleyre to Adelaide D. Thayer, July 19, 1909, Ishill Collection. Voltairine sent "kind regards to Mr. Thayer. I hope he doesn't suppose me to be a dangerous explosive!"

silently dropping away, bit by bit into the great current, where still the ships go up and down, as they
used, but not stopping as they used. At Sarnia, the
old convent is sold as an apartment house, the wide
grounds sold in lots here and there, and three ugly
dwelling houses built on them. But the building is
unchanged without—or almost. I did not try to go in.
At Windsor I found two of my old teachers from
the old place—two of the *good* ones—and was surprised to find how many little things they remem-
bered from those old, old days before I knew you;
Sister Médard told me she has one of my old compositions yet, and sometimes she sits and reads
those old things of long ago. She was the one little
sister who sympathetically kissed me when all the
rest were frowning, and I always had a soft spot for
her.

Well, I wanted to go there these many years, and
now I have been, and am satisfied, as you are when
you have visited a graveyard.[37]

From Sarnia Voltairine went on to St. Johns. There,
in the barren winter prairie, she saw "the glory of the
moon on the snow" once more and the "great watching stars." Her mother, now seventy-three, was in better health than the year before, when Voltairine had
made a brief visit. "I think her one disease is lonesome-
ness, outside of her old age," she wrote. "She'll be miserable when I go away, I know."[38] Voltairine was tempted

---

[37] Voltairine de Cleyre to Mary Hansen, December 6, 1909,
Ishill Collection. An incomplete version of this remarkable let-
ter appeared in *The Modern School*, February 1917, and in *Free
Vistas*, I (1933).

[38] *Ibid.* Of her previous visit Voltairine had written: "I found
my poor mother somewhat ill . . . and while she was somewhat better when I left, she was very unhappy at my going,
and quite broke down and cried, a thing I never saw her do in
my life before at my leave-taking. Her being alone there so,
and so infirm and old, haunts me day and night." Letter to

to linger a while instead of returning to Philadelphia. Back in her childhood surroundings, her life had come full circle. She felt, she told Mary Hansen, "as if I were far, far down a long black tunnel, with only un-known darkness before me, and a lot of immeasurable pain behind. And I looked back at you all, and thought over and over what going back means, and shook my head and went farther down the tunnel. And twice I resolved not to come back, and had decided to go on to Chicago for this winter, and then see what next."

As she reflected on her life in Philadelphia, memories of the past came rushing back:

It *is* a long time, isn't it, since those days when we met up in poor Foster's stable, among the weevils and the scrap-iron. Life didn't look over-buoyant even then, and we didn't see all the black things a coming. I remember also being very much exercised in my mind when you went to live with G. B. for fear he wasn't good enough! Did I ever tell you? We can all laugh about it now; but I'm still of the opinion he wasn't quite good enough. Did I ever tell you about that 4th of July, when you, he, Elliott, and I went down to 34th St. to look at the fireworks; and I saw, as you and he stood on the box, or chair was it? how he pulled your head over and kissed you there in the crowd? It was dark, and I think no one else saw but me. And I've always been glad, dear girl, that that time I was shot I was living with you, though it made you so much trouble, and was a little respon-sible for all that happened afterward—my going to Norway and all that.

I was always pig-headed about anything I wanted to do, and often when what I wanted to do wasn't of so much importance in itself either; I wish I hadn't been quite so pig-headed. I might have been able to

Jacob and Anna Livshis, December 8, 1908, Labadie Collec-tion.

see the relative importance of things better. But
that's all over and done. And things have come and
gone, come and gone, like the water running away
by the pier, under the moon-wash.

Do you remember the dog, Mary? The little black
dog that came into us on Brooks St., and sat down
as if he had always known us? And how we found
he was sick at last, and I carried him up to my
room, and laid him on the couch; and he *would* want
to be on my lap; so I held him as much as I could
till he was dying; and then laid him on the couch
and staid [*sic*] by him till he gave his last awful
gulp and stiffened out.

Do you remember my white kitten that I shut in
the coal bin for Gordon's sake, and then it broke
the window and got away. Poor little thing, I can see
his bright terrified eyes and his white paw trying
desperately to get back through the crack after I
had buttoned the coal-house door; and I never saw
him again! And I hated myself so, for forsaking
the cat that way. And you tried hard to find him,
for my sake next day, but never could, though the
other one was left.

Do you remember the morning on Newmarket
St. when Gordon had said something hard to me, and
you came up and found me half on the floor, and
asked me if he had struck me? Did I ever tell you
how both of us—both he and I—after we had a quar-
rel—went and took poison? And he came up in spite
of all (I had taken some of that morphine of
Tomsie's) and took me away to Dr. Morgan's, when
we had told each other; and Dr. M. sent me to Horn
and Hardart's for black coffee that made me vomit
terribly, and Gordon's own stomach was burned up
with some stuff he had taken—his lips were black
next day, and we were both like rags.

O Girlie, if we were to go on counting the old
things—the infinitely little things, that have left the

indelible mark. No one can ever be so much again, because we can't be young and live life through with them.

I sort of feel mostly bankrupt these last two years —bankrupt in a lot of things that I used to have plenty of—energy, interest, faith—oh the faith I *haven't got* is a large thing—like Stephens I have lived "to eat a good many of my theories and I guess I can swallow the rest." And I guess for a while I'd like to be let to rot in peace—that's how I feel.[39]

In the end, Voltairine resolved to return to Philadelphia. "I'm going back again next week or soon after," she told Mary Hansen, "and so I hope, old girl, we'll see each other soon again, for it never was a pleasant thought that I was going far from you, and you've played as big a part in my life as I have in yours."[40] By the end of December she was back in the city where she had lived for two decades, nearly all of her adult life. But she was deeply troubled. Her melancholy persisted. And she was unable to settle down to work. Thus ten months later she was to leave again, this time never to return.

[39] Voltairine de Cleyre to Mary Hansen, December 6, 1909, Ishill Collection.
[40] *Ibid.*

9. Chicago

What had kept Voltairine de Cleyre going in the past, for all her weariness and despair, was her dedication to anarchism, her Dominant Idea. Anarchism was the one fixed point, the sole anchor in her restless, unhappy life. But now even that was slipping away. And there was nothing to replace it. She was coming to believe that human ignorance and prejudice were so deeply ingrained that they might never be overcome. She was assailed by nagging doubts as to her own place in the movement for human liberation. Where was she? What did she believe? What had she accomplished? Had any of it been worthwhile?

In February 1910 *Mother Earth* announced that Voltairine de Cleyre would speak in New York the following month on the anniversary of the Paris Commune. Seeing the notice, Voltairine wrote the following letter to Alexander Berkman:

> Now, old boy, I said "I'll come if you'll tell me what to say, but I really have nothing to say." I didn't mean it in jest, dear; I was very, very earnest. I have nothing to say.
>
> It isn't for any such reasons as you imagine, or at least I infer you do, from what you write. It's not because of my views on progress, or because I find progress slow, or because I have any fault at all to find with comrades. The whole thing is purely subjective with me; *I have lost my compass*; I don't know where I myself stand; I have no heart to urge what I am altogether uncertain of. I don't know anything—*anything at all*. I get hold of a thought, and I run along with it an hour or two, maybe a few days, maybe a week, and then it suddenly appears foolish to me, and all the structure I build on it floats off into air. Then I am all in a hopeless confusion

for a few days; and then another idea crops up, and things begin to assemble themselves around that for a while, and take some sort of shape. Then *it* goes smash, and I am lost again. And I have come to grasp at all those little temporary periods of imitation order in my brain, as the only thing I am likely to get, and to hold on to them when I grasp them as a dreamer who knows he is in a dream and does not want to open his eyes, though he knows full well he must do it soon.

I cannot preach Anarchism now, because I do not believe it with any great force or strength. I have not "backslid." I believe in Gov't. no more than I ever did for 21 years. But I can't make a fervent gospel of Anarchism now. I can't honestly tell any one it's worth trying for. And I am rather displeased with the whole appearance of our work since 1887. I see we have steered the thing into such a theoretical channel, that if a direct struggle between capitalist and worker takes place, we must *keep out of it* because of our sympathy with the strikers! What a charming result! Our name is such a prejudice that we must save our friends from its contamination!

Now of course, Alex, you must understand that this, too, I am saying under the pressure of one of those temporary central thoughts, whereon I string my beads for the time being. In a little while the strings will break, and the beads fall off again, and I will be without an idea—only a whirling upset in my brain—for another week or so; then some new futility.

If as you say the spirit in which we speak is the thing, what kind of a spirit is this to speak with?

. . . Well good-bye, dear Alex. I feel quite sure (through all my doubting) that while my letter may surprise and grieve you, you are going to be grieved for me, who suffer, more than for the cause which doesn't need me, or any individual, to keep it alive.

You will not be angry at me, only sorry for me, I know.

I am sick of all my own words. How can I speak them?[1]

In the past it had been Voltairine who provided Berkman with moral support when he desperately needed it. Now their roles were reversed. Praising Voltairine's writing and speaking, Berkman urged her to leave the oppressive environment of Philadelphia and go on a lecture tour for the movement. Her response was negative: "As to lecturing, dear Aleck, you don't understand. You think it is easy for me to write, because my writing is beautiful. But if you knew with what agonizing effort it is written; if you knew how I had to force myself! And if you knew the doubt and bewilderment in my mind (these last two years). I am not sure of anything. I am not sure that liberty is good. I am not sure that progress exists. I do not feel able to theorize or philosophize or preach at all. . . . I can see no use in doing anything. Everything turns bitter in my mouth and ashes in my hands. . . . All my tastes are dying; I hardly care at all for music any more; never enough to play a new piece through."[2]

Joseph Cohen too prescribed a speaking tour as a way for Voltairine to break out of her melancholy. But she remained unmoved: "inwardly, *all is ruined in me.* For nearly two years now, all faith has been at an end in me. All ideas which for so many years were built up, were suddenly undermined. Little by little, every thing has fallen. My own straightforward, direct nature has crumbled in on itself. Things which were great and strong once have become broken pieces. I have no desire to tell any one to be anything. I turn

[1] Voltairine de Cleyre to Alexander Berkman, February 17, 1910, Berkman Archive.

[2] Voltairine de Cleyre to Alexander Berkman, June 24, 1910, Berkman Archive.

away from my own former words with an absolute
sense of loathing. I could not repeat that lecture on
Anarchism in literature without a sense of frightful
disgust at every sentence. And I have nothing—*nothing*
to say. I would like to finish my life in silence; if I
ever awoke from torpor, it would be to *do*, not to say."[3]

As the months passed, however, and her spirits failed
to revive, she began to reconsider. Perhaps a change of
location would, as her comrades suggested, lead her
out of the tunnel and give her life fresh purpose. But
where should she go? she asked Berkman in June 1910.
To Chicago? To New York? By August she had decided
on Chicago; and, despite her earlier misgivings, she
would present a course of lectures en route.[4]

Voltairine left Philadelphia on October 7, 1910. That
same evening she spoke in New York on "Literature,
the Mirror of Man" before the International Group, an
anarchist branch of the Workmen's Circle. After another lecture the following day, she headed upstate,
speaking at Albany, Schenectady, Rochester, and Buffalo on such subjects as "Anarchism and American
Traditions," "Modern Educational Reform," and "The
General Strike."

In Buffalo on October 13th, Voltairine addressed a
memorial meeting for Francisco Ferrer, the Spanish
pedagogue whose execution in the Montjuich fortress a
year before (on charges of fomenting rebellion) had
provoked an international outcry and inspired a movement, in the United States and in other countries, to

[3] Voltairine de Cleyre to Joseph J. Cohen, n.d. [1910], Cohen
Papers.

[4] Voltairine de Cleyre to Alexander Berkman, June 24, 1910,
Berkman Archive; Voltairine de Cleyre to Joseph J. Cohen,
August 22, 1910, Cohen Papers; Voltairine de Cleyre to Harriet
De Claire, August 30, 1910, Labadie Collection.

establish schools on the model of his Escuela Moderna in Barcelona, where instruction had been based on libertarian and rationalist principles. In New York a Francisco Ferrer Association was founded on June 3, 1910, and a Modern School was afterwards established, with Harry Kelly, Leonard Abbott, Emma Goldman, and Alexander Berkman among the participants. During 1910 and 1911, Ferrer Schools were started in other cities, including Seattle, Portland, Salt Lake City, Chicago, and Philadelphia, where the Radical Library opened a Sunday School in the fall of 1910, with Joseph Cohen as its driving spirit.

As a teacher of the poor, Voltairine de Cleyre felt a special sympathy for Ferrer, who was both a free-thinker and an anarchist like herself, and whose essay "The Modern School" she translated after his death.[5] She shared his hatred for the Catholic Church and its authoritarian educational methods, which they both had experienced at first hand. At the same time, she rejected the public school, which she considered an agent of government indoctrination, instilling a blind obedience and "revolting patriotism" in the minds of the children. For Voltairine, moreover, Ferrer's execution evoked the gallows of Chicago; and in her Buffalo speech she lashed out at the obscurantists, secular and ecclesiastical alike, who had "laid in the ditch of Montjuich a human being who but a moment before had been the personification of manhood, in the flower of life, in the strength and pride of a balanced intellect, full of the purpose of a great and growing undertaking —that of the Modern Schools." The average individual could "not believe it possible that any group of persons calling themselves a government, let it be of the worst

[5] Francisco Ferrer, "The Modern School," *Mother Earth*, November 1909, issued as a pamphlet the same year. Voltairine de Cleyre is identified as the translator by Leonard Abbott in *The Modern School* magazine, Autumn 1913.

and most despotic, could slay a man for being a teacher, a teacher of modern sciences, a builder of hygienic schools, a publisher of text-books."[6]

In her lecture "Modern Educational Reform," delivered the following evening, she called for an "integral" instruction which, as advocated by Ferrer and Kropotkin, would cultivate both mental and manual skills in a libertarian atmosphere, free from the domination of either church or state. And while she recognized the importance of the humanities and sciences, she felt that children, instead of being taught from books alone, should receive an active outdoor education amid natural surroundings and learn by doing and observing at first hand, a program that, once considered utopian, has since been endorsed by modern theorists of progressive education. Given her profound love of nature, it is not surprising that her ideal school should have been "a boarding school built in the country, having a farm attached, and workshops where useful crafts might be learned, in daily connection with intellectual training," a vision anticipating the experiment begun at Stelton, New Jersey, three years after her death.[7]

Voltairine's lectures on "Francisco Ferrer" and "Modern Educational Reform" were severely criticized in *The Buffalo Express*, a paper in which she had published several poems before becoming an anarchist. She replied with a strong letter, pointing out that her own education had not been in a radical institution but in the public school of St. Johns, Michigan, and in the Convent of Our Lady of Lake Huron, Order of the Holy Names of Jesus and Mary. "As to the responsibility

[6] Voltairine de Cleyre, "Francisco Ferrer," *Selected Works*, pp. 297-320.

[7] Voltairine de Cleyre, "Modern Educational Reform," *Selected Works*, pp. 321-41. Fittingly, as has been noted, the main thoroughfare of the Stelton Colony was called Voltairine de Cleyre Street.

for my opinions, neither institution is responsible, for I received the usual dose of patriotism in the one and of hell-fire threats in the other. That I am an independent thinker is due to neither, but to the experiences of life and natural bent of mind."[8] To another hostile paper, the Catholic *Buffalo Union and Times*, she wrote: "If you think that I, as your opponent, deserve the benefit of truth, but as a stranger you doubt my veracity, I respectfully request you to submit this letter to Sister Mary Médard, my former teacher, now Superioress at Windsor, or to my revered friend, Father Siegfried, Overbrook Seminary, Overbrook, Pa., who will tell you whether, in their opinion, my disposition to tell the truth may be trusted."[9]

Voltairine left Buffalo on October 18th, after a five-day visit. Her next stop was Cleveland, where she stayed with Adeline Champney, a contributor to both *Mother Earth* and *Liberty*, and her companion Fred Schulder, Benjamin Tucker's sales representative. Here, on October 21st, she addressed another Ferrer memorial, attended, in spite of a driving rainstorm, by 120 people, "*wet*," Voltairine reports, "but *enthusiastic*." A feature of the meeting was the singing of the old Irish revolutionary song "The Wearing of the Green" and of "Annie Laurie," around which, Voltairine writes, "floats forever the memory of Albert Parsons' voice." During her speech, a priest in the audience became so infuriated that he went out to get a policeman to arrest her, but he did not return. "I infer he was angry because I told the truth about the Catholic Church in Spain," Voltairine remarked, "of whose character he was likely ignorant." Two days later, she spoke before the Cleveland Free Thought Society, at which a number of Tuckerites in the audience exhibited "the old narrow excommunicative spirit" of their mentor, insist-

---

[8] *The Buffalo Express*, October 22, 1910.
[9] Quoted by Havel in *Selected Works*, pp. 10-11.

ing that no communist could be an anarchist. "It made me feel that I was living some twenty years back, in the days when we held that our own particular economic gospel was the only 'road to freedom,' and whosoever did not hold it was bound to the perdition of authority."[10]

After Cleveland came Toledo and Detroit (with a side trip to St. Johns) and finally Chicago, where Voltairine concluded her tour with her annual Haymarket address on November 11th. Settling in Chicago, still one of America's main centers of radicalism, she rented a room in the apartment of Jacob and Anna Livshis, with whom she had stayed on previous trips to the city. Here she lived for the next nineteen months, until her death in June 1912. Jake and Annie Livshis were Russian Jews of the type Voltairine knew so well in Philadelphia, simple, warm, dedicated. Despite their European origins, however, they were active primarily among the English-speaking anarchists who had gathered around *Free Society* at the turn of the century, and their home at 2038 Potomac Avenue was a center of the Chicago movement. According to a friend, Annie Livshis was "the epitome of everything magnificent in the human spirit: gentle, soft-spoken, devoted to her cause."[11] Like Mary Hansen in Philadelphia, she adored Voltairine and gave her the love and affection which she needed perhaps more than ever.

To support herself in Chicago, Voltairine gave private lessons, as she had done in Philadelphia. Word of mouth and an advertisement in the *Fraye Arbeter Shtime* brought her a growing clientele, whom she taught English, elocution, and mathematics. "My friend Fanny took English lessons from her in the eve-

[10] Voltairine de Cleyre, "Tour Impressions," *Mother Earth*, January 1911; Voltairine de Cleyre to Joseph J. Cohen, October 26, 1910, Cohen Papers.

[11] Interview with Jeanne Levey, December 19, 1972.

ning," recalls Gussie Denenberg, a former pupil. "I
went to her for a few math lessons. As she taught it,
it seemed so easy compared to public school. She was
rather tall, slim, pale, with a face you couldn't take
your eyes off. Not beautiful, but she had wonderful
eyes."[12] By February 1911 Voltairine was earning
$13.50 a week, and her income was still growing. Part
of this she sent to St. Johns, as in the past. "I gave
Mother and Gordon over $1,000 between them," yet
they consider me "impractical," she complained to
Addie. "Impractical! Hell!" Nevertheless, mother loves
us "as much as it is in her broken-down, aged, infirm,
and Puritan-poisoned soul" to do.[13]

Voltairine resumed her regular output of lectures
and articles, speaking to Wobblies and trade unionists
as well as to anarchists and freethinkers, and writing
for *Di Fraye Gezelshaft* and *Volné Listy* besides the
Fraye Arbeter Shtime and *Mother Earth*.[14] For two
months, moreover, from November 1910 to January
1911, she lectured to adults on Sunday afternoons at
the new Ferrer Modern School, "an intense speaker,"
recalls Gussie Denenberg, "overflowing with sympathy."
According to Jeanne Levey, "she was beautiful, she was
poetic, there was something mellifluous about her
voice," while Rebecca August found her a "more
philosophical" speaker than Emma Goldman. "I learned
an awful lot from her!"[15]

[12] Interview with Gussie Denenberg, Washington, D.C.,
March 20, 1973.

[13] Voltairine de Cleyre to Adelaide D. Thayer, August 15,
1911, Ishill Collection.

[14] Saul Yanovsky, who translated her essays into Yiddish,
considered her "one of the most intelligent women in America."
Yanovsky, *Ershte yorn fun yidishn frayhaytlikhen sotsializm*,
New York, 1948, p. 101.

[15] Interviews with Gussie Denenberg, March 20, 1973;
Jeanne Levey, December 19, 1972; and Rebecca August, June
20, 1974.

Voltairine did not, for the most part, teach young children, for whom, with a few exceptions (such as Emma Cohen and Marion Bell), she never had much patience. "I am not enthused about children," she had told Joseph Cohen in Philadelphia. "I am not interested in them. And I feel I'm in the wrong place dealing with them." On her way to Chicago she reemphasized the point: "The more I come into contact with small children, the more I find it is almost intolerable to me to be in their presence; they are mostly such monuments of aggression! And I cannot for the life of me interest myself in what they are interested in, nor pretend to."[16]

She was becoming, moreover, sharply critical of the Modern School experiments, at least of those with which she had personal contact. Dissatisfied with the vagueness of the pamphlets issued by the Ferrer Association in New York, she recommended the publication in English of the textbooks used by Ferrer himself in Barcelona. In the Philadelphia school, as she wrote to Cohen, she detected a "strong desire to accomplish something with no definite idea of *what* it is nor *how* to do it. *What* should a child learn? And *how* should he learn it? Can you answer? Does he need arithmetic? How much? Geography? How much? History? What kind? Gardening? Manual training? In what lines? What should we throw away and what add to the present system? I would want clear systematic replies."[17]

Two months of lecturing at the Chicago Modern School inspired similar doubts and reservations. The school, she wrote to Cohen, is "very unsatisfactory. Too much 'liberty' and too little orderly idea of work." To Yanovsky she complained of "chaos both financially

[16] Voltairine de Cleyre to Joseph J. Cohen, September 5 and October 26, 1910, Cohen Papers.

[17] *Mother Earth*, December 1910; Voltairine de Cleyre to Joseph J. Cohen, August 22, 1910, Cohen Papers.

and morally" produced by the administrators;[18] and in January 1911 she left. The following month she turned down an invitation from Alexander Berkman and Leonard Abbott to become Business Manager of the Ferrer Association in New York at fifteen dollars a week. "I very much fear," she told Berkman, "that I should not make a success as a Business Manager. I should do better as some one's 'office cat.' " Besides, she asked, what do people like Hutchins Hapgood and Emma Goldman ("with the inevitable attaché Reitman") know about organizing and running a school? Bayard Boyesen, a former English instructor at Columbia, "is the only teacher in the bunch; and he is probably merely good at his own specialty, just as I am." As for Leonard Abbott, although a good journalist, he has "never impressed me as a practical man" and seems "more or less hypnotized by Emma, to me."[19]

Two months later, Abbott wrote Voltairine for a copy of her lecture "Modern Educational Reform," explaining that everyone in the Ferrer Association seemed to be "misty" on the subject. "I told him that six months ago," wrote Voltairine to Joseph Cohen, "but he didn't seem to feel the force of it then. I really think he, like a good many others, got swept off their feet by Ferrer's death, and began to holler 'Mod. Ed.' without knowing what they were hollering about."[20] Finally, when Cohen himself planned to convert the Sunday School of the Radical Library into a full-fledged day school (a project which never materialized), Voltairine was not encouraging: "You cannot compete with the public schools in equipment; 30 kids are too many; and you

[18] Voltairine de Cleyre to Joseph J. Cohen, November 23, 1910, Cohen Papers; Voltairine de Cleyre to Saul Yanovsky, November 30, 1910, Ishill Collection.

[19] Voltairine de Cleyre to Alexander Berkman, February 7, 1911, Berkman Archive.

[20] Voltairine de Cleyre to Joseph J. Cohen, April 13, 1911, Cohen Papers.

must have them all about the same age or you will need
an unconscionable number of teachers and attend-
ants." She had lost her faith entirely in the Modern
School movement, she confessed. "I have grown convinced that the only way to do anything on those lines,
is to convert the teaching profession—to 'inoculate them
with the poison' within the gov't schools themselves."[21]

Behind her disenchantment was a return of the
feeling of malaise and emptiness which had gripped
her in Philadelphia. Moving to Chicago had done little to relieve her physical or emotional travail, the illness and pain and overwhelming desire for escape.
Eight months had passed since she left Philadelphia,
yet "there has never been a moment in all that time
that I have not felt like a piece of driftwood," she wrote
to Cohen in June 1911. Her thoughts were "always in
an invincible turmoil," which made it increasingly difficult to write, especially about anarchism. As she confided to Yanovsky: "It seems to me I have to put my
brains in a press and just *squeeze* every word out. I
tell you I feel spiritually and mentally bankrupt! . . .
The prolific confidence of old years has died; I am
possessed by barren doubts only." The trouble, she
repeated, was that "*I don't know at all what I believe*;
and when I try to find out, my mind crumbles down in
the effort; a terrible apathy comes over me, a mental
stupor; I sit staring at my own problems, like an idiot.
I *can't* drive myself to go on."[22]

Worn out with the accumulated fatigue from years
of illness and struggle, she was easily irritated and in
no condition, either physically or emotionally, to with-
stand the procession of visitors who bustled in and out
of the Livshis apartment. "Believe me," she wrote to
Cohen, "I feel, more than ever in my life, the horrors

[21] Voltairine de Cleyre to Joseph J. Cohen, June 7, 1911,
Cohen Papers.

[22] *Ibid.*; Voltairine de Cleyre to Saul Yanovsky, March 6 and
29, 1911, Ishill Collection.

of *communism*. These comrades are *natural communists*. Their house is everybody's house. Everybody is welcome in every corner of it; and there is never one moment where one can be comfortably alone."[23] At times the intrusions were so unbearable that she "went out of the house and walked the streets to get away from the turmoil." A visit by Ben Reitman was a particular source of annoyance. "Reitman has been doing his usual stunts," she wrote Alexander Berkman. "I am glad to know he is leaving soon, for he gets everybody by the ears, talks vulgarly at meetings, says untruths, and irritates everybody."[24]

Her letters of this period ache with a yearning for peace and quiet. "Do you know, Mary, I often and often long desperately for the quiet and order of convent life," she told her Philadelphia friend. "I suppose it would be intolerable if I got it, but for the last three or four years it has been a continually recurring feeling: 'Oh, if only I could be in a place of *order* and well-regulated peace, and silent tongues.' " To Joseph Cohen she wrote more despondently: "I think I am too old to be alive, and ought to die."[25]

During the spring of 1911, at the moment of her deepest despair, Voltairine's spirits were lifted by the swelling revolution in Mexico, and especially by the activities of Ricardo Flores Magón, the foremost Mexican anarchist of the time, whose Partido Liberal

[23] Voltairine de Cleyre to Joseph J. Cohen, December 10, 1910, and April 13, 1911, Cohen Papers. See also her letter to Peter Livshis, December 3, 1910, Labadie Collection.

[24] Voltairine de Cleyre to Alexander Berkman, December 31, 1910, Berkman Archive. Cf. her letter to Joseph J. Cohen, February 1, 1912: "We had a month's siege of Reitman, but are now relieved of him."

[25] Voltairine de Cleyre to Mary Hansen, June 3, 1911, Ishill Collection; Voltairine de Cleyre to Joseph J. Cohen, February 7, 1911, Cohen Papers.

Mexicano played an important part in rousing the workers and peasants against the Díaz dictatorship. Flores Magón's movement reached a climax in May 1911 when, under the banner of "Land and Liberty," the Magonista revolt in Baja California established revolutionary communes at Mexicali and Tijuana, taking for their theoretical basis Kropotkin's *Conquest of Bread*, a work which Flores Magón regarded as a kind of anarchist bible and which his followers distributed in thousands of copies.

Flores Magón's movement, with its headquarters in Los Angeles, fired the imagination of American anarchists and Industrial Workers of the World. Both Alexander Berkman and Emma Goldman spoke and wrote on its behalf, raising funds for its journal, *Regeneración*, and for lawyers and bail when Flores Magón and his associates were arrested. Additional money came from the Anarchist Red Cross in New York and Chicago, thanks in part to the efforts of Lucy Parsons. As for Voltairine de Cleyre, as Emma Goldman writes, the Mexican cause was a matter "of most vital consequence. She devoted herself entirely to it, writing, lecturing, and collecting funds."[26] It gave her a new lease on life; and her radical career, with its soaring hopes and plunging disappointments, began a new and vigorous phase of activity.

During the last year of her life, Voltairine was "filled with the spirit of direct action,"[27] which inspired her to greater effort than might have been thought possible. For here was the true plebeian resurgence she had been waiting for, a social revolution of the poor and disinherited, whose cause she could fervently embrace. "At last," she declared in *Mother Earth*, "we can see a genuine awakening of a people, not to political demands alone, but to economic ones—fundamentally

[26] Goldman, *Living My Life*, p. 505.
[27] Havel, Introduction to *Selected Works*, p. 13.

economic ones. . . . 'Events are the true schoolmasters,'
I hear the justified voice of my dead Comrade Lum
calling triumphantly from his grave."[28] The Mexican
upheaval, she believed, was "a social phenomenon
offering the greatest field for genuine Anarchist
propaganda that has ever been presented on this continent; for here was an immense number of oppressed
people endeavoring to destroy a fundamental wrong,
private property in land, not through any sort of governmental scheme, but by direct expropriation." The
Magonistas "just now *are doing things*," she wrote to
Joseph Cohen. They are engaged in "an actual death
struggle for what we anarchists pretend we believe
in. There is more genuine Anarchism in *Regeneración*
in a week's issue than the rest of our publications put
together!—fighting Anarchism, that means to do and
is doing something to smash this whole accursed system."[29]

Voltairine's deepest sympathies had always been
with the simple, unspoiled rural folk who lived and
worked close to nature. She idealized the Mexican
peons who were seizing the land without help from the
"theory-spinners" of the cities. For no change could
be accomplished "except by the mass of the people.
Theories may be propounded by educated people,
and set down in books, and discussed in libraries, sit-
ting-rooms and lecture-halls; but they will remain
barren, unless the people in mass work them out." And
with that "clear and direct perception of the needful
thing to do which lettered men, men of complex lives,
nearly always lack, being befogged by too many lights,

[28] Voltairine de Cleyre, "The Mexican Revolt," *Mother Earth*,
August 1911. The upheaval in Mexico, she wrote Mary Hansen
on June 3, 1911, "is a genuine economic revolt, with the red
flag for its standard."
[29] *Mother Earth*, April 1912; Voltairine de Cleyre to Joseph
J. Cohen, October 30, 1911, and March 28, 1912, Cohen Papers.

they move straight upon their purpose, hew down the landmarks, burn the records and title-deeds."[30]

What Voltairine felt for the Mexican peasant was expressed with glowing eloquence in a series of essays in 1911 and 1912, one of which appeared in *Volné Listy*, the Czech anarchist paper in New York: "The Indian's 'laziness' is proverbial among white men; but, far from its being what the white man thinks it is, it is rather the intense protest of a free soul against a useless and degrading waste of life. He wishes to feel himself a child of the sun and sky, a being through whom moves the breath of life, a thing of the soil and the air, and not a tool for the aimless production of heaps of goods at someone else's orders. The half-breeds, on the white side again, are the descendants of Latins; and, while the Latin peoples work, they have never hungered and thirsted after purely commercial gain as have Northern nations; they have always preserved a devotion to the beautiful (even the useless beautiful) and the mere joys of life—song, dance and festival—unknown to the Anglo-Saxon. Add to all this the enervating climate of much of Mexico, and you have an understanding of what our grab-and-get system of life stigmatizes as 'Mexican laziness.' These people want the land; they do not want to live in cities; they want to use the land in their own way, according to their inherited communal customs. Time and time again they have rebelled, and their rebellions have been murderously put down, but this instinctive hunger for the free field of life is so essentially a part of their being that the only way to kill it is to kill the entire agrarian population. At the present time it has risen up more invincible than ever; and, although the people are ignorant—less than 20 per cent being able to read

[30] *Mother Earth*, August 1911, December 1911-February 1912.

and write—they need no book learning to convince them that the land is theirs by right."[31]

For the next few months the Mexican Revolution absorbed Voltairine's complete attention. In July 1911 she became the Chicago correspondent of *Regeneración* and, with her half-breed friend Honoré Jaxon, organized the Mexican Liberal Defense Conference (later called the Chicago Mexican Liberal Defense League), serving as treasurer from her room in the Livshis apartment. In *Mother Earth* and the *Fraye Arbeter Shtime* she published an appeal for funds, which were forwarded to W. C. Owen, a British-born anarchist who edited the English page of *Regeneración* and was one of Flores Magón's principal supporters. In addition, she made a personal appeal to the Radical Library, now Branch 273 of the Workmen's Circle, of which she was still a dues-paying member. "Once at a meeting at 424 Pine Street," recalls a member of the group, "Joseph Cohen read us a letter from her in Chicago asking for a collection, so we sent $100."[32]

At picnics, mass meetings, and private gatherings, Voltairine de Cleyre defended the "blood-red banner on the burning soil of Mexico," as she put it in a speech of October 29, 1911,[33] and distributed thousands of copies of *Regeneración* and of W. C. Owen's pamphlet *The Mexican Revolution*. She lectured at the Scandinavian Liberty League, the Open Forum, I.W.W. Local 85, and other radical and working-class groups. By April 1912 some $250 had been collected and dis-

[31] Quoted in W. C. Owen, *The Mexican Revolution*, Los Angeles, 1912, p. 6. Cf. Owen to Emma Goldman, June 28, 1926, Goldman Archive. There is a similar passage in her speech on "The Mexican Revolution," *Mother Earth*, February 1912, reprinted in *Selected Works*, pp. 269-70.

[32] Interview with Harry Melman, Philadelphia, November 28, 1971. Cf. Voltairine de Cleyre to Joseph J. Cohen, January 12, 1912, Cohen Papers.

[33] *Selected Works*, p. 275.

patched to Owen in Los Angeles. Yet Voltairine was
not satisfied. She wondered how "the mass of those
who are sympathetic in idea with libertarian movements can continue to prattle about 'art,' 'literature,'
the latest imported violinist, and the aesthetic beauty
of the concepts of Anarchism! While these men fight
the battle, with starvation as companion."[34]

In the course of these activities, Voltairine met a
young Bohemian anarchist named Joseph Kucera,
who became her last lover. Tall, fair, and good-looking,
Kucera was a machinist by trade and a frequent contributor to *Volné Listy* (his articles included a sympathetic treatment of Czolgosz, in the January 1903
issue). Like Garside and Gordon before him, however,
he appears to have been wanting in character. According to Emma Goldman, who seldom admired Voltairine's lovers, he was "one of the many anarchist
idealists so long as he felt the pinch in his stomach.
Once he ascended to a certain amount of power and
money his idealism was left by the roadside."[35] Yet he
never treated Voltairine as shabbily as her previous
lovers had done; and he worked closely with her on
behalf of Flores Magón, publishing a pamphlet in
Czech on the Mexican rising, possibly with her help.[36]

[34] Voltairine de Cleyre, "Report of the Work of the Chicago
Mexican Liberal Defense League," *Mother Earth*, April 1912.
See also her "Chicago Workers Show Sympathy," *Regenera-
ción*, July 1, 1911.

[35] Emma Goldman to Leonard Schwartz, September 8, 1932,
Goldman Archive. Cf. Goldman to Joseph Ishill, September 8,
1932, Ishill Collection: "I never thought much of him and
therefore never permitted him to enter my life too closely."
Kucera afterwards married the daughter of a wealthy manu-
facturer and left the movement. He died in New York around
1930.

[36] Josef Kučera, *Revoluce v Mexicu*, New York, 1912, pub-
lished by the "Volné listy" press. See also Kucera to Rudolf
Grossmann, November 17, 1911, Ramus Archive, International
Institute of Social History.

In the heat of her enthusiasm for the Mexican revolutionaries, Voltairine began to study Spanish and, in September 1911, prepared to go to Los Angeles to be near the scene of the struggle. But illness intervened, and Kucera went in her place. Her last poem, "Written—in—Red," was dedicated to her Mexican comrades. It appeared in *Regeneración* six months before her death:

Illumine the message: "Seize the lands!
Open the prisons and make men free!"
Flame out the living words of the dead
Written—in—red.[37]

[37] Voltairine de Cleyre, "Written—in—Red (To Our Living Dead in Mexico's Struggle)," *Regeneración*, December 16, 1911; reprinted in *Selected Works*, p. 75.

10. Light upon Waldheim

The last year and a half of Voltairine de Cleyre's life, before the onset of her final illness, was perhaps the most militant period of her career. Shedding the vestiges of her former pacifism, she fastened her hopes on social revolution as the road to human liberation. She issued appeal after appeal for "direct action," delivering her most eloquent lecture on the subject on January 21, 1912. Published as a pamphlet by the Mother Earth press, it was distributed at anarchist and working-class gatherings in thousands of copies.[1]

Apart from the Mexican Revolution, it was the increasingly violent labor struggle in America itself which drove her further to the left. She felt a strong kinship with the Industrial Workers of the World, the Anarcho-Syndicalists, and other labor militants, with their uncomplicated philosophy of action and uncompromising opposition to capitalism. Writing to Alexander Berkman during the McNamara case of 1910-1911, she affirmed her belief in "the class-war, in 'class-consciousness.' "[2] For the bombing of the Los Angeles Times Building (for which the McNamara brothers were tried and imprisoned) she blamed the paper's owner, Harrison Gray Otis, a die-hard opponent of organized labor in the mold of Henry Clay Frick. "I'm only confoundedly sorry McNamara didn't hit *him* instead of the building, with the poor 20 scabs," she wrote to Saul Yanovsky.[3]

Like Berkman and Emma Goldman, she continued

[1] Voltairine de Cleyre, *Direct Action*, New York, 1912. A Yiddish translation appeared in the *Fraye Arbeter Shtime* between March 2 and April 6, 1912.

[2] Voltairine de Cleyre to Alexander Berkman, December 31, 1910, Berkman Archive.

[3] Voltairine de Cleyre to Saul Yanovsky, March 6, 1911, Ishill Collection.

to defend the McNamaras even after their admission of guilt, turning her wrath upon Samuel Gompers, Morris Hillquit, and others who, in violation of labor solidarity, had demanded severe punishment for the defendants: "Who cries vengeance for the criminals who killed the workers in the Cherry mine? or the Johnstown and Austin floods? or the victims of the 1907 panic, which Wharton Barker, the banker, tells us was connived by Theodore Roosevelt? Who now are the criminals responsible for the 200 miners buried alive at this moment at Briceville? Every day they murder more, calmly and cold-bloodedly, than did the Times disaster. And let them cease their hypocrisy. And let our people hurl back at them their own cry: 'Murder is murder.' Let them understand who are the fundamental criminals, and what is their fundamental crime. Let them ask not indeed for vengeance, but the abolition of this scheme of property right for some in what belongs to us all, whereby we are brought to this horrible war, and driven to conclude that there is no way of getting any meager portion of what is ours but by violence."[4]

Voltairine's indignation was equally aroused by the treatment of anarchists and Wobblies during the San Diego free-speech fight in the spring of 1912. "Did you read how 100 I.W.W.'s have been made to kneel and kiss the flag in California?" she asked her young comrade, Ben Capes. "Glorious land of liberty! 'They all said they were anarchists.' 45 constables and a large body of armed citizens enforced it. I don't know, but I rather think I'd have said 'You better shoot: I'll not do it.'"[5]

Throughout this period of social turmoil, Voltairine maintained an extremely heavy schedule of work. "Like

[4] Voltairine de Cleyre, "The McNamara Storm," *The Agitator*, January 15, 1912.

[5] Voltairine de Cleyre to Ben Capes, April 5, 1912, Goldman Archive.

an anchorite," noted Sadakichi Hartmann, "she flayed her body to utter one more lucid and convincing argument in praise of direct action." On March 18, 1912, she addressed a Paris Commune memorial sponsored by the Chicago Bohemian Group. "It was the most beautiful meeting I can remember," she told Joseph Cohen, "but it meant a lot of work writing letters, arranging programs, and preliminary meetings."[6] In the succeeding weeks, she helped with the arrangements for a May First celebration, corrected the proofs of Berkman's *Prison Memoirs*, and spent many hours translating the memoirs of Louise Michel, a task which she "cherished and longed to complete" but never did. On free afternoons she would go to the Waldheim Cemetery with Peter Livshis, Jake and Annie's deaf and dumb son, to place flowers at the Haymarket tomb.[7]

By the middle of April Voltairine was worn out with fatigue. Only forty-five years old, she was broken in health and had little strength to carry on. A prisoner of her decaying body, she remained in chronic discomfort and pain. "My ears and nose," she wrote, "are always in a terrible state of irritation." She told the Livshis family that "the noise of cars, trains, and furious pounding of iron with a hammer" were nothing as compared with the noise that constantly pounded in her head.[8] Her move to Chicago had solved none of her problems. Her illness had not subsided. The climate was disagreeable, being too cold in winter and too hot in summer. "Chicago was never so hot, in all its history," she had complained to Yanovsky in July 1911. "I felt like jumping in the lake last night, but as my

[6] *Mother Earth*, April 1915; Voltairine de Cleyre to Joseph J. Cohen, March 28, 1912, Cohen Papers.

[7] Navro manuscript, Ishill Collection; Peter Livshis to Emma Goldman, June 5, 1926, Goldman Archive.

[8] Voltairine de Cleyre to Joseph J. Cohen, November 23, 1910, Cohen Papers; Peter Livshis to Emma Goldman, June 5, 1926, Goldman Archive.

religious friends say I should then go to a still hotter place, I forebore." Away from Philadelphia, she felt "a wanderer and a stranger," as she wrote to Joseph Cohen. "Some way, I cannot get used to living in Chicago; my heart is always back there in Phila.; and it seems to me my work will never be any good except there." Longing for "the old places and the old faces," she decided to return at the nearest opportunity.[9]

On April 14, 1912, Voltairine made her last public appearance in Chicago, reciting Freiligrath's "Revolution" in the West Side Auditorium for the benefit of the Anarchist Red Cross. Three days later she was overcome by a severe attack of the sinuses. A doctor was called and diagnosed the trouble as otitis media, or inflammation of the middle ear. When her condition worsened, she was removed to St. Mary of Nazareth Hospital. The infection, it was found, had penetrated her brain, and an immediate operation was performed. Rallying momentarily, she wrote to her mother that she was still alive, although "the whole back of my nose seems to be decayed."[10]

Before long she suffered a relapse, and a second operation was required. Her son and Nathan Navro came from Philadelphia to be at her side. Having lost her power of speech, she used signs to make herself understood. As she lay there, immobile and voiceless, a priest passed her room and she grimaced to show her displeasure. By now her strength was broken, and life was ebbing away. After nine weeks of "horrible suffering," there remained the consolation that the peace she so desperately craved, the mournful peace of her

[9] Voltairine de Cleyre to Saul Yanovsky, July 5, 1911, Linder Archive, International Institute of Social History; Voltairine de Cleyre to Joseph J. Cohen, May 8 and June 7, 1911, Cohen Papers.

[10] Note from J. P. Pfeifer, M.D., April 22, 1912; Cohen Papers; Voltairine de Cleyre to Harriet De Claire, n.d. [May 1912], Labadie Collection.

poems, was soon to come. She died on Thursday morning, June 20, 1912, just after 11 o'clock.[11]

On Sunday, June 23rd, she was buried in the Waldheim Cemetery, beside the graves of the Haymarket anarchists whose martyrdom had inspired her life. Two thousand mourners attended, among them representatives of the Workmen's Circle, the Bohemian Bakers' and Turners' Unions, the Jewish Cabinetmakers' Union, the Women's "Progress" Society, and the English, Hungarian, Czech, and Italian branches of the I.W.W. (including William D. Haywood, Vincent St. John, and William Trautmann). Voltairine's mother and sister came from St. Johns to attend the burial. "As my sister lay in her casket," Addie recalls, "Mrs. Lucy Parsons stood beside her and arranged a spray of red carnations on it; and a hush fell on the crowd." A small simple stone marks her grave, inscribed with her name and dates; and when comrades visit the Haymarket monument, "they lovingly remember Voltairine de Cleyre."[12]

On the evening of the funeral, a memorial meeting was held in Philadelphia, arranged by the Radical Library, with George Brown and Chaim Weinberg among the speakers. On the stage hung a large picture of Voltairine decorated in red and black. The next day, a similar gathering took place on the Lower East Side in New York, where Alexander Berkman, Harry Kelly, and Saul Yanovsky addressed a hushed audience. In Los Angeles, *Regeneración* declared that "the Mexican peon has lost a true and powerful friend."[13]

[11] Harry de Cleyre to Agnes Inglis, October 12, 1947, and March 4, 1950, Labadie Collection; *Why?*, August 1913.

[12] Adelaide D. Thayer to Joseph Ishill, December 1, 1937, Ishill Collection; Goldman, *Voltairine de Cleyre*, p. 27. See also Kucera's letter in the *Fraye Arbeter Shtime*, June 29, 1912; and "Voltairine de Cleyre," *Freedom*, August 1912.

[13] *Fraye Arbeter Shtime*, June 29 and July 6, 1912; *Regeneración*, June 22, 1912.

Emma Goldman, returning from a lecture tour in the West, stopped in Chicago and went to Waldheim with Annie Livshis, who had nursed Voltairine to the last and seen to her burial. On her grave they placed carnations and geraniums, "the only monument she ever wanted." "There she lies," wrote Emma, "whose body had never known respite from pain, whose soul had never tasted peace, and who yet never relaxed, until the end, in her zeal, her wonderful zeal, for the ideal she loved so well—Anarchism, the redeemer of the human race." Her death affected Emma deeply: "As I stood beside Voltairine's grave, in the shadow of the monument dedicated to the memory of our comrades, I felt that another martyr had been added to them. She was the prototype of the sculptured Waldheim figure, beautiful in her spiritual defiance and filled with the revolt of a flaming ideal."[14]

In July 1912 *Mother Earth* published a memorial issue to Voltairine de Cleyre, with selections from her writings and tributes to her by Harry Kelly, George Brown, Mary Hansen, and Alexander Berkman. Many know of her courage and sacrifice, said Brown, "but few know how sweet a companion she was, how staunch a friend." In Chicago, Annie Livshis issued a small brochure, *In Memoriam: Voltairine de Cleyre*, with poems, a portrait, and her favorite song. To Harriet De Claire Annie sent Voltairine's fur cap and soon received a note of thanks: "It was what she wore the last sight I had of her living face. The dearest daughter that ever a woman had. I shall love you always because you were good to her."[15] In the fall of 1912, a committee of Voltairine's friends, consisting of Leonard Abbott, Harry Kelly, Joseph Kucera, Saul Yanovsky, Hippolyte Havel, and Perle McLeod, was formed to collect and

[14] *Mother Earth*, August 1912; Goldman, *Living My Life*, pp. 504-505.
[15] Harriet De Claire to Anna Livshis, December 30, 1912, Labadie Collection.

publish her works. Edited by Alexander Berkman, with a biographical sketch by Havel, the *Selected Works of Voltairine de Cleyre*, "an arsenal of knowledge for the student and soldier of freedom," appeared in 1914 under the imprint of the Mother Earth Publishing Association.

For the next few years memorial meetings were held in New York, Chicago, Philadelphia, and Los Angeles on the anniversary of Voltairine de Cleyre's death. Her poem "The Hurricane" was set to music by George Edwards, who had offered Emma Goldman the use of his Musical Institute of San Diego during the free-speech fight of 1912. Leonard Abbott included Voltairine in his lecture course on radical literature at the Ferrer Center in New York. And her poems were recited at children's entertainments at the Ferrer Colony in Stelton, whose main street was named in her honor.[16] "She has left the stage," said her Chicago comrade Jay Fox, "but her memory will linger long, like the odor of a fragrant rose crushed at full bloom; like the impress of a great thought flashed on the mind." The most moving tribute, however, came from Will Duff in Glasgow: "Voltairine, I am pleased to have been your friend and comrade, for you were one of the bravest, truest, and sweetest women that ever lived. You need no stone nor funeral bell; you are tombed in the true hearts that loved you well."[17]

[16] *The Modern School*, July 1, 1914; July 1918.
[17] *The Agitator*, July 15, 1912; *The Herald of Revolt*, September 1913.

Chronology

1901 Social Science Club started in Philadelphia. September 6: Leon Czolgosz shoots President McKinley. Isaaks arrested in Chicago.

1902 March 21: letter to Senator Hawley. December 19: shot by Herman Helcher.

1903 Trip to Norway and Britain. Meets Kristofer Hansteen, Rudolf Rocker, Errico Malatesta. *Crime and Punishment.*

1904 Severe illness; enters hospital.

1905 Attempts suicide. Russian Revolution.

1906 Partial recovery of health. March: founding of *Mother Earth.* May 27: death of father in Milwaukee. Meets Alexander Berkman.

1908 February 20: Broad Street Riot. Arrest, trial, acquittal.

1909 Free-speech campaign. June 30: address at Cooper Union. Visits Port Huron and Sarnia. *Anarchism and American Traditions.*

1910 October: lectures in New York, Ohio, Michigan. Moves to Chicago. Teaches at Ferrer Sunday School. *The Dominant Idea.*

1911 Founds Mexican Liberal Defense Conference. Campaigns for *Regeneración* and Ricardo Flores Magón. Meets Joseph Kucera.

1912 March 18: addresses last Paris Commune meeting. *Direct Action.* April: onset of final illness. June 20: dies in St. Mary's Hospital. June 23: buried in Waldheim Cemetery.

Bibliography

ARCHIVAL MATERIALS

The Labadie Collection, University of Michigan. The best
collection of anarchist literature in the United States, it
contains many of Voltairine de Cleyre's letters, manuscripts, and related documents, as well as letters from
her mother, sister, and son. In addition, it possesses a
good collection of photographs and a wealth of printed
sources, including many of the rare anarchist and free
thought publications in which Voltairine de Cleyre's
writings appeared. But for the efforts of Joseph A.
Labadie, founder of the collection, and of Agnes Inglis,
its curator until her death in 1952, much of this material
would have been lost to posterity.

*The Joseph Ishill Collection, Houghton Library, Harvard
University.* Like Jo Labadie and Agnes Inglis, Joseph
Ishill (1888-1966) was a dedicated preserver of anarchist literature, and the Ishill Collection is among the
richest libertarian archives in the United States, contain-
ing a wide range of manuscript and printed sources in
many languages. The publisher of artistic, hand-printed
works on Peter Kropotkin, Elie and Elisée Reclus,
Benjamin Tucker, and other prominent anarchists, Ishill
intended to issue a multivolume collection of the writings of Voltairine de Cleyre, a project which unfortunately was never realized. His archives, however,
contain a large quantity of her manuscripts and letters
(to Mary Hansen, Saul Yanovsky, and William and
Margaret Duff, among others) gathered for this purpose,
as well as correspondence from her family and friends
(including Dyer D. Lum) and recollections of her by
Nathan Navro, Olav Koringen, and Walter Starrett. The
Ishill Papers at the University of Florida, Gainesville,
though a much smaller collection than the one at
Harvard, has additional documents of importance,
among them further letters and an autobiographical
sketch by Dyer Lum.

The International Institute of Social History, Amsterdam. Houses the foremost anarchist collection in the world, thanks largely to the Austrian historian of anarchism Max Nettlau, who died in 1944. Important letters from Voltairine de Cleyre to Alexander Berkman are preserved in the Berkman Archive and other letters and manuscripts in the archives of Emma Goldman and Solo Linder. Pertinent materials are also to be found in the archives of Nettlau, Josef Peukert, Pierre Ramus (Rudolf Grossmann), Rudolf Rocker, and the Socialist League. In addition, the Institute possesses an outstanding collection of anarchist books, pamphlets, leaflets, journals, and photographs.

Other Libraries and Archives. Voltairine de Cleyre's letters to Joseph Cohen are preserved in the Bund Archives of the Jewish Labor Movement, New York. The Archives of Labor History and Urban Affairs at Wayne State University, Detroit, have one Voltairine de Cleyre letter (to William Armistead Collier, Jr.), as does the Tamiment Collection of New York University (to John B. Andrews). There is also one letter to Benjamin Tucker in the Tucker Papers, New York Public Library. Further documentary and printed sources are to be found in the Modern School Collection, Rutgers University; the George A. Schilling Papers, University of Chicago; the Ben L. Reitman Papers, University of Illinois, Chicago Circle; the Baskette Collection, University of Illinois, Urbana; the State Historical Society of Wisconsin, Madison; the Columbia University Library, New York; the YIVO Institute of Jewish Research, New York; and the Centre International de Recherches sur l'Anarchisme, Geneva.

Private Collections. The following private collections contain letters, photographs, or other pertinent materials: the Thomas H. Bell Papers, Los Angeles; the Leonard D. Abbott Papers, New York; the Moses and Lillian Harman Papers, San Francisco; the Harry Kelly Papers, New York; the William Wess Papers, London; and the papers of Voltairine de Cleyre's granddaughter, Mrs. G. R. Buckwalter, Cincinnati.

Works by Voltairine de Cleyre

In addition to her unpublished manuscripts in the above archival repositories, Voltairine de Cleyre contributed hundreds of poems and articles to a wide range of journals between 1885 and 1912 (see Periodicals section below). I have not attempted to itemize all of these here, though many are cited in the reference notes. What follows, rather, is a list of her printed books and pamphlets. Individual essays and poems are included only if they were published as separate titles.

Anarchism and American Traditions. New York, Mother Earth Publishing Association, 1909. Originally published in *Mother Earth*, December 1908 and January 1909. A new edition was published by the Free Society Group of Chicago in 1932, with an extract from Hippolyte Havel's Introduction to the *Selected Works of Voltairine de Cleyre.* The essay was reprinted in the Silverman and Veysey anthologies listed under Related Works. An Italian translation (by Maria Rovetti Cavalieri) appeared in Milan in 1909, reprinted from Luigi Galleani's journal *La Cronaca Sovversiva.* A Russian translation was published in *Probuzhdenie,* August 1930; and a Yiddish translation was made by Joseph Cohen, but I have not located a printed edition.

Det Anarkistiske Ideal. Christiania [Olso], Social-Demokraten, 1903. A Norwegian translation of her lecture "The Anarchist Ideal," delivered in Christiania on August 18, 1903.

Anarquismo. Buenos Aires, La Antorcha, 1929. A Spanish translation of her speech on "Anarchism," delivered in Philadelphia and published in *Free Society,* October 13, 1901. A Russian translation appeared in *Probuzhdenie,* May 1930. The Spanish edition includes Havel's biographical sketch from the *Selected Works of Voltairine de Cleyre.*

Betrayed (poem), n.p., n.d.

Crime and Punishment. Philadelphia, Social Science Club, 1903. A lecture to the Social Science Club, March 15, 1903. Translated into Danish and Swedish.

Direct Action. New York, Mother Earth Publishing Association, 1912. A lecture delivered in Chicago, January 21, 1912. A Yiddish translation (probably by Saul Yanovsky) appeared in the *Fraye Arbeter Shtime* between March 2 and April 6, 1912, and was reprinted in pamphlet form in 1914 by the Broyt un Frayhayt Group of New York.

The Dominant Idea. New York, Mother Earth Publishing Association, 1910. A French translation (by E. Armand) appeared in 1911 and was reissued in 1917 and 1933.

The Drama of the Nineteenth Cenutry. Pittsburgh, R. Staley & Co., n.d. [1889]. A lecture to the Pittsburgh Secular Society, December 16, 1888.

The Gods and the People (poem). London, Liberty Press, 1897. Published also by William Duff in Glasgow, 1898, as Solidarity Leaflet no. 1, and by Abe Isaak in San Francisco, n.d. [1898?].

In Defense of Emma Goldmann [sic] *and the Right of Expropriation.* Philadelphia, The Author, 1894. A lecture delivered in New York on December 16, 1893 (misdated in the pamphlet as 1894). Also London, Liberty Press, 1894. Serialized in the London *Liberty* from November 1894 to January 1895. Reprinted in *The Herald of Revolt*, September 1913.

McKinley's Assassination from the Anarchist Standpoint. New York, Mother Earth Publishing Association, 1907. Reprinted from *Mother Earth*, October 1907.

The Mexican Revolt. New York, Mother Earth Publishing Association, 1911. Reprinted from *Mother Earth*, August 1911.

Nameless (poem). n.p., n.d.

The Past and Future of the Ladies' Liberal League. Philadelphia, Ladies' Liberal League, 1895. Serialized in *The Rebel* from October 20,1895 to January 1896.

Selected Stories. Seattle, The Libertarian Magazine, 1916. Contains "The Heart of Angiolillo," "At the End of the Alley," and "Where the White Rose Died." Special issue (in pamphlet form) of *The Libertarian Magazine*, July 1916, edited by Cassius V. Cook.

Selected Works of Voltairine de Cleyre. Edited by Alexander Berkman with a biographical sketch by Hippolyte

Havel. New York, Mother Earth Publishing Association, 1914. Reprinted by the Revisionist Press, New York, 1972. An abridged Chinese edition appeared in Canton and Shanghai in 1915.

Vi azoy men vert poter fun krizisen [How we shall rid ourselves of crises]. New York, Anarchist Federation of America, n.d.

The Worm Turns (poems). Philadelphia, Innes & Sons, 1900.

Besides the translations noted above, a number of Voltairine de Cleyre's speeches, essays, poems, and stories appeared in Italian, German, Yiddish, Russian, Czech, and other languages. Examples are "The Chain Gang" (translated by Max Sartin and Virgilia D'Andrea) and "Dyer D. Lum" (translated by Max Sartin) in *L'Adunata dei Refrattari*; "Francisco Ferrer" and "On Liberty" (translated by Gustav Landauer) in *Der Sozialist*; "At the End of the Alley" (translated by Saul Yanovsky) in *Di Fraye Gezelshaft*; "Literature, the Mirror of Man" and "The Philosophy of Anarchism" in the *Fraye Arbeter Shtime*; and "The Hurricane" in *Rabochaia Mysl'* and *Volna* (both published in New York).

Works about Voltairine de Cleyre

Abbott, Leonard D. "A Priestess of Pity and Vengeance," *The International* (New York), August 1912; reprinted in *Mother Earth*, September 1912. See also Abbott's letter on Voltairine de Cleyre in *The American Freeman* (Girard, Kans.), July 1949.

———. "Voltairine de Cleyre's Posthumous Book," *Mother Earth*, October 1914.

Cohen, Joseph J. "Voltairine de Cleyre," *Fraye Arbeter Shtime*, June 29, 1912.

Constan, P. [Ahrne Thorne]. "Tsum fertsigstn yortsayt nokh Voltairine de Cleyre," *Fraye Arbeter Shtime*, January 2, 1953.

Duff, William. "Voltairine de Cleyre," *The Herald of Revolt*, September 1913 (a special Voltairine de Cleyre issue).

———. "Voltairine de Cleyre's Tour in Scotland," *Freedom* (London), November 1897.

Elwell, Mary. "The Worm Turns," *Lucifer*, June 9, 1900.

Fox, Jay. "Voltairine de Cleyre," *The Agitator*, July 15, 1912. See also his speech in *The Syndicalist*, July 1, 1913, delivered in Chicago on the first anniversary of her death.

Frumkin, Abraham. "Voltairine de Cleyre," in his *In friling fun yidishn sotsializm*, New York, A. Frumkin Jubilee Committee, 1940, pp. 223-60 (originally published in the *Fraye Arbeter Shtime*).

Galleani, Luigi. "Voltairine de Cleyre, 1866-1912," *La Cronaca Sovversiva*, July 27, 1912. Reprinted in his *Medaglioni: figure e figuri*, Newark, L'Adunata dei Refrattari, n.d. [1930], pp. 110-18; and in *L'Emancipazione* (Oakland, Calif.), June 15, 1932.

Goldman, Emma. *Voltairine de Cleyre*. Berkeley Heights, N.J., Oriole Press, 1932.

Hapgood, Hutchins. "A Famous Unknown," *The Globe and Commercial Advertiser* (New York), June 21, 1912.

Hartmann, Sadakichi. "Voltairine de Cleyre," *Mother Earth*, April 1915.

Havel, Hippolyte. Introduction to the *Selected Works of Voltairine de Cleyre*, New York, Mother Earth Publishing Association, 1914, pp. 5-14.

Heyman, Porter. "Voltairine at Waldheim" (poem), *Man!*, July-August 1937.

In Memoriam: Voltairine de Cleyre. Chicago, Annie Livshis, 1912.

Kelly, Harry. "Voltairine de Cleyre," *Mother Earth*, June 1913.

Koringen, Olav. Untitled manuscript on Voltairine de Cleyre's visit to Norway (1903), with notes by Max Nettlau, Ishill Collection, Harvard.

Kucera, Joseph. "Voltairine de Cleyre (A Character Sketch)," *Why?*, August 1913.

Leighton, Marian. "Voltairine de Cleyre: An Introduction to American Left-Wing Anarchism," *Black Rose* (Somerville, Mass.), no. 2, Spring 1975, pp. 1-7, with Voltairine de Cleyre's "The Making of an Anarchist," pp. 8-15.

Muñoz, Vladimiro. "Una cronología de Voltairine de Cleyre," *Reconstruir* (Buenos Aires), no. 60, May-June 1969, pp. 51-58.

Navro, Nathan. Untitled manuscript on Voltairine de Cleyre, Ishill Collection, Harvard.

Nettlau, Max. "En recuerdo de Voltairine de Cleyre, anarquista americana (1866-1912)," *La Protesta* (Buenos Aires), supplement, March 31 and April 16, 1928.

Parker, S. E. "Voltairine de Cleyre: Priestess of Pity and Vengeance," *Freedom* (London), April 29, 1950.

Perlin, Terry M. "Anarchism and Idealism: Voltairine de Cleyre," *Labor History*, XIV (Fall 1973), 506-20.

Rexroth, Kenneth. "Again at Waldheim" (poem), *Retort* (Bearsville, N.Y.), Winter 1942.

Starrett, Walter [W. S. Van Valkenburgh]. Untitled manuscript on Voltairine de Cleyre, Ishill Collection, Harvard.

"Voltairine de Cleyre," *Freedom* (London), August 1912. Probably by John Turner or Thomas H. Keell.

"Voltairine de Cleyre," *Regeneración*, June 22, 1912. See also "Voltairine Dead," in English page of same issue, probably by W. C. Owen.

"Voltairine de Cleyre (1866-1912)," *Equality* (Evansville, Ind.), I:2, n.d. [February 1976].

"Voltairine de Cleyre: A Tribute," by Harry Kelly, George Brown, Mary Hansen, and Alexander Berkman, *Mother Earth*, July 1912 (a special Voltairine de Cleyre issue).

Yanovsky, Saul. "Voltairine de Cleyre," *Fraye Arbeter Shtime*, June 22, 1912.

RELATED WORKS

Books, Pamphlets, and Articles

Adelman, William J. *Haymarket Revisited*. Chicago, The Illinois Labor History Society, 1976.

Ashbaugh, Carolyn. *Lucy Parsons: American Revolutionary*. Chicago, Charles H. Kerr Publishing Company, 1976.

Avrich, Paul, ed. *The Anarchists in the Russian Revolution*. Ithaca, N.Y., Cornell University Press, 1973.

———. *The Russian Anarchists*. Princeton, N.J., Princeton University Press, 1967.

Berkman, Alexander. *Now and After: The ABC of Communist Anarchism*. New York, Vanguard Press, 1929.

Berkman, Alexander. *Prison Memoirs of an Anarchist.* New York, Mother Earth Publishing Association, 1912.

A Catechism of Anarchy. Philadelphia, Social Science Club, n.d. [1902?]. Probably written by Voltairine de Cleyre.

The Chicago Martyrs: The Famous Speeches of the Eight Anarchists in Judge Gary's Court; and Altgeld's Reasons for Pardoning Fielden, Neebe and Schwab. San Francisco, Free Society Library no. 1 (series 2), 1899. Introduction by William Holmes.

Cohen, Joseph J. *The House Stood Forlorn.* Paris, "E. P.," 1954.

————. *In Quest of Heaven.* New York, Sunrise History Publishing Committee, 1957.

———— and Alexis C. Ferm. *The Modern School of Stelton.* Stelton, N.J., Modern School Association of North America, 1925.

————. *Der Urshprung fun gloybn.* Tel Aviv, Fraye Gedank, 1950.

————. *Di yidish-anarkhistishe bavegung in Amerike.* Philadelphia, Radical Library, 1945.

David, Henry. *The History of the Haymarket Affair.* New York, Farrar & Rinehart, 1936.

Drinnon, Richard. *Rebel in Paradise: A Biography of Emma Goldman.* Chicago, University of Chicago Press, 1961.

Eastman, Max. *Enjoyment of Living.* New York, Harper & Row, 1948.

Eyges, Thomas B. *Beyond the Horizon: The Story of a Radical Emigrant.* Boston, Group Free Society, 1944. Introduction by Harry Kelly.

Ferrer y Guardia, Francisco. *The Modern School.* New York, Mother Earth Publishing Association and Francisco Ferrer Association, n.d. [1909]. Translated from the French by Voltairine de Cleyre. Originally published in *Mother Earth,* November 1909.

Flexner, Eleanor. *Century of Struggle: The Woman's Rights Movement in the United States.* Cambridge, Mass., Harvard University Press, 1959.

————. *Mary Wollstonecraft.* New York, Coward, McCann, 1972.

Foner, Philip S., ed. *The Autobiographies of the Haymarket Martyrs*. New York, Humanities Press, 1969.

Frost, Richard H. *The Mooney Case*. Stanford, Calif., Stanford University Press, 1968.

Goldman, Emma. *Anarchism and Other Essays*. New York, Mother Earth Publishing Association, 1911. Biographical sketch by Hippolyte Havel.

————. *Living My Life*. New York, Alfred A. Knopf, 1931.

———— and Alexander Berkman. *Nowhere at Home: Letters from Exile of Emma Goldman and Alexander Berkman*. Ed. by Richard and Anna Maria Drinnon. New York, Schocken Books, 1975.

Gordin, Abba. *Sh. Yanovsky: zayn lebn, kemfn un shafn, 1864-1939*. Los Angeles, Sh. Yanovsky Memorial Committee, 1957.

Gordon, Samuel H. *Revolution: Its Necessity and Its Justification*. Philadelphia, Knights of Liberty, 1894. A lecture before the Ladies' Liberal League, March 27, 1894.

Graham, Marcus, ed. *An Anthology of Revolutionary Poetry*. New York, The Editor, 1929. Introduction by Ralph Cheyney and Lucia Trent.

————, ed. *Man! An Anthology of Anarchist Ideas, Essays, Poetry and Commentaries*. London, Cienfuegos Press, 1974.

Grave, Jean. *Moribund Society and Anarchy*. San Francisco, A. Isaak, 1899. Translated from the French by Voltairine de Cleyre.

Guérin, Daniel. *Anarchism*. New York, Monthly Review Press, 1970.

Havel, Hippolyte, ed., *The Revolutionary Almanac, 1914*. New York, Rabelais Press, 1914.

Holmes, William T. *The Historical, Philosophical and Economical Bases of Anarchy*. Columbus Junction, Iowa, E. H. Fulton, 1896, Liberty Library no. 1.

How to Get Rid of the Tramp. Philadelphia, Social Science Club, 1902. Reprinted from *Free Society*, June 23, 1901. Probably by Voltairine de Cleyre.

Ishill, Joseph, ed. *Free Vistas: An Anthology of Life and Letters*. 2 vols., Berkeley Heights, N.J., Oriole Press, 1933-1937.

Ishill, Joseph, ed. *The Oriole Press: A Bibliography*. Berkeley Heights, N.J., Oriole Press, 1953.

———, ed. *Peter Kropotkin: The Rebel, Thinker and Humanitarian*. Berkeley Heights, N. J., Free Spirit Press, 1923.

James, C. L. *Anarchy: A Tract for the Times*. Eau Claire, Wis., The Author, 1886.

———. *Origin of Anarchism*. Chicago, A. Isaak, 1902.

Joll, James. *The Anarchists*. London, Eyre & Spottiswoode, 1964.

Kelly, Harry. "Roll Back the Years: Odyssey of a Libertarian." Unpublished autobiography, ed. by John Nicholas Beffel, Beffel Papers, Tamiment Collection, New York University.

Krimerman, Leonard I. and Lewis Perry, eds. *Patterns of Anarchy*. Garden City, N.Y., Anchor Books, 1966.

Kučera, Josef. *Revoluce v Mexicu*. New York, Volné listy, 1912.

Lum, Dyer D. *A Concise History of the Great Trial of the Chicago Anarchists in 1886*. Chicago, Socialistic Publishing Co., n.d. [1886?].

———. *The Early Social Life of Man*. Boston, White & Co., 1872.

———. *The Economics of Anarchy*. New York, Twentieth Century Publishing Co., 1890.

———. *In Memoriam, Chicago, November 11, 1887: A Group of Unpublished Poems by Dyer D. Lum*. Berkeley Heights, N.J., Oriole Press, 1937. Introduction by Voltairine de Cleyre (her obituary of Lum in the London *Freedom*, June 1893).

———. *Philosophy of Trade Unions*. New York, Baker's Journal, 1892. Reprinted Washington, D.C., American Federation of Labor, 1914.

———. *Social Problems of Today: or The Mormon Question in Its Economic Aspects*. Port Jervis, N.Y., The Author, 1886.

———. *The "Spiritual Delusion": Its Methods, Teachings, and Effects*. Philadelphia, Lippincott, 1873.

———. *Utah and Its People*. New York, Ferrier, 1882.

———. "Why I Am a Social Revolutionist," in *The "Why I*

Ams": An Economic Symposium. New York, Twentieth Century Publishing Co., 1892.

Macdonald, George E. Fifty Years of Freethought. 2 vols., New York, Truth Seeker, 1929-1931.

Mackail, J. W. The Life of William Morris. 2 vols., London, Longman's, Green, 1899.

Mackay, John Henry. The Anarchists: A Picture of Civilization at the Close of the Nineteenth Century. Boston, Benjamin R. Tucker, 1891. Translated from the German by George Schumm.

Madison, Charles A. Critics and Crusaders: A Century of American Protest. 2nd edn., New York, Frederick Ungar, 1959.

Maitron, Jean. Le mouvement anarchiste en France. 2 vols., Paris, Maspero, 1975.

Martin, Alberto, Vladimiro Muñoz, and Federica Montseny. Breve historia del movimiento anarquista en Estados Unidos de America del Norte. Toulouse, Ediciones Cultural Obrera, 1973.

Martin, James J. Men Against the State: The Expositors of Individualist Anarchism in America, 1827-1908. Revised edn., Colorado Springs, Colorado, Ralph Myles, 1970.

Mendelsohn, Crystal Ishill. "A Complete Checklist of the Publications of Joseph Ishill and His Oriole Press," The American Book Collector, xxv (September 1974-February 1975).

The Modern Inquisition in Spain. Philadelphia, 1897. Published as a supplement to The Firebrand, July 11, 1897.

Morris, May. William Morris: Artist, Writer, Socialist. 2 vols., Oxford, Shakespeare Head Press, 1936.

Morris, William. The Letters of William Morris to His Family and Friends. Ed. by Philip Henderson. London, Longman's, Green, 1950.

Morton, James F., Jr. The American Secular Union. Chicago, American Secular Union, n.d. [1910 or 1911].

Muñoz, Vladimiro, ed. Antología ácrata española. Barcelona, Ediciones Grijalbo, 1974.

Nettlau, Max. La anarquía a través de los tiempos. Barcelona, n. d. [1935 or 1936].

———. Bibliographie de l'anarchie. Brussels and Paris, Les Temps Nouveaux, 1897.

Nettlau, Max. "Die erste Blütezeit der Anarchie (1886-1894)," Volume Four of his seven-volume history of anarchism, of which only the first three have been published. Volumes Five, Six, and especially Seven (all untitled) also contain pertinent material. Housed in International Institute of Social History, Amsterdam.

Owen, William C. *The Mexican Revolution: Its Progress, Causes, Purpose and Probable Results.* Los Angeles, Regeneración, 1912.

Parsons, Albert R. *Anarchism: Its Philosophy and Scientific Basis as Defined by Some of Its Apostles.* Ed. by Lucy E. Parsons. Chicago, Mrs. A. R. Parsons, 1887.

Perry, Lewis C. *Radical Abolitionism: Anarchy and the Government of God in Antislavery Thought.* Ithaca, N.Y., Cornell University Press, 1973.

Reichert, William O. *Partisans of Freedom: A Study in American Anarchism.* Bowling Green, Ohio, Bowling Green University Popular Press, 1976.

Rocker, Rudolf. *Johann Most: das Leben eines Rebellen.* Berlin, Der Syndikalist, 1924. Foreword by Alexander Berkman.

———. *The London Years.* London, Robert Anscombe, 1956.

———. *Pioneers of American Freedom.* Los Angeles, Rocker Publications Committee, 1949.

Rowbotham, Sheila. *Women, Resistance and Revolution: A History of Women and Revolution in the Modern World.* London, Allen Lane, 1972.

Schuster, Eunice M. *Native American Anarchism: A Study of Left-Wing American Individualism.* Northampton, Mass., Smith College, 1932.

Sears, Hal D. *The Sex Radicals: Free Love in High Victorian America.* Lawrence: The Regents Press of Kansas, 1977.

Silverman, Henry J., ed. *American Radical Thought: The Libertarian Tradition.* Lexington, Mass., D. C. Heath, 1970.

Sprading, Charles T. *Liberty and the Great Libertarians.* Los Angeles, The Author, 1913.

Stepniak [S. M. Kravchinsky]. *Underground Russia.* London, Smith, Elder, & Co., 1883.

Symes, Lillian, and Travers Clement. *Rebel America: The Story of Social Revolt in the United States.* New York, Harper & Row, 1934.

Tarrida del Mármol, Fernando. *Les Inquisiteurs d'Espagne: Montjuich, Cuba, Philippines.* Paris, Stock, 1897.

Thomas, Edith. *Louise Michel, ou la Velléda de l'anarchie.* Paris, Gallimard, 1971.

Thompson, E. P. *William Morris: Romantic to Revolutionary.* London, Lawrence & Wishart, 1955.

Tucker, Benjamin R. *Instead of a Book.* New York, Benjamin R. Tucker, 1893.

Van Ornum, W. H. *Fundamentals in Reform.* Columbus Junction, Iowa, E. H. Fulton, 1896, Liberty Library no. 5.

Veysey, Laurence. *The Communal Experience: Anarchist and Mystical Counter-Cultures in America.* New York, Harper & Row, 1973.

————, ed. *Law and Resistance: American Attitudes Toward Authority.* New York, Harper & Row, 1970.

Wardle, Ralph M. *Mary Wollstonecraft: A Critical Biography.* Lawrence, University of Kansas Press, 1951.

Warren, Sidney. *American Freethought, 1860-1914.* New York, Columbia University Press, 1943.

Weinberg, Chaim. *Fertsig yor in kamf far sotsialer bafrayung.* Los Angeles, Weinberg Book Publishing Committee, and Philadelphia, Radical Library, 1952.

Wolff, Adolf. *Songs of Rebellion, Songs of Life, Songs of Love.* New York, Albert and Charles Boni, 1914.

Woodcock, George. *Anarchism: A History of Libertarian Ideas and Movements.* Cleveland and New York, World Publishing Co., 1962.

————, and Ivan Avakumović. *The Anarchist Prince: A Biographical Study of Peter Kropotkin.* London and New York, T. V. Boardman, 1950.

Yanovsky, S. *Ershte yorn fun yidishn frayhaytlikhen sotsializm.* New York, Fraye Arbeter Shtime, 1948. Introduction by Dr. Herman Frank.

Periodicals

L'Adunata dei refrattari. New York, 1922-1971. Edited by Max Sartin *et al.*

The Agitator. Home, Wash., 1910-1912. Edited by Jay Fox.

The Alarm. Chicago and New York, 1884-1889. Edited by Albert R. Parsons and Dyer D. Lum.

The Alarm. Chicago, 1915-1916. Edited by Lucy E. Parsons and Aaron Baron.

Altruria. New York, 1907-1908. Edited by Dr. William J. Robinson.

L'Ami des ouvriers. Hastings, Pa., 1894-1895. Edited by Louis Goaziou.

Der Anarkhist (Yiddish). Philadelphia, 1908.

Der arme Teufel. Detroit, 1884-1900. Edited by Robert Reitzel.

The Beacon. San Diego and San Francisco, 1889-1891. Edited by Sigismund Danielewicz.

The Blast. San Francisco and New York, 1916-1917. Edited by Alexander Berkman.

The Boston Investigator. Boston, 1831-1904.

Broyt un frayhayt. Philadelphia, 1906. Edited by Joseph J. Cohen.

The Commonweal. London, 1885-1894. Edited by William Morris *et al.*

La Cronaca Sovversiva. Barre, Vt., and Lynn, Mass., 1903-1919. Edited by Luigi Galleani.

The Demonstrator. Home, Wash., 1903-1908. Edited by James F. Morton, Jr.

Discontent. Home, Wash., 1898-1902. Edited by Charles L. Govan *et al.*

El Esclavo. Tampa, Fla., 1894-1898. Edited by Pedro Esteve.

The Firebrand. Portland, Ore., 1895-1897. Edited by Abe Isaak *et al.*

The Firebrand. Mount Juliet, Tenn., and Sweden, Tex., 1902-1905, 1909-1910. Edited by Ross Winn.

Fraye Arbeter Shtime. New York, 1890-　　　　Edited by Saul Yanovsky *et al.*

Di Fraye Gezelshaft (new series). New York, 1910-1911. Edited by Saul Yanovsky.

Free Society. San Francisco, Chicago, and New York, 1897-1904. Edited by Abe Isaak.

Free Society. New York, 1921-1922. Edited by Marcus Graham and Hippolyte Havel.

Freedom. London, 1886-1927. Founded by Peter Kropotkin *et al.*

Freedom. New York and Chicago, 1890-1892. Edited by Lucy Parsons.

The Freethinkers' Magazine. Buffalo and Chicago, 1882-1894. Edited by H. L. Green.

Freethought. San Francisco, 1888-1890. Edited by Samuel P. Putnam and George E. Macdonald.

Freiheit. New York, 1882-1910. Edited by Johann Most (published in England and Switzerland, 1879-1882).

The Herald of Revolt. London, 1910-1914. Edited by Guy A. Aldred.

The Independent. New York, 1848-1928.

The Individualist. Denver, 1889-1890. Edited by Frank Q. Stuart.

The Labor Leader. Boston, 1887-1897.

The Liberal. Chicago, 1890-1926.

The Libertarian Magazine. Seattle, 1915-1917. Edited by C. V. Cook.

Liberty. Boston and New York, 1881-1908. Edited by Benjamin R. Tucker.

Liberty. London, 1894-1896. Edited by James Tochatti.

Lucifer. Valley Falls, Topeka, and Chicago, 1883-1907. Edited by Moses Harman.

The Magazine of Poetry. Buffalo, 1889-1896.

Man! San Francisco and Los Angeles, 1933-1940. Edited by Marcus Graham.

The Modern School. New York and Stelton, N.J., 1912-1922. Edited by Leonard D. Abbott, Harry Kelly *et al.*

The Monist. Chicago, 1890-   . Edited by Paul Carus.

Mother Earth. New York, 1906-1918. Edited by Emma Goldman and Alexander Berkman.

The Open Court. Chicago, 1887-1936. Edited by Paul Carus.

The Pennsylvania Nationalist. Philadelphia, 1880s-1890s.

Probuzhdenie. Detroit, 1927-1939. Edited by E. Z. Moravsky and M. I. Rubezhanin.

The Progressive Age. Grand Rapids, Mich., 1880s. Edited by Voltairine de Cleyre. I have been unable to locate this journal.

The Radical Review. Boston, 1877-1878. Edited by Benjamin R. Tucker.

The Rebel. Boston, 1895-1896. Edited by C. W. Mowbray, Harry Kelly, and N. H. Berman.

Regeneración. Los Angeles, 1910-1918. Edited by Ricardo Flores Magón.

Revolt. New York, 1916. Edited by Hippolyte Havel.

The Rights of Labor. Chicago, 1886-1893.

The Road to Freedom. Stelton, N.J. and New York, 1924-1932. Edited by Hippolyte Havel and Walter Starrett.

Solidarity. New York, 1892-1898. Edited by F. S. Merlino and J. H. Edelmann.

Der Sozialist (new series). Berlin, 1909-1915. Edited by Gustav Landauer.

The Syndicalist. Chicago, 1913. Edited by Jay Fox.

Les Temps Nouveaux. Paris, 1895-1914. Edited by Jean Grave.

Truth. Pittsburgh, 1889-1890.

The Truth Seeker. New York, 1873-1922. Edited by E. M. and George E. Macdonald.

Twentieth Century. New York, 1888-1898. Edited by Hugh O. Pentecost.

Volné listy. New York, 1890-1917. Edited by V. Rejsek.

Why? Tacoma, Wash., 1913-1914. Edited by Samuel T. Hammersmark, Eugene Travaglio *et al.*

The Woman Rebel. New York, 1914. Edited by Margaret Sanger.

Index

Library of Congress Cataloging in Publication Data

Avrich, Paul.
   An American anarchist.
   Bibliography: p.
   Includes index.
   1. De Cleyre, Voltairine, 1866-1912.
2. Anarchism and anarchists—United States—
Biography. 3. Feminists—United States—
Biography.   I. Title.
HX843.A97   335'.83'0924 [B]   78-51153
ISBN 0-691-04657-3